Mothers and meaning on the early modern English stage

Manchester University Press

Mothers and meaning on the early modern English stage

Felicity Dunworth

Manchester University Press
Manchester and New York
Distributed in the United States exclusively
by Palgrave Macmillan

Copyright © Felicity Dunworth 2010

The right of Felicity Dunworth to be identified as the author of this work has been asserted by her in accordance with the Copyright, Designs and Patents Act 1988.

Published by Manchester University Press
Oxford Road, Manchester M13 9NR, UK
and Room 400, 175 Fifth Avenue, New York, NY 10010, USA
www.manchesteruniversitypress.co.uk

Distributed in the United States exclusively by
Palgrave Macmillan, 175 Fifth Avenue,
New York, NY 10010, USA

Distributed in Canada exclusively by
UBC Press, University of British Columbia, 2029 West Mall,
Vancouver, BC, Canada V6T 1Z2

British Library Cataloguing-in-Publication Data is available

Library of Congress Cataloging-in-Publication Data is available

ISBN 978 0 7190 8846 9 paperback

First published by Manchester University Press in hardback 2010

This paperback edition first published 2012

The publisher has no responsibility for the persistence or accuracy of URLs for any external or third-party internet websites referred to in this book, and does not guarantee that any content on such websites is, or will remain, accurate or appropriate.

Printed by Lightning Source

For my sisters Katie, Sarah, Charlotte and Caroline

In memory of my mother Elizabeth and my daughter Clare

And, especially, for Helen

Contents

	Acknowledgements	*page* ix
	Introduction	1
1	The transformation of tradition in the sixteenth century	19
2	Motherhood and the classical tradition	52
3	Motherhood and history	79
4	'Pleasing punishment': motherhood and comic narrative	111
5	Motherhood and the household: domestic tragedy and city comedy	143
6	Typology and subjectivity in *Hamlet* and *Coriolanus*	167
7	Dead mothers among the living	196
8	Conclusion	222
	Bibliography	228
	Index	245

Acknowledgements

I first wrote about motherhood in my doctoral thesis and I remain grateful for the support that I received from colleagues at the University of Kent during the long genesis of that work, especially Andrew Butcher, Marion O'Connor, Lyn Innes, Kate McLuskie, Sue Wiseman and the late Sasha Roberts. Catherine Belsey took the trouble to send me some images. I was fortunate to be examined by Darryll Grantley and Elaine Hobby, both of whom offered invaluable advice and encouragement. Extracts from the thesis were published in *Paragraph* (21), edited by Jan Montefiore, and in *The Body in Late Medieval and Early Modern Culture*, edited by Darryll Grantley and Nina Taunton (Ashgate, 2000). In reconsidering the subject for this book I have been supported with infinite patience by staff at Manchester University Press.

    I must thank Jen Wyatt, Sharon Smith, Stuart Goodall and Sue Piotrowski, who have in different ways made it possible for me to keep writing. Sue Ball, Claire Bartram, Kirsten Cooke, Dave Cummings, Rob Duggan, Michelle Keown, Moira Mitchell, Gearóid O'Flaherty, Anastasia Valassopoulos, Jonathan Wilde and my lifelong and much missed chum Tim Walton all helped me in different ways. The wonderful Wainers know what I owe them and how much I love them for it. Catherine and Justin Richardson have offered consistent support, as have my sisters, Katie, Sarah, Lottie and Caroline, who are, as ever, stars.

    Brian Dillon, my incomparable partner, read some of the chapters for me. His wisdom, patience and love have sustained me more than I can say and I thank him with a lot of love and all my heart. My darling daughter Helen, who cannot recall a time when I was not writing about motherhood, found the cover illustration for me. Through her I have learned what motherhood really means.

Introduction

> The breaking of tradition does not at all mean the loss or devaluation
> of the past: it is, rather, likely that only now the past can reveal itself
> with a weight and an influence it never had before.[1]
>
> Giorgio Agamben

The significance of motherhood in early modern drama resonates beyond the boundaries of any individual theatrical characterisation. Its influence is evident, for example, in a subtle reference to a wife and mother in Shakespeare's *The Merchant of Venice*:

> *Shylock:* Out upon her! Thou torturest me Tubal, it was my turquoise, I had it of Leah when I was a bachelor: I would not have given it for a wilderness of monkeys. (3.1.111–113)[2]

The mention of the hitherto unknown Leah at a crucial moment in the play becomes a significant and complicating factor in the audience's understanding of both Shylock and Jessica. The brief suggestion of a wife and mother in the context of the giving of a significant gift hints at a complex 'background' to the relationships enacted upon the stage. Motherhood here operates to suggest what Julia Kristeva has called, in a different context, 'a sacred beyond', for although Leah has nothing to do with the plot, the fact that an audience is made to imagine her existence, and ponder the meanings of that existence, provokes some complex adjustments in their reading of Shylock and his daughter.[3]

Motherhood as a signifier has always been overdetermined in ways that have been remarkably consistent in western European culture, where its complicated emotional, social and political implications attest to continuities of meaning. Certain qualities (of selflessness, of unconditional love, for example) are traditionally associated with motherhood in such a way that they have become understood as natural and universal. This is borne out by a consideration of the paradigms through which the concept has been read; from before Augustine to after Freud, assumptions are revealed which routinely dehistoricise and universalise motherhood as instinctive and natural: as a given.[4] This continuity of meaning is essential to the construction of the mother figure in dramatic and other discourses from the second half of the sixteenth and early seventeenth centuries because it enables her to offer a consistent emotional focus throughout the political, religious and social changes of the period.

If motherhood operates as a relatively unchanging idea, however, it is also especially subject, in terms of the interpretation and presentation of that idea, to the influences and constraints of culture, politics and religion. During the period covered by this book, dramatists chose to emphasise different aspects of motherhood according to the demands of genre and theatre and in response to contextual pressures. The significance of the mother figure became particularly important in a drama which was self-consciously fashioning and refashioning itself in relation to the shifting preoccupations of the society from which it emerged.

The dramatised mother operates emblematically as a rhetorical and visual signifier of a complex set of ideas: she is the embodiment of conflicting discourses, re-presenting them as spectacle. Francis Bacon described emblems as figures that reduce 'conceits intellectual to images sensible', and Michael Bath shows that the sixteenth-century emblem was, in general, a synthesis of classical, humanist and scriptural topoi – a useful corollary to the argument made in this book that the mother figure drew her range of signification from a similar synthesis.[5] For Martha Hester Fleische 'an image is an emblem, in short, if it is devised and viewed with an emblematic eye'. Fleische shows that the concept of the emblem as theatrical can be traced back to at least 1569 when the emblem book *A Theatre for Worldlings* was translated from French and published in English.[6] The concept of the emblem offers an appropriate way to describe the function of the dramatised mother in the period, working as she does to elucidate complex meaning, even as that meaning includes both continuity and change. Motherhood therefore functions to affect an audience's understanding of a narrative through the mother's capacity to complicate, destabilise and mediate. Shakespeare's assertion of Leah is a rhetorical rather than a visual image, but it nevertheless elicits a complex, difficult reaction, which interrogates the moral structure of the play.

Introduction

For much of the twentieth century, criticism of the representation of mothers in early modern drama centred upon Shakespeare, tended to the conservative and the personal and was apt to confuse early modern 'interest' in maternity with the representation of a particular kind of mother figure appropriate to the critic's own perceptions of what motherhood should mean. For example, Maynard Mack:

> There is amazingly little interest in either mothers or mothering in most of Shakespeare, and the comparatively few mothers who are brought to our attention as mothers, though they include such exemplary mothers as the Countess of Roussillon, Lady Macduff, Virgilia and Hermione, include also Tamora, cruel Queen of the Goths in *Titus Andronicus*, Gertrude in *Hamlet*, Lady Macbeth (a mother at least by her own testimony), Volumnia in *Coriolanus* and the poisoning Queen in *Cymbeline*, mother of the clod Cloten. Not – one may perhaps reasonably conclude – a puff for radiant Elizabethan motherhood.[7]

The implication here appears to be that mothers who cannot be categorised as 'exemplary' are not really mothers at all. An earlier, famous example is A. C. Bradley's account of the final cause of Hamlet's psychic disintegration – 'it was a moral shock of the sudden ghastly disclosure of his mother's true nature' – that similarly depends upon romantic, conventional assumptions about what a proper mother should be.[8] This approach has occasionally driven critics to extreme lengths in order to accommodate early modern 'interest' in mothers of a less than exemplary nature: 'If differently placed, Lady Macbeth might not have been a bad mother', suggests one, though there is nothing to suggest that Lady Macbeth was a bad mother despite her terrifying fantasy of infanticide at a tense narrative moment in Shakespeare's play.[9] Such readings have been criticised for a lack of rigour and for sentimentality (Bernard Shaw rightly pointed out that Lady Macbeth 'says things that will set people's imaginations to work in the right way: that is all') but not necessarily for the assumptions about the nature of motherhood that tend to inform them.[10] Bradley and Mack, whatever the limits of their respective readings, raised questions about the complications and challenges of representing motherhood in early modern drama that are still engaging critics.[11]

The dramatised mother thus tended to be understood by reference to a consistent set of ideas informed by fixed notions of what a mother should be. Bradley's assertion of Gertrude's 'true nature' is telling; it suggests a link between an understanding of good motherhood and what is 'natural'. The power of this persistent tradition in history, historiography and criticism is acknowledged by the historian Elisabeth Badinter, even as she challenges it:

> It is pointless to maintain that maternal behaviour is not grounded in instinct as long as people persist in regarding a mother's love for her child as so strong and seemingly universal that it must somehow owe something to nature. Despite the change of vocabulary, the old notion endures, and it all becomes a question of semantics.[12]

Writing from another perspective, the psychoanalyst Rozsika Parker acknowledges 'the imperative that there is only one way to be a good mother', and observes: 'Our culture permits flexibility in other activities that involve intimacy, some heterogeneity, some diversity of style, but hardly any at all when it comes to mothering'.[13]

In their discussion of psychoanalytic approaches to motherhood, Janice Doane and Devon Hodges conclude, as does Parker, that the psychoanalytic paradigm itself tends to assume that 'mother' is ahistorical and is thus in danger of replicating that same traditional notion that motherhood is linked to nature and instinct: 'Object-relations theories tell us to "Cherchez la mère": we advise a close scrutiny of this imperative, an imperative that has done more to maintain than to challenge the norms of patriarchal culture'.[14] This is also acknowledged by Karen Newman, writing on Renaissance drama from a new historicist perspective, who argues that this consistency has both a political function and political implications as a means by which patriarchy is constantly asserted and reaffirmed.[15] Mary Beth Rose likewise reveals a 'thematically determining omnipresence of patriarchalism' in early modern drama, specifically Shakespeare's plays, and argues that 'feminist inquiries must involve a full scrutiny of the discourses distinctive to, and the options available in Renaissance England' to understand the ideological context for dramatic texts.[16] Rose finds an entrenched conservatism in Shakespeare's comedies which has 'an evident structural analogue in the anachronistic discourses of Vives, and in his tragedies', leading her to conclude that 'the Shakespearean text comes down decidedly in the conservative camp, allying itself with more traditional discourses' in the treatment of the mother figure.[17] For Rose, the dramatic potential of the mother figure is – in Shakespeare's plays at least – circumscribed by the weight of conservative, patriarchal, tradition.

This book takes a different perspective from critics like Rose and Karen Newman, who have been concerned, in Newman's words, to 'explore how the feminine subject is constructed'.[18] Rather than consider the dramatised mother in terms of subjectivity, this book explores her dramatic function in terms of the effect that the complex of meanings she embodies brings to the dynamics of dramatic narrative and structure. In her persuasive interpretation of Shakespeare's later tragedies, Janet Adelman describes the mother as a locus of anxious fantasies of power and discovers a patriarchal assumption that 'women must pay the price for the maternal powers invested in them'.[19] Kathryn Schwarz, paraphrasing Newman, argues that 'women's reproductive bodies become metonyms for the ways in which patriarchy works' in the early modern period, so that meaning is privileged over subjectivity in terms of representation.[20] For Newman this figurative function of the maternal body ensures that 'the social is presented as natural and therefore unchangeable, substantiated, filled with presence'.[21] The phrase 'the ways in which patriarchy works' suggests, in its generality, unbounded possibilities for the mother figure: a limitless set of potential meanings. In another analysis, Julia Kristeva's assertion of 'motherhood's impossible syllogism' – 'it happens, but I'm not there' – attests to this, contemplating the mother as a kind of cipher, offering out endless meaning but present only as an absence of self. This concept of motherhood as a kind of meaningful absence is addressed another way by Susan Robin Suleiman, who quotes Helen Deutsch's assertion that 'mothers don't write, they are written'.[22]

In drama, this frees up meaning. Untrammelled by subjectivity the mother figure has the potential to be read, as Susan McLoskey argues, as a 'cipher for all the play's main characters', and though this has sometimes been read as a negative quality, symptomatic of a subjectivity to be recovered, mothers are unique in the potential they offer to create a particular kind of complex narrative.[23] The meanings engendered by motherhood focus the mother figure as a constellation of ideas and points of reference: consistent and enduring, certainly, but also in constant flux as the significance generated by those fixed meanings shifts in response to the influence of changing circumstances. The interplay between the mother's fixed meanings and their shifting significance allows her a set of multifaceted representational functions which were well understood and exploited by those writing for the Elizabethan and Jacobean theatre.

It is perhaps this very complexity that accounts for the much-noted absence of the mother in early modern plays. The 'amazingly little interest' in mothering that Mack acknowledges has been addressed by Carol Thomas Neely, who offers historical explanations for this problematic absence:

> The rarity of mothers [in Shakespeare's plays] may reflect or confirm demographic data showing that Renaissance women frequently died in childbirth. It may embody the social reality that patriarchal culture vested all authority in the main parent; making it both logical and fitting that he alone should represent that authority in the drama. It may derive ... from generic conventions: the uncommonness of mature women in the genres of comedy, history play and tragedy. Or it may result from a scarcity of boy actors capable of playing mature women in Shakespeare's company.[24]

Neely alerts us, importantly, to the possible dangers of focusing too closely upon 'the phenomenon of absent mothers' for evidence of the sort of misogyny ('the best mother is an absent or dead mother') that Mary Beth Rose discovers, by offering the demands of theatrical convention and dramatic form as modifying possibilities.[25] Neely's account remains rather open ended – 'the nature and significance of this phenomenon and the relative significance of the factors accounting for it probably vary from genre to genre or even from play to play' – but her insistence upon the unique dynamic of each individual play is nevertheless important to any discussion of the specificity of meaning with which the mother figure colours the texts that she inhabits.[26]

By the sixteenth century, motherhood was a complex and fluid notion, available in a variety of discourses for ends that are interestingly diverse. As a type, an emblematic device, a metaphor and a symbol, the fluidity of the mother image was pervasive and complicated. In Christian and classical tradition the mother figured the church or the state or nature, offering a variety of allegorical possibilities. Her significance as a metaphor on the grand scale coexisted unproblematically with the more commonplace and practical, so that, for example, Raynalde's translation of Rösslin's obstetric manual *The Byrthe of Mankynde*, which became a standard, regularly revised, publication for over a century from 1545, discusses female fertility in relation to the propagation of beans and corn, and suggests remedies for infertility and gynaecological problems based upon the use of germinating crop seeds either in the making of medicines and lotions or by virtue of sympathetic healing.[27] The womb is described, both in its physiological aspect and its generative potential, as a 'purse', which encapsulates the currency of future generations. At the same time an individual freak baby, a 'monstrous birth', could be understood as having prophetic significance for the entire nation, as in the dismal prognostications of the clergyman Stephen Batman, whose *The Doome Warning all men to the Iudgement* 'produced an extensive chronicle of every prodigy and monstrous birth in every book he had read'.[28]

The qualities of motherhood might transcend gender as they had for much earlier devotional literature. St Anselm had written of both St Paul and Jesus in terms of their maternal qualities and there was an influential iconographic tradition that envisioned Christ the nurse, described androgynously as a bridegroom with breasts.[29] A secular version of this drew on Plato, whose argument in the *Symposium* that love and poetry have similar procreative functions had become a common conceit, deployed, for example, by Philip Sidney in his preface to *Astrophel and Stella*, where the mother's body becomes an exotic metaphor for literary creativity in a description of 'the labouring streames' of the womb that engenders his poetry. Sidney translates in similar vein from Plato's *Symposium*: 'Those who are pregnant in the body only betake themselves to women and beget children – this is the character of their love . . . but souls which are pregnant – for there certainly are men who are more creative in their souls than in their bodies – conceive that which is proper for the soul to conceive or contain'.[30] Elizabeth Sacks quotes John Lyly's witty account of 'monosexual literary parenthood' in his preface to *Euphues and his England* (1580): 'the paine I sustained for him in travaile, hath made me past teeming, yet doe I think myself very fertile, in that I was not altogether barren'. Of his book's relationship with his previous publication he wryly asserts, 'Twinnes they are not, but yet brothers, the one nothing resembling the other, and yet as all children are now-a-daies, resembling the father'.[31]

Lyly self-consciously combines the maternal and paternal experiences of labour and fatherhood respectively, in a metaphor which has an analogue in childbed scenes, for example in *A Chaste*

Maid in Cheapside, where anxieties about paternity are raised in a scene featuring the childbed as a central image. Such scenes are predominantly populated by women figures; that is, by boys playing women. The erotic potential of theatrical cross dressing seems likely to be suppressed, when boys play mothers in such plays, in favour of the production of a kind of irony similar to that deployed by Lyly, the paternity joke gaining resonance from the impersonation of mature women by young men. Generally though, in contrast to the quickenings, groans, pangs and teemings that decorated so many written prefaces, the traumatic and frequent experience of real childbirth receives little attention in the Elizabethan theatre. Births, where they happen in the drama, tend to take place off stage with the usual commonplace references to labour pains as a matter of convention.

Discourses that placed the mother in relation to her husband and children tended to bring together practical knowledge, ideology and myth. Conventional obstetrics confirmed that the married mother was incubator of her husband's children, facilitating the development of his seed (her genetic contribution not being properly understood), 'reproducing' her husband through her maternity and thus providing emotional satisfaction, dynastic stability and some insurance for old age.[32] Historians vary in their assessment of the extent to which childlessness or infertility carried any social stigma for either parent, but childless women were perhaps incorporated into the social milieu associated with motherhood through their support at the confinements of their peers. Lady Margaret Hoby attended at several confinements and clearly played an important part in that of an unnamed 'wiffe' with whom, after arriving at 6 a.m., she says, 'I was busy tell 1 a Cloke, about which time, She bing delivered and I having praised God, returned home'. Lady Margaret did not find her childlessness a barrier to her offering advice to other parents either, on occasion offering instruction to neighbours on 'divers nedful dutes to be knowne: as of parence Chousinge for their children'.[33] Elaine Hobby suggests that ladies like Lady Margaret may also have taken the gentlewomanly task of reading the relevant sections of childbirth manuals and advice books to those in their care, among other duties.[34]

The pregnant woman was understood to bear responsibility for her child, both in her own right and because her duty to her husband designated the obligation. This began at conception. Ideas were abundant and confusing regarding the baby in its mother's womb; there are common references to abortive pregnancy as a kind of divine punishment for parental (especially maternal) misdeeds, particularly sexual incontinence. Deformed babies might result from the mother's intercourse with beasts or devils, sex during menstruation or misbehaviour or fright during pregnancy.[35] Once a child was born, the nursing mother was traditionally considered ideal though breastfeeding was paradoxically also described as a demeaning and bestial practice. From humanists like Erasmus and More to the authors of Protestant conduct books a century later, writers placed a consistent emphasis upon the virtues and advantages of maternal nursing.[36] Nevertheless women of the upper and, increasingly across the period covered by this study, middle classes were less likely to feed their young than their poorer sisters, and their husbands seem often to have been actively involved in their decision whether to nurse or not.[37] The problematic double significance of breastfeeding, the desirability of the mother's continued social, economic and sexual activity and the perceived need for large numbers of children at a time when many of them would probably die before the age of ten (breastfeeding is a contraceptive practice) contributed to a situation where many families who could afford it often resorted to the employment of a wet nurse. Dorothy Maclaren has shown how misguided such reasoning was and demonstrates that women who nursed their own babies probably had healthier children and the prospect of greater longevity.[38]

The relationship between the idea of motherhood and Christianity has been well documented. Although new – or new variants of old – ideas about motherhood emerged during the period after the Reformation, they tended to add to, rather than change, the complex of meanings that motherhood could offer. Certain conventional notions and practices remained embedded in popular culture although their significance might be altered. Erasmus argued against professional wet nursing by reference to the 'tyrant', 'King Custom' in his colloquy 'The New Mother'.[39] The tradition of 'churching', or ritual purification of women after childbirth, had been considered essential before a woman could be received back into her community. Keith Thomas refers to the popular belief that a woman who died in childbed before the rite had been performed should not have Christian burial.[40] By the beginning of the seventeenth century, though, the Protestant church appears to have been emphasising the celebratory aspect of the ceremony. Some Puritans ridiculed the whole thing and families seem to have used it mainly as the opportunity for a party, although in a recent essay Kathryn McPherson has discovered that different Protestant groups 'disagreed sharply about the justification, value, location and phrasing of churching'.[41] Nevertheless the familiar paradox prevailed: childbirth was a blessing upon the family but at the same time despoiled the mother; motherhood was on one hand an elevated status to which women should aspire, exemplified by the mother of Jesus, while at the same time the bestial act of giving birth constituted an enactment of the punishment of Eve whose guilt is evident in the tragedy that to be born is to have to die. Thus death is inscribed in the condition of motherhood itself.

The dramatised mother was therefore, in Barthes's formulation, polysemous in early modern theatre, her meaning endlessly modified and challenged in response to the rapidly changing conditions of Elizabethan and Jacobean society and politics.[42] Her discursive complexity has provoked readings that have brought to bear upon her a range of disciplines and theoretical approaches. Psychoanalysis, history and anthropology, for example, all offer potential interpretations of the meaning of motherhood, just as theoretical perspectives from cultural materialism to feminism and deconstruction provide a range of tools with which to inform such interpretations. This study aims to acknowledge that range through a flexible approach to its subject, reflecting the way in which the mother figure is always open to rereading and re-presentation. While it is not possible to discuss all perspectives all of the time, the study aims to show the value of different approaches in illuminating the mother figure. It has been argued in a different context that the successful representation of generic figures 'depends heavily upon the public's capacity to respond ritualistically to ... historical, religious or psychological motifs' and it is with a similar breadth of possible readings in mind that this book shapes its discussions of the dramatised mothers that are its subject.[43] The aim is to rediscover the mother figure as a successful and dynamic dramatic construct operating at the interface between audience and performance; between culturally and socially constructed notions of what motherhood is and the dynamics of dramaturgy and narrative. The challenge is to begin to disentangle the dramatic, circumstantial and ideological factors which intersect to produce the mother as a figure that is simultaneously constant and always subject to reinterpretation and to explore her influence upon narrative and dramatic structure; to discover what the idea 'mother' meant as the boy playing the woman stepped on stage.

The ways in which motherhood bridges and fills the spaces between moral, spiritual and concrete experience, and its tendency to focus a series of complicated and shifting meanings in a continuous process of development, transmission and appropriation, endows the image of the mother with a powerful range of affective and intellectual potentialities. The title of this chapter emphasises the transformation of tradition. Tradition is taken here to refer to a set of meanings which were ratified and developed through their usage over centuries, so that their significance and complexity was well understood. But tradition also refers to the process of passing on, of conveyance, of delivery or even of surrender.[44] Both meaning and process are important in the ensuing discussion, which explores not only the significance which usage had donated to motherhood up to and including the opening years of the sixteenth century, but also the transmission of that usage: what Giorgio Agamben has called 'the living act of tradition'.[45] The book attempts to describe both the accumulation of ideas that made available a set of understood meanings for the concept 'mother', and the transmission (and transformation) of those meanings through figurations of that idea during the political and cultural shifts of the Reformation, Counter-Reformation and the establishment of Protestant England.

The book begins by tracing literary and dramatic traditions associated with the representation of motherhood from the medieval period; a time when much playing was informed by liturgical conventions and religious practices that operated in a constant dialogue with the political and social concerns of the wider world. Chapter 1 considers the representation of figures such as Noah's wife, Eve and the Virgin in relation to the typology that is established through their paradigm stories. Religious and literary texts such as the writings of Julian of Norwich and Margery Kempe and the poems *Piers Plowman* and *The Romance of the Rose* demonstrate the complexity and reflexivity of motherhood in a range of genres that in turn influence dramas such as the later court plays *Wisdom* and *Nature*. Focusing upon the mother figure in terms of function rather than subject, the chapter traces the utility of motherhood as a dramatic trope, arguing for its importance as a carrier of a complex and resonant typology that has emerged out of, and has been simultaneously enriched by religious, political and cultural concerns. This richness of meaning ensures that the mother figure is integral to a reformulation of ideology during the process of Reformation. Her importance as an emblem is demonstrated by reference to two polemical plays written during the Reformation and its aftermath, the Protestant *Kyng Johan* and its Catholic rejoinder, *Respublica*. The appropriation and reappropriation of the mother figure is explored as evidence of a religious and political struggle to monopolise and colonise the mother as emblem. This gained a new and important currency with the accession of a female monarch. Both Mary and Elizabeth made shrewd political use of the idea of motherhood and its meaning, establishing an inextricable link between those ideas and the promotion of monarch and state which inevitably has implications for the representation of the mother on the stage.

The second chapter considers the influence of classical drama. English theatre had always combined entertainment with the transmission of moral, Christian and political ideas and had developed its conventions accordingly. The rediscovery of classical dramatic texts for use in grammar schools and the advent of cheap printing made possible the writing and dissemination of translations and imitations that had a significant effect upon drama. Models that addressed the mother in new ways became available as the works of Greek and Roman dramatists appeared in translation throughout the second half of the sixteenth century. Familiar conventions were revisited and reworked to deploy new ideas. The mother figure was measured against her counterparts in newly available and popular narratives, notably the work of Seneca. The two plays discussed in this chapter, *Gorboduc* and *Jocasta*, show the dramatised mother enriched and complicated by this collision of early and classical dramatic forms. The mother's dramatic potential, notably in court plays that refer obliquely to the Succession, is radically extended by attention to classical drama. A consequence of this combining of form is a reinforcement of the link between violence and the typology of motherhood that was already present in the sufferings of Mary and the machinations of her antitype, through attention to figures like Medea, Jocasta and Clytemnestra. This is evident in Elizabethan versions of classical plays, often mediated through Italian and Italianate translations and imitations. In a discussion of the Latin play *Roxana*, Shakespeare's *Titus Andronicus*, Kyd's *The Spanish Tragedy* and Marlowe's *Tamburlaine*, connections between maternity and the depiction of violence are traced to show how an assertion of the maternal, both in rhetoric and through dramatic spectacle, serves to emblematise both the causes and consequences of conflict and to elicit an affective response that invites reconsideration of the political in the light of the personal.

Chapter 3 extends this concern by considering the place of the mother figure in the representation of history, exploring the typology adumbrated in the first two chapters as a quality of narrative in late sixteenth-century history plays. Elizabethan chronicles imply a teleology that offers a reading of history in terms of a grand scheme structured around causes and events. This chapter suggests that motherhood in history plays operates against the dynamics of teleology to offer alternative readings of historical episodes. The meanings carried by the mother bisect chronology to assert a mythic and macrocosmic history, which insists upon an alternative context for the reading of the play as 'story'. Beginning with Dr Legge's Latin play *Richardus Tertius* and followed by a discussion of Peele's *Edward I* and finally with an examination of the role of Queen Margaret in Shakespeare's *Henry VI* plays, it is argued that motherhood works as a kind of narrative *event*, plotted as an intervention in the iteration of chronologically organised occurrences to complicate the dramatic representation, and thus the political and moral implications of history.

The fourth chapter draws upon the readings of motherhood in the previous chapters to explore the importance of the physical specialness of the mother's body to her dramatic value. The dramatised mother differentiates herself from other female types when she invites consideration of her past, present or future physical potential to be pregnant or to lactate, often by drawing attention to what the audience should 'see'. Taking two plays about Patient Griselda written forty years apart (by Phillip and Dekker) and Shakespeare's *Romeo and Juliet*, this chapter suggests that the body of the mother was subjected to an increasingly voyeuristic public scrutiny not only on the stage but in contemporary culture and practice, as maternity was increasingly exposed and controlled through state legislation and the processes of commodification. The discursive tensions created by an ambivalent appreciation of motherhood – sexual and creatural; spiritual and noble; endowing death as it gives life – are contained through performance. Theatre spectators were thus free to take pleasure in the spectacle of the maternal body and of its scrutiny and control.

The production of obstetric manuals and also of domestic conduct books where the mother's role is clearly adumbrated is symptomatic of an increased emphasis upon motherhood as a fundamentally *social* function which is important in ensuring stability in the wider world. Chapter 5 considers the mother's physical presence in relation to spaces; to the geography that signifies and comprises her social function and status. The focus is upon the representation of domesticity in domestic tragedies, which turn upon the dangerous potential of motherhood in an uncertain Protestant world, and city comedies, which farcically expose the tensions and hypocrisies of an environment where social and economic considerations are shown to predominate. The complex social structures in such a world are clearly adumbrated in *A Warning for Fair Women*, *A Yorkshire Tragedy* and *A Chaste Maid in Cheapside*, where the family is the smallest unit of an integrated society that is based upon the importance of geographic locality and economic interdependence. In such conditions maternity is vulnerable and with it, the fragile stability of the social structures that depend upon it.

Chapter 6 explores that vulnerability and the danger for the family that proceeds from it in the context of high tragedy, through readings of *Hamlet* and *Coriolanus*. Both plays, in their complex dealings with a son's relationship to his mother, demonstrate a reworking of typology to take account of shifting ideological preoccupations. In both plays, the mother has a public and political role that is dangerous and that makes her son vulnerable in a fragile political world. The mother as characterised may be sympathetic, but her maternity is destabilising, provocative of violence and a disturbance of family structure. The mother figure is here no longer a pathetic signifier of the personal consequences of political action; rather, she infects the political and creates danger through her own agency: an unhappy collision between her personal desires, her condition as mother and matters of state. The penultimate chapter extends this by considering a connection between Jacobean drama and contemporary discourses concerning the Protestant family and its relation to the state. Taking such diverse texts as Gouge's *Of Domesticall Duties* and King James's writing on government, as well as the popular genre of mothers' legacies, the chapter proposes that the representation and reception of motherhood in drama is coloured by shifts in religious and political pressures rather than because of a new celebration of affective family relations. Shakespeare's *The Winter's Tale* and Webster's *The Duchess of Malfi* revisit the focus upon motherhood and meaning treated in the first chapter. In the sixteenth century the dramatised lived experience of allegorical mother figures attested to a political urgency for reform; a need to rescue beleaguered motherhood and to reinstate the mother figure in proper relation to her monarch and the state. In these later plays written at a time when there is a social, religious and political need to consolidate and calm, the mother's meaning becomes transcendent and unchanging. Celebrated in terms of her domestic and private successes, the mother's meaning can only be broadcast by separating life from meaning and making an icon of her; by celebrating her in statues and on tombs; by publishing her words and by sharing her writings. In different ways, the potency of the mothers in *The Winter's Tale* and *The Duchess of Malfi* is, to quote Hermione, 'preserv'd' and memorialised so that motherhood transcends mortality to offer the unthreatening and unthreatened reassurance of everlasting and unconditional love. The book concludes by suggesting that what Patrick Collinson once termed the 'turning inward' of later Protestantism has its analogy in these changes in the meaning of the mother at the end of the period covered by this study.[46]

Notes

1 Giorgio Agamben, *The Man Without Content*, trans. Georgia Albert (Stanford: Stanford University Press, 1999), p. 108.
2 William Shakespeare, *The Merchant of Venice*, ed. W. Moelwyn Merchant (Harmondsworth: Penguin, 1985).
3 Julia Kristeva, 'Motherhood According to Giovanni Bellini', in Julia Kristeva, *Desire in Language: A Semiotic Approach to Literature and Art*, trans. L. Roudiez (Columbia: Columbia University Press, 1980), p. 237.
4 See Janice Doane and Devon Hodges, *From Klein to Kristeva: Psychoanalytic Feminism and the Search for the 'Good Enough' Mother* (Ann Arbor: University of Michigan Press, 1992) for psychoanalytic approaches to motherhood after Freud.
5 See Michael Bath, *Speaking Pictures: English Emblem Books and Renaissance Culture* (London and New York: Longman, 1994), pp. 2–3 and p. 48 for the quotation from Bacon.
6 Martha Hester Fleische, *Iconography of the English History Play* (Salzburg: Institut für Englische Sprache and Literatur, Universität Salzburg, 1974), pp. 2–3. Also Rosemary Freeman, *English Emblem Books* (New York: Octagon Books, 1966).
7 Maynard Mack, *Rescuing Shakespeare* (Oxford: International Shakespeare Association at Oxford University Press, 1979), p. 7.
8 A. C. Bradley, *Shakespearean Tragedy*, ed. John Russell Brown (Basingstoke: Macmillan, 1986), p. 94.
9 Sarup Singh, *Family Relationships in Shakespeare and the Restoration Comedy of Manners* (Oxford: Oxford University Press, 1983), p. 198.
10 Bernard Shaw, *Shaw on Shakespeare*, ed. E. Wilson (London: Cassell, 1961), p. 142. Also, L. C. Knights, *How Many Children Had Lady Macbeth?* (Cambridge: Minority Press, 1933).

11 For example, Kathryn M. Moncrief and Kathryn R. McPherson, eds, *Performing Maternity in Early Modern England* (Aldershot: Ashgate, 2007).
12 Elisabeth Badinter, *The Myth of Motherhood: An Historical View of the Maternal Instinct*, trans. Roger DeGaris (London: Souvenir Press, 1981), p. xxii. See also Adrienne Rich, *Of Woman Born: Motherhood as Experience and Institution* (London: Virago, 1977).
13 Rozsika Parker, *Torn in Two: The Experience of Maternal Ambivalence* (London: Virago, 1995), pp. 1–2.
14 Doane and Hodges, *From Klein to Kristeva*, p. 78.
15 Karen Newman, *Fashioning Femininity and English Renaissance Drama* (Chicago: University of Chicago Press, 1991), intro. and p. 62. See also Naomi J. Miller in 'Mothering Others: Caregiving as Spectrum and Spectacle in the Early Modern Period', in Naomi J. Miller and Naomi Yavneh, eds, *Maternal Measures: Figuring Caregiving in the Early Modern Period* (Aldershot: Ashgate, 2000), pp. 1–25.
16 Mary Beth Rose, 'Where are the Mothers in Shakespeare? Options for Gender Representation in the English Renaissance', *Shakespeare Quarterly* 42:3 (1991), 291–5. Rose refers to the work of John Knox and Juan Luis Vives, neither a direct product of early modern England though Knox's work was available in print and translations of Vives were accessible from 1529. See also Valerie Wayne, 'Advice for Women from Mothers and Patriarchs', in *Women and Literature in Britain 1500–1700*, ed. Helen Wilcox (Cambridge: Cambridge University Press, 1996), p. 64.
17 Rose, 'Where are the Mothers in Shakespeare?', pp. 304 and 313.
18 Newman, *Fashioning Femininity*, p. xix.
19 Janet Adelman, Suffocating Mothers: Fantasies of Maternal Origin in Shakespeare's Plays (London: Routledge, 1992), pp. 4 and 10.
20 Kathryn Schwarz, 'Mother Love: Clichés and Amazons in Early Modern England', in Miller and Yavneh, *Maternal Measures*, p. 294.
21 Newman, *Fashioning Femininity*, p. 4.
22 Kristeva, 'Motherhood According to Giovanni Bellini', p. 237. Susan Robin Suleiman, 'Writing and Motherhood', in *The Mother Tongue: Essays in Feminist Psychoanalytic Interpretation*, eds Shirley Nelson Garner, Claire Kahane and Medelon Sprengnether (Ithaca and London: Cornell University Press, 1985), p. 356.
23 Susan McLoskey, quoted by Laurie A. Finke in 'Painting Women: Images of Femininity in Jacobean Tragedy', *Theatre Quarterly* 36:3 (1984), 357–70.
24 Carol Thomas Neely, *Broken Nuptials in Shakespeare's Plays* (New Haven: Yale University Press, 1985), pp. 171–7.
25 Rose, 'Where are the Mothers in Shakespeare?', p. 301. Also Lisa Jardine, *Still Harping on Daughters: Women and Drama in the Age of Shakespeare* (Brighton: Harvester Press, 1983).

26 Neely, *Broken Nuptials*, p. 171.
27 J. W. Ballantyne, 'The Byrthe of Mankynde' – the Text, *Journal of Obstetrics and Gynaecology of the British Empire*, vol. XII (1907), 269–71. As I write, Elaine Hobby's eagerly awaited edition, *The Birth of Mankind, Otherwise Named The Women's Book*, is forthcoming (Aldershot: Ashgate, 2009).
28 Keith Thomas, *Religion and the Decline of Magic* (London: Weidenfeld and Nicolson, 1971), p. 109.
29 From Caroline Bynum, *Jesus as Mother: Studies in the Spirituality of the Higher Middle Ages* (Berkeley: University of California Press, 1982).
30 Dorothy Connell, *Sir Philip Sidney: The Maker's Mind* (Oxford: Clarendon Press, 1977), p. 46. The preface to Sir Philip Sidney, *Astrophel and Stella*, 1591, is quoted in C. Gebert, *An Anthology of Elizabethan Dedications and Prefaces* (New York: Russell and Russell, 1966), p. 72.
31 Elizabeth Sacks, *Shakespeare's Images of Pregnancy* (London: Macmillan, 1980), p. 8.
32 See Audrey Eccles, *Obstetrics and Gynaecology in Tudor and Stuart England* (London: Croom Helm, 1982).
33 *The Diary of Lady Margaret Hoby*, ed. Dorothy M. Meads (London: Routledge, 1930), pp. 63, 191, 195.
34 Elaine Hobby discusses the role of the gentlewoman reader at confinements. See Elaine Hobby, ed., *The Midwives Book, or the Whole Art of Midwifry Discovered* (Oxford: Oxford University Press, 1999), p. xv. Hobby gives a history of early modern obstetric manuals in her introduction.
35 Thomas, *Religion and the Decline of Magic*, p. 106.
36 Desiderius Erasmus, *The Colloquies of Erasmus*, 'The New Mother' (1526, Basel), trans. Craig R. Thompson (Chicago: University of Chicago Press, 1965), p. 283.
37 Dorothy Maclaren, 'Fertility, Infant Mortality and Breast Feeding in the Seventeenth Century', *Medical History* 22 (1978), and by the same author, 'Marital Fertility and Lactation', in *Women in English Society 1500–1800*, ed. M. Prior (London: Methuen, 1983), pp. 211–32. Also Linda Pollock, *Forgotten Children* (Cambridge: Cambridge University Press, 1983); Alan MacFarlane, *The Family Life of Ralph Josselin* (Cambridge: Cambridge University Press, 1970), p. 85; Patricia Crawford, 'The Sucking Child', in *Continuity and Change* I (1986), 23–54, 83–84; and J. W. Ballantyne, 'The Byrthe of Mankynde – Its Authors and Editions', in *Journal of Obstetrics and Gynaecology of the British Empire*, 10:4 (1906). Fig. XV shows how references to nursing increase in later editions of Raynalde's *Byrthe of Mankynde*.
38 Dorothy Maclaren's argument in 'Fertility, Infant Mortality and Breast Feeding'.
39 Erasmus, The Colloquies of Erasmus, p. 270.
40 Thomas, Religion and the Decline of Magic, p. 38.

41 See Kathryn R. McPherson, 'Dramatising Deliverance and Devotion: Churching in Early Modern England', in *Performing Maternity in Early Modern England*, p. 133. Also Peter Clark, 'The Alehouse and the Alternative Society', in *Puritans and Revolutionaries*, eds Keith Thomas and Donald Pennington (Oxford: Clarendon Press, 1978), p. 63.
42 Roland Barthes, 'Rhetoric of the Image', in *Image, Music, Text* (London: Fontana, 1977), pp. 38–9.
43 Quoted by Adrian P. Tudor in 'Talking Pictures: Performance on the Page', in *Acts and Texts: Performance and Ritual in the Middle Ages and the Renaissance*, eds Laurie Postlewate and Wim Hüsken (Amsterdam: Rodopi, 2007), p. 151.
44 In ancient usage this passing can imply a kind of surrender, or even betrayal. See the *Oxford English Dictionary*, vol. 18, 2nd edn (Oxford: Clarendon Press, 1989), 353–4. See also Howard Caygill, 'Benjamin, Heidegger and the Destruction of Tradition', in *Walter Benjamin's Philosophy*, eds Andrew Benjamin and Peter Osborne (London: Routledge, 1994), pp. 1–31, esp. p. 12. Caygill recalls that the Latin *traditio* was a legal term which meant 'delivery', 'conveyance' or 'surrender' and he suggests that the sense of tradition as 'handing down' came later. All usages appear to have operated in complicated tandem during the sixteenth century though the latter was increasingly usual.
45 Giorgio Agamben, *The Man Without Content*, trans. Georgia Albert (Stanford: Stanford University Press, 1999), p. 107.
46 Patrick Collinson, *From Iconoclasm to Iconophobia* (Stenton Lecture, 1985; Reading: University of Reading, 1986).

1

The transformation of tradition in the sixteenth century

> This fine and lovely word Mother is so sweet and so much its own that it cannot properly be used of any but Him, and of her who is his own true Mother – and ours. In essence, motherhood means love and kindness, wisdom, knowledge, goodness.[1]
>
> Julian of Norwich

Motherhood and meaning

Julian of Norwich, whose meditation is quoted above, was one of several late medieval Christian mystics who used maternity as a complicated and flexible concept, informed by a tradition of exegesis that allowed her to describe spiritual experience that was both deeply affective and intellectually sound. The aim of this chapter is to explore the operation and significance of this 'fine and lovely' word 'mother' in the dramatic expression of popular and affective piety in pre-Reformation England to show that, by the beginning of the fifteenth century, motherhood had accumulated a complex range of meanings that had already become established as dramatic tradition. This multiplicity of meanings ensured that motherhood developed as an important trope in the polemical strategies of religious and political reform in England. The dramatic deployment of the mother figure in Catholic theatre and its appropriation by Protestant propagandists attests to its central function in a battle to assert political and religious ideology which appealed on the basis of intellectual rigour and emotional satisfaction.

From at least the fourteenth century the processes of reform engendered and enriched an awareness of tradition that was fundamental in the construction and representation of proto-Protestant and, later, Reformation and Counter-Reformation ideology. For early reformers such as Wycliffe, 'veyn tradicioun' referred to an outmoded and morally dubious system of belief.[2] Under pressure from both this use of the term to derogate, alongside reformist pressure for biblical evidence to support ecclesiastical 'tradition', the term was, according to Alister McGrath, later understood to refer also to 'a separate, distinct source of revelation, in addition to scripture'. Such revelation was in a continuous process of transmission, 'a stream of unwritten tradition, going back to the apostles themselves [which] was passed down from one generation to the next within the Church'.[3] Tradition, then, and the means of its transmission, was both contested and appropriated long before the Reformation.[4] Meanings and representations of motherhood were central in this. Motherhood had become a traditional focus of religious and political meaning; asserted by conservatives, alienated, ironised and challenged by reformers, yet simultaneously appropriated by each to promulgate their competing ideologies.[5]

Julian's concern to fix maternal meaning upon the figure of Jesus reminds us that 'mother' asserts a human figure as much as a metaphysical idea. The word always foregrounds its material meaning – the individual person, the mother *figure*; so that 'mother' is always signifier as much as signified. This quality had informed an allegorical tradition which allowed the concept of motherhood both to focus and to represent a complicated and shifting set of meanings. Christian veneration of the mother of Christ had led to a celebration of the Holy Virgin as a maternal archetype from which, as Marina Warner has shown, a typology of divine maternity developed that combined Mary's incarnations as Virgin, Bride and Mother into one flexible whole that was, as Ann Astell says, 'primarily maternal in orientation'.[6] Astell shows, importantly, how this is the consequence of 'the fusion of two histories': that of the evangelical biography of Mary, and the literal meaning in the *Song of Songs*, leading to the construction of a figure where the literal bleeds into the allegorical, enhancing her affective power. Thus in twelfth-century exegesis Mary the holy mother was the garden where God sowed the seed that bore Jesus as fruit. She was also described as the holy fleece soaked with dew from heaven at the moment of the Conception.[7]

Mary's body, which had housed Jesus, also figured the church through the personification Ecclesia, the bride of Christ. Warner describes fourteenth-century Hildegarde of Bingen's vision of the mother church as 'the "image of a woman" of large size, as big as a great city, with a crown on her head and splendour falling from her arms like sleeves': a fascinating version of the trope which imagines the mother of God in terms of a flourishing city and an image which accommodates secular, as well as religious, power.[8] Cycle plays of the story of Noah use similar flexibility of meaning. In the Chester *Noah's Flood*, the ark with its boundless capacity represents mother church, but it is also the image which dominates the celebration of a secular community of townsfolk who work together towards both material prosperity and spiritual salvation. The allegory of church as mother is enhanced in this and similar plays by the presence of her comic antitype, Noah's wife, who works against both God and community by refusing to enter the ark in favour of the society of drunken gossips.[9]

Mary is also the queen of heaven, a status which endows her with powers of intercession and mediation and especially with the authority to be what Astell calls a 'maternal *informatio*',[10] a good and reliable guide. In the Chester *Purification* play, for example, it is Mary who instructs Joseph that Jesus must be taken to the temple because 'I wote well that it is Godes will', and it is she who determines the subsequent action.[11] Such typology operates in the poem *Piers Plowman* where, in the narrator's apocalyptic dream vision, Lady Holy Church descends from a castle dressed in white linen to address him as her 'sone' and to teach him about charity and truth, in a powerful combination of bride, instructress and mother. M. Teresa Tavormina draws attention to the importance of the trinity which is present not only in the three qualities of Holy Church above, but in the 'loving Unity' of 'Christ and Christendom and Holy Church the mother'.[12] But motherhood is double-edged in this text. The world of Will's dream is turned upside down in both political and religious terms, and Holy Church is under attack.[13] Maternity is thus associated not only with power, but, paradoxically, with vulnerability; the mother figure acts as protectress but is also in need of protection for herself and for her children. The meaning of 'mother' insists upon literal humanity as well as metaphysical transcendence, so that the mother figures frailty as much as she figures authority. The paradox is dramatised at the end of the Wakefield *Second Shepherd's Pageant* where, following Mary's authoritative exposition of the nativity to her visitors, one shepherd notices how Jesus 'lies full cold' in anticipation of the Passion and Mary's bereavement.[14] The pageant *Herod the Great* in the same cycle demonstrates maternal vulnerability most clearly when the desperate and brave defence of the mothers of the innocents is ineffectual against the policy and the might of Herod's men in their 'armour full bright'.[15] Here, the mothers' humanity is shown to be inadequate in their physical inability to fend off attack. This exposes a crucial aspect of maternal frailty: the mother is vulnerable because she is always human, because 'mother', whatever else it signifies, always also refers to the physicality and vulnerability of the maternal body. The mothers of the innocents provoke an affective response from audiences by reformulating the consequences of evil and of public conflict in terms of private and personal experience and grief and by figuring the tragedy that is inscribed in the condition of being merely human.

The limits (and the complexity) of this paradox are clear in a need to emphasise the extraordinariness of Mary's maternity, particularly in relation to those aspects of the maternal body which offer a troubling reminder of original sin. In the *N-Town* Nativity a version of the apocryphal story of the doubting midwife makes explicit the gap between the blessed human flesh of the Virgin and that of all other mothers.[16] In this tale, the Virgin is attended by two midwives, one of whom insists upon a detailed physical examination of the post-parturate Virgin because she does not believe in the immaculate birth. She is inflicted with a withered hand when she touches Mary's body to investigate. Her immediate repentance is rewarded by the arrival of a new hand, brought down from heaven by an angel. Jesus is born, extraordinarily, 'withouten spot or any pollution'. And yet Mary's milk – another indication of her humanity – is associated with her cleanliness and purity. Both physical phenomena offer related expressions of her holiness and her important difference:

> Be-holde the brestys of this clene mayd
> Full of fayr mylke how thei be;
> And her chylde clene as I fyrst sayd,
> As other ben, nowth fowle arayd,
> But clene and pure, bothe modyr and chylde.[17]

Mary's body is shown to be absolutely material and ordinarily fleshly. She invites the midwives in turn to undertake an intimate investigation of her body: 'I am clene mayde and pure virgyn; / Tast with your hand your-self al-on'.[18] That this is done in full view of the audience is evident from the stage direction that follows, '*Hic palpat Zelomy Beatam Mariam Virginem*'. Simultaneously, though, Mary's apparently fleshly body is mystifying; it is, and is not, like 'others'. This is emphasised by the second midwife's challenge to Mary's proclamation of her purity, which draws attention to the gap between what the midwife understands motherhood to mean, and what Mary is:

> *Maria*: Yow for to putt clene out of dowth,
> Towch with your hand and wele a-say,
> Wysely ransake and trye the trewthe owth,
> Whethyr I be fowlyd or a clene may.
> *Hic tangit Salome Marie et cum arescerit manus eius ululando et quasi flendo dicit.*
> *Salome*: Alas, Alas, and wele a-waye!
> For my grett dowth and fals beleve
> Myne hand is ded and dre as claye.[19]

The tension in this and other versions of the nativity in this genre is structurally generated by the juxtaposition of a kind of comic realism alongside explicit symbolism, setting the mythic against the material (and one aspect of the maternal body in contest with another). The universalising significance of the event is placed in tension with the dangerous ignorance of the midwife who cannot distinguish between the fact of the blood, leakage and mess of human childbirth, and the symbolism of this mother's full breasts.[20] Mary's body becomes the site of both a promise of eternity and a premise of tragedy, highlighting the gap between human understanding and the ways of God, emphasised by a typology which read the nativity as a prefiguration of the passion. The Virgin's lactating body figures God's mercy by reference to Christ's blood; her function is thus to symbolise both the power of an omnipresent Father-God and the sacrifice of his Son: the ultimate objectives of such representations.[21] The doubting midwife is, of course, associated typologically with other comic female challengers to God's authority from Eve to Noah's wife in all existing versions of the flood pageant and the alewife who remains in hell after the harrowing in the Chester cycle.

The corporeal qualities of motherhood are celebrated in another way in the early fourteenth-century *Romance of the Rose* by Jean de Meun, where Dame Nature represents, according to Warner, 'the biological necessity of the race to reproduce, the carnality and consequent inferiority of females as members of the species'.[22] Warner is arguing here that the carnality which caused the Fall informs a concept of the maternal (as an aspect of postlapsarian sexualised femininity) as inevitably flawed. Motherhood always signifies mortality, and the relation between maternity and the personification of Mother Nature required careful adumbration if the 'natural' – that is, fleshly and human – qualities that constitute part of the mother's meaning tend to imply physical and spiritual frailty and failure. In an essay which discusses the personification of nature in the *Romance of the Rose*, Sarah Kay suggests that the idea of motherhood as this 'natural' state was conditioned by an acknowledgement that nature required the moderating influence of patriarchal reason if its qualities were to contribute to spiritual satisfaction. Kay shows how Nature 'constantly invokes the need for the interpretation and control of her own gifts by the operation of reason'.[23] Kay's essay confirms that patriarchal interventions are crucial adjuncts to the assertion of 'nature', a term that, like the concept of maternity with which it is so closely allied, can be benevolent or malignant depending upon the rational, patriarchal controls that are brought to bear upon it.

Such control is apparent in medieval clerical exegesis, which both explains and appropriates some 'natural' qualities of the maternal. St Bernard's famous exploration of the *Song of Songs* discovers a discourse upon the motherly aspects of Jesus, explaining references to breasts and milk in the *Song* in relation to the nurturing relationship between Christ and the individual soul and also to the administrative relationship between an abbot and his monks.[24] Bernard habitually brings together images of the yearning bride, the caring mother, the nurturing Christ and the caring abbot, as an excerpt discussed by Caroline Bynum demonstrates:

> Take not however that she [the bride] yearns for one thing and receives another. In spite of her longing for the repose of contemplation she is burdened with the task of preaching; and despite her desire to bask in the bridegroom's presence she is entrusted with cares of begetting and rearing children. [Just as once before, she is reminded that] she [is] a mother, that her duty [is] to suckle her babes, to provide food for her children . . . we learn from this that only too often we must interrupt the sweet kisses to feed the needy with the milk of doctrine.[25]

Bernard's assertion of maternity was safely displaced on to the male body of Jesus, or, indeed, of himself, so that its 'natural' corporeal manifestations are appropriated safely into a mystical signifier of the paradox of the Incarnation.²⁶ And St Anselm carefully differentiated between spiritual and corporeal maternity: 'Do, mother of my soul, what the mother of my flesh would do'. He describes St Paul as 'a nurse who not only cares for her children but also gives birth to them a second time by the solicitude of her marvellous love'.²⁷ For Bernard and Anselm there is a celebratory emphasis upon the material and emotional qualities of motherhood once brought under male control. 'Mother' here operates to bring together concepts of spiritual perfection and natural bounty by reference to perfect maternity, and thus offers a metaphor for exemplary union between the body and the soul.

Anselm and Bernard were both likely influences upon female visionaries such as Julian of Norwich, who devotes a long meditation to the mystery of 'our sweet, kind and ever-loving Mother Jesus; Jesus, our true Mother, feeds us not with milk but with himself, opening his side to us and calling out all our love'.²⁸ For Julian, Jesus is 'our Mother in nature, working by his grace in our lower part for the sake of the higher'.²⁹ The traditional vulnerabilities of the female are thus reformulated by Julian as necessary conditions for piety.³⁰ Julian's reformulation finds eloquent expression in the devotions of Margery Kempe, who, upon revealing her religious experiences to her confessor, was told that she was 'sucking even at Christ's breast' and who imagined herself as an intimate assistant to St Anne at the birth of the Virgin and to the Virgin at the birth of Christ.³¹ In this, Kempe draws upon her own understanding of motherhood to imagine both herself and Christ in terms of the maternal.³² Her initial visions seem to have been precipitated by her own first experience of motherhood. The illnesses that she endured through pregnancy, and the trauma of childbirth, were followed by a series of revelations that affected the rest of her life and informed her mystical experiences. Her meditations are coloured by a lifelong desire for celibacy, despite the fact that she bore another thirteen children. Kempe's visit to Julian of Norwich seems to have affirmed for her the link between her own aspirations to chastity and Christ's potential as a mother. Christ's interest in Margery's own maternity was crucial to her. He told her when she was pregnant and after the birth of one of her later children he instructed her to have no more and instead to visit the anchoress Julian for guidance.³³ Michel Foucault discusses in more general terms a 'transformation of sex into discourse' through the practice of confession in terms of power relations and the construction of 'truth', a transformation which, in the case of Margery Kempe, is coloured by its transmission through a woman whose own sexual and maternal experiences made her tend to reformulate connections between piety and the activities of reproduction.[34]

This reformulating of concrete sexual and maternal experience into affective piety turned attention back to the materiality of motherhood in terms of Mary's humanity. Kempe imagined herself feeding the grieving Virgin with caudle, a food used specifically for the sick and for women in childbed. However such an act might be read symbolically, Gail MacMurray Gibson shows that Kempe's inclusion in her book of the recipe for her caudle (gruel and spiced wine) attests to a shrinking of the gap between human experience and the imagination of ideal maternity.[35] She also refers to Kempe's fascinating story of the Christ-child doll which was presented to women to be petted and kissed.[36] Gibson shows how close piety comes here to sympathetic magic: what she later describes as 'a very narrow line between religious icon and reassuring talisman'.[37] It is, however, as important to note the difference between the Christ-doll ritual and magic, as it is to note the similarities here; the doll is imbued with meaning which makes it an appropriate object for devotion – it concretises the numinous for those who engage with it, and allows them, too, to experience, however imperfectly, the motherhood (in both senses) of Christ.

The diversification of the mother figure into the allegorical personae of expositionary texts such as *Piers Plowman* thus developed alongside both the 'commemorative reconstruction' of biblical tradition in the mystery plays, and the appropriation of tropes of maternity into the discourses of affective piety.[38] Later fifteenth-century and early sixteenth-century moral drama extended the figure's potential range of meanings in plays 'designed to convey and comment upon a selection of doctrine and to recommend certain patterns of choice and action'.[39] *Wisdom* (c.1469) represents the soul, Anima, in terms of the mother/bride familiar from exegesis of the *Song of Songs* and combines this potential with the vulnerability of the mothers of the Innocents. The play celebrates the relation between Christ (figured in the play as Wisdom) and the soul of man in terms of explicit sexual passion – 'how amiable / to be halsyde and kyssyde of Mankynde' – in an allegory which demonstrates, as Happé shows, 'that Anima, the human soul, may find salvation by accepting a role as the Bride of Christ'.[40] But it also exposes human, fleshly, frailty in the figure of Anima, whose potential perfection, signified by her white dress, is compromised by the 'derke schadow I bere of humanyte', emblematised by a black mantle. Pamela King sees this costume as confirming that 'Wisdom represents the essential duality of Christ as God and man imperfectly mirrored in the soul', here represented as his bride.[41] W. A. Davenport discovers a similar duality linking Anima's costume to the medieval idea of the 'sensible' soul as separate from the 'rational' soul, a distinction which he traces back to Aristotle (but which must also owe something to Aquinas). Lois Potter describes the dress (in a way that catches its visual effect) as 'the cloud which the body casts over the soul'. For all these critics, Anima embodies meanings in tension; she is vulnerable because she is constructed out of oppositions.[42]

Anima's frailty, figured partly through her costume, is most strongly focused through an association with maternity. Her vulnerability to infection by evil is demonstrated by seven small demons that run out from under her skirt and then back under it. These little devils who colonise Anima's body like bad children – and they would have been played by small children – affirm a typological opposition between the perfect mother/bride, who is the Virgin through the *Song of Songs*, and the inadequate, corrupted mother/prostitute Mary Magdalene, accommodating both type and antitype.[43] This typology may have been emphasised in performance if David Bevington's analysis of the doubling of roles is correct. He suggests that the actor who plays Christ/Wisdom would, significantly, double as Lucifer, externalising the psychomachia which informs the play. But only one actor would play Anima, who embodies and interiorises the oppositions that centre upon her.[44]

Peter Happé shows how *Wisdom* operates by dramatising a conflict between Reason and Sensuality at the heart of humanity.[45] Henry Medwall's *Nature* treats the same opposition. His eponymous heroine associates herself with the material, natural, fleshly world, but, like Dame Nature in the *Romance of the Rose*, emphasises the controlling operation of God's providence upon even the most sensual aspects of her activities.[46] Both plays emphasise the value of a life lived in the world, where the demands of the soul and of the body, the intellect and the senses, compete: a conflict accommodated painfully in *Wisdom*, or more benignly in *Nature*, in the figure of the mother.[47]

The concept of motherhood thus accommodated differences between moral, spiritual and concrete experience in late medieval and early Tudor culture, offering a focus for a series of complicated and shifting meanings, which were always in a continuous process of development, transmission and appropriation. Its utility was enhanced by the ability of the maternal to indicate the physical, real and human: the mother figure literally embodies complex and conflicting ideas, donating form and mediating meaning. She spectacularly brings together the figurative and the corporeal; the symbolic and real human experience. This endows the stage mother with a powerful affective and intellectual potential that became important to the reformulation of ideology during the Reformation, and explores its operation in the political drama of the middle years of the sixteenth century.

The Reformation and the appropriation of tradition

Following the Act of Supremacy in 1534, the politicians and clerics who masterminded the Reformation in England were faced with the task of restructuring a sense of national unity which had been fragmented by conflict and speedy and radical change. Reformers were faced with the problem of 'traditions' that no longer suited the new political and religious circumstances, which were seen as threatening to the fragile new establishment. Marina Warner has noted that 'the conflict between Protestants and Catholics inspired a struggle to monopolise the rhetorical image', and it is clear that an awareness of the value and power of traditional concepts led to a determined policy of reformulation.[48] Familiar images were endowed with a new significance which was driven home by a concerted propaganda effort. The appropriation and extension of the allegorical potential of the mother was central to that effort, both in contemporary political rhetoric and in the drama which was produced to support it. The iconography and ideology of motherhood was re-presented to promote the idea of the mother nation, a reworking of the allegory which was intended to excite an affective, as well as a reasoned, response.

This policy was one of containment as much as of propaganda. The mother was a dangerous figure to leave hanging in ideological mid-air, particularly because of her identity with that most Catholic icon, the mother of Christ, and her consequent ability to articulate and demonstrate the effects of political evil in terms of personal pain and loss. Her subversive potential in drama seems to have been real enough during the Reformation, particularly because, according to Seymour Baker House, street drama had become an important location for 'debate over religious issues involving politics at the highest level' in the early sixteenth century.[49] Gail McMurray Gibson suggests, for example, that there was 'furious debate' over plays depicting the Assumption of the Virgin Mary during the Reformation, citing a range of evidence:

> The missing initial page of the 'Last Judgement' in the Wakefield cycle – evidently lost when a censored Assumption play was removed from the play register; by the York purification play that was hastily inserted at the end of the manuscript, out of proper sequence; by the missing play of Mary's Assumption performed by the town wives of Chester, and probably by the Assumption play written on different paper and by a different hand that was added to the N-town manuscript.[50]

The N-town play is an example of the potential for subversion contained in this form of drama. It is one of a potentially controversial series of dramatisations from the life of Mary which begins, according to Matthew Kinservik, with episodes that focus 'upon [Mary's] obviously pregnant body which contains the conflict of Mosaic law with the new Word'.[51] The potential danger of the Assumption play to the Henrician reformers is clear. Mary is condemned by devilish bishops and princes for inciting rebellion, 'thorow here fayre speche oure lawes they steyn'.[52] The interests of the Virgin and her supporters are contested by a bishop and three princes who are acutely aware of her subversive potential: 'Yif we slewe hem, it wolde cause the comownys to ryse'.[53] The possible correspondence between the circumstances of this play and the situation of the popular Katharine of Aragon, both before and after her death, suggests that the play, new or not, had the potential to transform the familiar religious iconography of the final days of the Holy Virgin through an emotional appeal to public opinion.[54] Indeed, H. C. Gardiner links the disappearance of plays about Mary specifically to the Dissolution, adding weight to David Bevington's assertion that the suppression of such plays was perhaps due to 'the hazards of political analogy'.[55]

The dramatic potential of ideal motherhood was thus at the centre of a struggle between Catholic and Protestant factions as they competed to regain the religious and moral high ground. The Catholic iconography of the Virgin, and the doctrine that it promulgated, was appropriated and transformed into a new version of transcendent maternity. Jacqueline A. Vanhoutte has shown how Thomas Cromwell's chief propagandist, Richard Morison, attempted to reformulate a national identity for Protestant

England by re-presenting the mother as a figure of England in published tracts which depend upon affective appeals to nationalism as much as upon rational argument. Vanhoutte sees Morison as the primary force behind a concerted drive to construct a new nationalist ideology from, she says, existing notions of 'community, religion, family, honour and sexuality'.[56] Motherhood, inscribed at some level in each of these concepts, thereby became crucial. Morison, writes Vanhoutte, extended the connection between mother and state to embrace the traditional connection between the maternal and nature, an analogy that enabled him to stress an emotional relation between the nation and her people: 'the country had "nourished" the English and ... therefore they are bound to love it'.[57] The figure of the mother nation thus became central to polemical strategies, most notably in the political drama which was a vital part of Cromwell's drive to consolidate his reforms despite the unwillingness of what Christopher Haigh characterises as 'a reluctant majority'.[58] Morison employed John Foxe's great friend John Bale throughout the 1530s as a propagandist specialising in the production of drama, and he funded Bale's own company of actors.[59] Bale followed and developed Morison's strategy in focusing upon the representation of the nation as mother in his most influential play: the interlude *Kyng Johan*.

The play was originally performed before Archbishop Cranmer's court during Christmas 1539.[60] Written at a point in the English Reformation when Henry VIII appeared to be losing his enthusiasm for reform, *Kyng Johan* brings together the concerns of God and king in a polemical play which seeks to represent the twelfth-century English monarch as a hero and martyr to the Protestant cause. Quarrels between the historical John and the pope had led to an interdict over England, and Bale dramatises the historical confrontation between church and state as a moral play in which an embattled English king struggles against an evil Catholic empire, ultimately suffering a martyr's death at the hands of a monk. The play is structured according to the conventions of traditional morality drama and so reflexively draws attention to itself as both a continuation of the plays that in the past had promoted the interests of the traditional church, and as a break from past practice: reworking of old tropes in terms of a new ideology.[61]

In *Kyng Johan* England is figured by Bale as a mother abused by her subject-children and bereaved through the wickedness of the pope. This embodiment of the nation as mother enables the dramatist to pattern bereaved Widow Englande upon a dramatic typology which associates her thematically and visually with the vulnerable mothers of the mystery plays. By emphasising continuities with the structures of traditional Catholic drama Bale is able to transfer the affective function of earlier maternal types on to the body of the nation as figured by his heroine. His abused Widow Englande is thus constructed to promote what Vanhoutte calls a 'shift in ways of imagining community'. She presents a capacity to embody the spiritual and civic qualities of a combined church and state, set against a demonised version of Catholicism led by a bestial pope.[62] Like her Catholic precursor, Ecclesia, Englande is ideally unified with God, for, as she tells the king, her true husband is 'God hym selfe', cruelly estranged from her by the machinations of the clergy.[63] The underlying assumption is clearly that a nation once whole has been divided, that a 'natural' configuration of father, mother and children is undermined by the operation of 'unnaturall' evil. Bale's aim is to provoke nostalgia for a mythic, healthy and unified England. Vanhoutte argues that the device of projecting 'a duality on a nation which is always already one' can be seen in the theatricality of state executions for heresy, citing the example of Friar Forest, whose torture and death were staged to demonstrate the divisive nature of his crime, so that the scaffold bristled with representatives of the state who supervised the annihilation of the divisive Catholic traitor.[64] Foxe's later descriptions of the Marian martyrs tended to emphasise the vicious disruption of godly Protestant families by persecution. John Rogers, for example, is said to have expressed fear at the last for his wife and eleven children, 'all my little souls', after previous attempts to ensure their security while he was under house arrest which had involved sending his pregnant wife 'many times' to plead with Bishop Stephen Gardiner.[65] In this and other examples, the Catholic authorities are repeatedly depicted, as D. Andrew Penny says, as 'both anti-scriptural and anti-family'.[66] At the level of nation, as at that of the family, the reformers sought to demonstrate how evil operates to disrupt what is 'natural', to the point where the flesh and the spirit are divided against each other, both within the consciences of individual martyrs (Foxe quotes Rawlins White confessing to 'a great fighting between flesh and spirit' before his death) and within the nation.[67]

The spectacular quality of the opening scene of Bale's play, particularly the debilitated figure of Englande, who enters ragged and physically weak, endorses visually the recent transformation of John's realm from health to disease. King John, a well-meaning but bewildered protagonist, barely recognises her in her shockingly diminished condition: 'I mervyll ryght sore how thow commyst chaunged thus'.[68] The suggestion that her transformation has been recent and sudden works well in the context of the rapid changes and polarising of allegiances that the Reformation brought about in the 1530s, and the need for Cromwell's increasingly beleagured faction to show this to be the consequence of the disturbing effects of Catholic treachery rather than Protestant change. This is achieved by an immediate identification of Englande as mother through an account of her relationship with her 'children', some of whom she rejects, accusing them of abuse: 'Nay, bastardes they are, unnaturall by the rood! / Sens ther begynnyng they ware never good to me'.[69]

The dramatisation of the familiar allegorical scheme which posits a benevolent but vulnerable maternity in opposition to the forces of evil allows the dramatist to promote a terror of Catholic sedition through Englande's rejection of her children as 'bastards'. The implication that the mother has been raped by a tyrannical power allows treason to be figured as the worst kind of personal, as well as political, violation. Intimacy between mother and child here figures the proper relationship between subject and state just as that between husband and wife is analogous to that between the nation and God. Such relationships are shown to be 'natural', playing upon that word's meaning as 'legitimate', alongside an appeal to complex traditional allegorical links between nature and maternity. Intimacy, then, is recast through metaphor as a 'natural' loyalty to the nation that has been violated here by the criminal introduction of seditious 'children' into the very body of the realm.[70] The allegory is followed through to its furthest dramatic potential in the generic figure of blind Commynalte, England's faithful but unseeing child, who is terrorised by the Catholic church in the person of Cardinal Pandwlfus into a position where the child is in conflict with his mother. Nation and church fight out a kind of psychomachia for the soul of the common man; a confrontation represented by the forces of evil tearing a mother and child apart. When Englande cries to her child, 'If thow leve thy kyng take me never for thy mother' the cardinal laconically responds, 'Tush, care not for that, I shal provyd the another'.[71] The cardinal connives at the rupture of the relationship between Englande and Commynalte, ready with his own manufactured alternative to what is 'naturall'. Signified in this way, the disintegration of the bond between mother and child becomes an especially apt motif for inducing an affective response in an audience that must be engaged emotionally if the serious matter of the drama is to be appropriately received.

Vanhoutte shows how Bale echoes Morison's polemic strategy, quoting Morison's tract *A Lamentation in Which is Showed what Ruin and Destruction Cometh of Seditious Rebellion*, in which a personified England bemoans the rupture that treason has wrought: 'I am one, why do you make me twain? Ye are all mine; how can any of you, where none ought so to do, seek the destruction of me ... Thus England might say, and much more, which I will say for her'.[72] Anti-Catholic polemic is expressed in terms of the mother's personal agony so that the mother figure is able to promote partisan notions through a direct and emotional appeal to the audience. Bale makes the figure of Englande the site where problems of both religious and civic allegiance are articulated, utilising the mother figure as an emblem through which emotional responses generated by both are mediated. Her reality as a dramatic figure, her engaging vitality, even though expressed through despair, preserves and promotes Bale's message. As Vanhoutte observes, 'the struggle to represent England is ... for Bale, a struggle to find a common ground which will allow for a re-unification of the intensely divided body politic'. This struggle is played out in *Kyng Johan* upon, and by, the mother.[73]

Mary I and the royal body natural

On the first of February 1554, in the face of Wyatt's revolt at her prospective marriage to the Catholic Phillip of Spain, Queen Mary Tudor addressed the lord mayor of London and the aldermen at the Guildhall, promising that the liaison would not take precedence over her loyalty to her realm. Her words were recorded by John Foxe:

> I am your Queen, to whom at my coronation, when I was wedded to the realm and laws of the same (the spousal ring whereof I have on my finger, which never hitherto was, nor hereafter shall be, left off), you promised your allegiance and obedience unto me ... And I say to you, on the word of a Prince, I cannot tell how naturally a mother loveth the child, for I was never the mother of any; but certainly, if a Prince and Governor may as naturally and earnestly love her subjects as the mother doth love the child, then assure yourselves that I, being your lady and mistress, do as earnestly love and favour you. And I, thus loving you, cannot but think that ye as

heartily and faithfully love me; and then I doubt not but we shall give these rebels a short and speedy overthrow.[74]

Even Foxe, the Protestant polemicist, acknowledges her oration to be a political success, wryly complimenting Mary upon her performance: 'she seemed to have perfectly conned [her speech] without book'.[75] It emphasised Mary's authority as a monarch while at the same time taking advantage of her gender to assert an emotional relationship between the queen and her subjects, to great effect. By making herself mother of her nation, Queen Mary deftly placed herself within a familiar literary and iconographic tradition which described an allegorical relationship between the figure of the mother and the imagination of those power structures that were most dominant: the church and the state. Such intelligent handling of familiar ideas was crucial at a moment when both were perceived to be under threat. Queen Mary and her advisers had developed a rhetoric suited to the circumstances of female monarchy, allying the power of the queen's position to conventional allegorical practices which associated the mother figure with the representation of both religious and secular authority.[76] Queen Mary's speech at the Guildhall promoted her as a mother to her people, engaging head on with the propaganda of the Protestant reformers who had preceded her.

Mary's ability to assert her gender to reclaim the mother trope for her own political advantage was initially a propaganda success to which even her Christian name contributed. On his return from exile in 1554, Cardinal Pole publicly and pointedly saluted Mary at Whitehall with the words of the *Ave Maria*, 'Hail Mary full of grace', neatly combining the familiar Catholic trope, the status of the English queen and the notion of idealised motherhood in an emphatic celebration of her religious and political triumph. The metaphor was not lost upon sympathetic spectators, whose accounts often perpetuate the rhetorical focus upon the queen as mother. When Pole arrived in England, Mary's welcome was described by an Italian courtier as that of a 'mother towards her son whom she had long given up as lost'.[77] At this early and optimistic moment in her reign, the queen, on the eve of her marriage, was potentially a biological mother too, something which, cleverly, she obliquely and coyly refers to in her speech at the Guildhall, offering through her physical body the welcome possibility of political and religious stability through an established succession.

With a young, Catholic, queen on the throne the concept of motherhood acquired a new political potential. The powerful allegorical mother-queen exploited by Morison and Bale, locating the mother as a central point of stability to be simultaneously defended and depended upon, was reappropriated by the Catholic faction and shown to be, in a sense, real; personified and exemplified by Mary. The figure offered a coincidence of ideology and actuality which offered unprecedented opportunities for propaganda and which also, according to one biographer, seems to have appealed to Mary's own rather romantic model of her role as queen.[78] This model was perhaps encouraged by her court. For example, in the year of her accession she was presented with what is now known as the *Queen Mary Psalter*, a medieval text notable for its celebration of motherhood, which, as Anne Rudloff Stanton shows, promotes an appreciation of mothers, including both the biblical Bathsheba and the mother of St Thomas Becket, who are shown to 'actively protect and champion their children'.[79] The entangled political and personal value of such a text to the new queen is touchingly evident in the choice of binding. This displays the pomegranate badge which Mary adopted upon accession from her own mother, Katharine.[80] This gift, with its detailed depiction of the life of Becket, whose tomb at Canterbury had been desecrated by her father's reformers, offered the queen a potent symbol which brought together her own personal, and her realm's political, past and future.[81] The mothers it depicted were shown to be active agents of change for the better and the text can be seen as an encouragement to Mary to act, as mother to her people, as a potential mother to heirs, and in celebration of her own mother, to fulfil what is here demonstrated to be part of a divine pattern.[82]

The writer of the interlude *Respublica* – anonymous, but probably Nicholas Udall – which was put on at court during the Christmas celebrations of 1553, took full advantage of the new significance of the allegory of motherhood, and of Mary's personal investment in its value.[83] The play was performed at a politically difficult time, with Mary's betrothal to Phillip causing widespread anxiety, and news of Wyatt's intended rebellion coming through, and it was important to settle nerves at court. The play, despite its self-confessed function as political allegory, displays an awareness of its royal audience which clearly influences the structure of the drama.[84] From the opening prologue – which combines the argument of the play with a thanksgiving that Mary, who figures as 'oure most wise / and most worthie Nemesis' (Prologue, l. 53), has now arrived to put the country right – to the closing celebration of a potentially long and successful reign, the play associates the mother, the nation, the Catholic church and, only a little more subtly than Cardinal Pole, the person of Mary herself. In many ways it reads as a direct response to *Kyng Johan* (though I can find no evidence for a direct link between the two), for it utilises a similar structure which is based upon an allegorical mother-nation figure whose distress at an unnatural rupture in her relationship with her children/subjects can only be resolved by firm religious and political guidance from the reigning monarch. In Bale's play the monarch is present as a character upon the stage, presenting King John as the historical model for a Protestant monarch and though the play was seen by persons of influence, there is no record that Henry actually saw it. It is sufficient that its effect lay in its promotion of a particular blueprint for kingship. In a fascinating extension of this operation of theatre as polemic, however, *Respublica* depends for maximum effect upon the presence, in the audience, of Queen Mary.

Glynn Wickham has noted that both *Respublica* and *Kyng Johan* combine the distinct religious or social preoccupations of previous plays in an adapted moral framework to political effect: 'This blurring of the centre of focus, itself a product of the times, [was] calculated to heighten both tensions and tempers in the mid sixteenth century'.[85] David Bevington has shown how 'the playwright's specific delicate task is to reconcile Mary's courtiers to her program of reform, and at the same time to caution the Queen gently about extremism in punishing or disenfranchising minor offenders', so that the play must necessarily display a great deal of tact if it is to succeed.[86] By making the heroine a mother and so drawing upon the multidetermined nature of such a figure, the dramatist seems to score a political success comparable to Mary's achievement at the Guildhall. The combination of benign authority and nurture that is suggested by ideal motherhood is exploited through a series of appeals to the emotional power that is inevitably invested in the mother figure.

As in Bale's play, the mother's deviant children plot to damage her in a shocking subversion of the ideal relationship between mother and child. Their sinful greed – 'Respublica shall feed the tyll thowe wilt saie hoo' (1.3.300) – acknowledges the ideal mother's capacity for boundless giving but also emphasises her feminine fragility, as an unprotected and thus vulnerable woman.[87] Such cynical exploitation of this – 'Respublica hath enough to fill all oure lappes' (1.3.321) – shows that the mother's lap, seat of plenty, has been appropriated by children whose greed will render her unable to sustain all those to whom she is parent (1.3.321). The distressing implications of this are modified by the balancing assertion of an alternative kind of mother–child relationship in the generic figure, People ('we Ignoram people whom itche doe perzente') who first appears in the play at the beginning of the third act (3.3.648). People clings to 'Rice puddingcake' (3.3.636) until forcibly separated from her: a childlike and vulnerable figure who is, says Bevington, designed to tap into Mary's own understanding of the commons in terms of 'paternalistic (or maternalistic) fondness . . . of endearing concern for a population that is supposed to know its place and respond with affectionate concern to a strong, compassionate leadership'.[88] The deceived Respublica's rejection of the advice that this good child offers – 'we ignoram people beeth not zo blinde' (3.3.665) – and the resulting violent rupture of their relationship by her enemies are made doubly upsetting because of the way in which the image resonates with ideas about the family and, simultaneously, the state. The effect of this upon Mary, who had personally experienced such rejection, and upon a court audience which was well aware of her personal history, and simultaneously conscious of their place in political history, must have been powerful. When the two are reunited in a short scene which focuses exclusively upon their reconciliation, Respublica's language is that of a mother comforting a hurt child in an emotional reconciliation between mother and child and queen and country: 'Shrinke not backe from me, but drawe to me my deare frend. And how ys it with you now? Better than it was?' (5.7.1595). Mary, as Nemesis who will 'reforme thabuses which hithertoo hath been' (Prologue, l. 50), is finally welcomed by Veritas on to the stage to embrace Respublica in a satisfyingly emblematic finale which plays upon Mary's chosen motto, *Filia Temporis Veritas* (5.10.1814). In its assertion of the personal as the political, and the person of the queen as the figure of the nation, the embrace which concludes *Respublica* celebrates the joyful coming together of monarch, nation and true faith as an event full of promise.

John Proctor, writing to promote Mary's reforms, similarly linked the return of Catholicism to national prosperity by reference to an allegorised maternal body:

Come, come lovinge countree men, For the passion of Christ, make haste and come . . . Beholde your lovinge mothers armes are open to receive you, her busom unlashed, her brestes bare to feede you with the sweete milke of trye knowledge, although ye have ungentle delte with her in forsakinge her.[89]

The importance of the queen's body, both material and symbolic, as demonstrated in the union of the physical body of the queen and the figure of Lady Respublica, has its echoes in the legal theory of the constitution that was being developed during the period. The notion that the monarchy in fact constituted two bodies, the 'body natural' and the 'body politic', was developed, says Marie Axton, by primarily Catholic lawyers in response to the problems of succession which bedevilled the English crown.[90]

> The body politic was supposed to be contained within the natural body of the Queen. When lawyers spoke of this body politic they referred to a specific quality: the essence of corporate perpetuity. The Queen's natural body was subject to infancy, infirmity, error and old age; her body politic, created out of a combination of faith, ingenuity and practical expediency, was held to be unerring and immortal.[91]

The theatrical union of Mary and Respublica, then, represents the monarchy at its most complete; the unification of the political and personal, as the body natural of the reigning queen contains the actor representing the body politic within her arms.

The highly affective tenor of much of the polemic of the early years of Mary's reign was crucial to its initial successes, as Mary's Guildhall speech, quoted above, indicates. At court it is evident in entertainments like *Respublica*, but also in ceremonial occasions designed to provoke a public show of powerful personal feeling. Christopher Haigh describes, for example, the celebrations for the return of Cardinal Pole, a few months after *Respublica* was performed: 'on 30th November, at Whitehall, Pole absolved the members of both Houses, "with the whole realm and dominions thereof, from all heresy and schism"; the absolution was received with great emotion, and hard-bitten politicians wept as they called "Amen! Amen!"'[92] In scenes such as these, political and personal aspirations are depicted as unified as all those taking part seek to demonstrate their pleasure at political and religious change through a massed public exhibition of individual emotional experience. In terms of the rhetoric shared and fought over by agents of both Reformation and Counter-Reformation, what has been wickedly divided has now been made whole again.

The transformation of tradition

The potential of the queen's body natural to contain and to express her body politic outside the allegorising world of the drama, though, resided in the possibility of a pregnancy which would secure a Catholic succession. Maternity remained a central concept in the political battles of the 1550s, focused upon the body of the queen herself. Mary was aware that the greatest chance she had for the continuation of her policies was to produce a child and when rumours of a pregnancy began to circulate in September 1554 they seem to have had a 'calming and beneficial effect' in London, according to Loades.[93] The unpopularity of the Spanish marriage was contained, perhaps, by publicity which accounted for Mary's intentions in terms of pure patriotism and religious duty, as in Pole's oration:

> Thou Lorde ... thou knowest that thy servant never lusted after man, never gave her selfe to wanton company, nor made her selfe partaker with them that walke in lightnes: but she consented to take an husbande with thy feare, and not with her luste. Thou knowest that thy servant toke an husband, not for carnall pleasure, but only for the desired love of posteritie, wherein thy name may be blessed for ever and ever. Give therefore unto thy servauntes, a male issue.[94]

A parallel polemical strategy revealed Mary's supposed pregnancy as the result of divine intervention, ensuring an explicit association with the life of the Virgin. John N. King tells of Dr Chadsey's sermon which compared the queen's condition with the Annunciation, 'in a sermon on the *Vulgate* text "*Ne timeas Maria, invenisti enim gratiam apud Deum*" (*Luke* 1–30)' after which 'A *Te Deum* was sung and a solemn procession was made'.[95] The event was similarly celebrated at a secular level in the circulation of ballads which joyfully link the promise of political stability with the return of the Catholic faith, through a focus upon Mary's expectant body: 'Now singe, nowe springe, oure care is exil'd / Oure vertuous Quene is quickened with child'.[96]

By the beginning of the following year, Mary's physical appearance seemed to confirm her expected confinement, and by May there were a number of false reports of the birth of a son, as well as darker rumours concerning a substitution plot. By July it was 'being tacitly acknowledged [that] Mary had been the victim of sickness and her own desires'.[97] Mary thought herself pregnant again at the beginning of 1558, eight months after she had last seen her husband, though her news was greeted with some private derision, and was soon proved to be false.[98] She died in November of that year, acknowledging her mistake in a codicil to her will: 'I then thought myself to be with child [and] did devise and dispose the Imperial Crown . . . unto the heir issues and fruits of my body begotten' before bequeathing the throne to her Protestant younger sister.[99] The skilful propagandist manipulation of the queen's potential maternity which had characterised the optimistic early years of her reign had been impossible to sustain as it became increasingly obvious that the queen could not produce a Catholic heir. Propaganda appears to have been quietly abandoned in favour of a pragmatic approach which characterised a gradual recognition of the Protestant Elizabeth's claim by the court, despite some resistance from Mary herself.[100]

The beginning of Elizabeth's reign, too, demonstrates the development of a propaganda strategy which takes as its central focus the gender of the new monarch, this time characterised by a determined retreat from the celebration of the potential 'natural' maternity offered in the body of the female monarch, which had informed the propaganda of her sister's reign. The association with the Holy Virgin lingered on, enhanced by two fortunate coincidences of date: first that Elizabeth's accession took place two days before the feast of St Elizabeth, the Virgin's mother; secondly that the queen's own birthday fell on the eve of the birth of Jesus's mother.[101] Allison Heisch shows how both occasions developed as festivals as Elizabeth's reign progressed, a fact which, she says: 'disturbed both some Catholics, who felt that the Accession Day and the Queen's birthday were being taken more seriously than the official holy days, and some members of the Protestant right wing, who viewed the ceremonies as idolatrous'. Yet, Heisch points out, 'despite Elizabeth's capacity to enrage both extremes of the Christian spectrum, the celebrations continued and the Queen's birthday became part of the church calendar'.[102]

The fact that, despite misgivings on both sides, these celebrations became absorbed into the Elizabethan calendar without too much trouble indicates a subtle shift in the appropriation of the paradigm of holy motherhood by state propagandists. These celebrations appear to have been essentially civic, playing down the Marian desire to identify the monarch with the Virgin, and promoting the idea of Elizabeth as mother to the state. In other words, Elizabethan propaganda appropriated the iconic qualities of holy maternity that had been deployed by the previous administration, but turned them to political and civic ends. From the Reformation, motherhood had been deployed to signify both civic and spiritual qualities. In Elizabeth's reign there is a shift of emphasis that incorporates the significance of the religious paradigm but redirects it towards a vision of Elizabeth as mother to her subjects, promoting what Heisch characterises as 'a kind of collective maternity'.[103] The implications of such an analogous relationship between family and state were spelled out in the homilies published in 1562, such as 'Against Willful Rebellion': 'for first, the rebels do not only dishonour their Prince, the parent of their country, but also do dishonour and shame their natural parents, if they have any, do shame their kindred and friends, do disinherit and undo forever their children and heirs'.[104]

In a different approach from that of her sister, Elizabeth and her supporters deflected attention from the reproductive potential of the queen's natural body towards a celebration of the body politic of which she was the temporary custodian. Marie Axton has shown how this led to the queen and her parliament negotiating through a complicated game of metaphor. Elizabeth's determined emphasis upon her function as a governor – 'I am but one bodye naturallye considered though by his [God's] permission a bodye politique to governe' – allowed her to divert attention from the sexual and maternal potential of her biology and to subordinate the meanings of her body natural (the provision of a successor) to the promotion of her incarnation as body politic:

> I am already bound to an Husband, which is the kingdome of England, and that may suffice you: and this, (quoth shee) makes mee wonder, that you forget yourselues, the pledge of this alliance which I have made with my kingdome. (And therwithall, stretching out her hand, shee shewed them the Ring with which shee was giuen in marriage, and inaugurated to her kingdome in expresse and solemne terms.) And reproch mee no more (quoth shee) that I haue no children: for euery one of you, and as many as are English, are my Children, and Kinsfolkes.[105]

The political success of this ploy depended upon the queen promoting herself as a mother of her collective subjects as an alternative to marriage, 'And so I assure you all that though after my death you may have many stepdames, yet shall you never have any a more naturall mother than I mean to be unto you all', so that the allegory of the mother is appropriated into a rhetoric which is reproduced at every level of propaganda.[106] Prayers authorised by the church ask that Elizabeth should be a 'true nourisher and nurse': a 'mother', a nurse 'to thine afflicted flock'; a prayer written by Foxe describes her as 'a Queen so calm, so patient, so merciful, more like a natural mother than a princess'.[107]

Helen Hackett shows how this construction of Elizabeth as mother owed much to a Protestant reading of Isaiah 49.23, which she calls 'a key Biblical text for the Protestant reformers'.[108] The verse, in the Geneva Bible, runs 'And kings shalbe thy nourcing fathers, and Quenes shalbe thy nources', and is glossed, notes Hackett, 'meaning that kings shalbe converted to the gospel and bestow their power and autoritie for the preservation of the Church'.[109] This reading offered an alternative, satisfyingly Protestant, point of reference for the mother metaphor, one based, moreover, upon text rather than iconography. Hackett demonstrates the political and religious importance of this alternative, which offered a reconciling motif to absorb both Calvinist pressures and 'to encourage Protestant loyalty to the new Queen'.[110] Further, Hackett shows, it allowed Elizabeth's propagandists to underscore a crucial difference between the new queen and her Catholic sister. John Aylmer, bishop of London, said that Elizabeth 'commeth in ... lyke a mother, and not lyke a stepdam' and followed this with a neat reworking of typology to associate Mary with what he suggests is the nation's fall from grace:

> ... as for thys losse we haue nowe, I doubte not, but as the olde fathers are wonte to saye, that as by a woman came death: so by a woman was broughte fourthe life. In like manner as bi a woman (whether negligence, or misfortune, I wote not) we have taken this wound, so by a nothers diligence and felicitie, we shal have it againe healed.[111]

Any intimation that such an analogue might refer to the maternal potential of the queen's physical person here – and in 1559 Aylmer may have intended such a reading, if obliquely – is undercut at the end of the text, where emphasis is firmly replaced upon the metaphor. Elizabeth is associated with 'Mother England' (in a reassertion of the trope of Morison's Henrician polemic), who claims that 'Out of my wombe ... [came] Ihon Wyclefe, who begate Husse, who begat Luther, who begat Truth'.[112] The difference is that this mother is no longer under attack. What is formulated here is a forward-looking propaganda which celebrates England and Elizabeth in terms of maternal bounty – 'I will fill your busoms and your mouthes, your wyves and your children, with plentie' – maintaining a focus upon the political power of the public monarch and deflecting attention away from the physical potential of the private woman.[113]

Throughout the sixteenth century, then, the dramatised mother figured energetic and sustained political and religious debate, though the emphasis of that debate shifted from Reformation to succession. The mother's dramatic power was enhanced by the encompassing qualities of the mother figure – at a time when 'religious opinion was political opinion' her ability to signify both, and to embody their attendant conflicts and crises, attests to her importance.[114] The mother figure offered dramatists the opportunity to organise and to configure the representation of conflict. By depicting her anguish, redolent of both love and grief, the mother is the focus of an emotional account of political concerns. If, as anthropologists suggest, a function of emotion is to create the right conditions for action, then the dramatised mother proves to be an effective means of provoking in an audience an affective response which is designed to incite an active engagement with the topical matter at the centre of the drama.[115]

Notes

1 Julian of Norwich, *Revelations of Divine Love*, trans. C. Wolters (Harmondsworth: Penguin, 1966), p. 169.
2 *Oxford English Dictionary online* (Oxford: Oxford University Press, 1989), *tradition, n*, para. 6.
3 Alister E. McGrath, *Reformation Thought: An Introduction* (Oxford: Blackwell, 1993), p. 136.
4 Heiko Oberman, in *Masters of the Reformation* (Cambridge: Cambridge University Press, 1991), discusses the ambiguity of tradition during the European Reformation. 'Custom', a concept allied to 'tradition', was interrogated as part of the Reformation agenda. The substitution of new customs (with a play on 'costume') for old is the subject of the Interlude *New Custom*. See J. S. Farmer, ed., *Anonymous plays, comprising Jack Juggler, King Darius, Gammer Gurton's needle, New custom, Trial of treasure* (Guildford: Charles W. Traylen, 1966).
5 Giorgio Agamben distinguishes between a 'traditional system' where 'an absolute identity exists between that act of transmission and the thing transmitted', and 'non-traditional societies' which are characterised by 'the accumulation of culture'. Giorgio Agamben, *The Man Without Content*, trans. Georgia Albert (Stanford: Stanford University Press, 1999), p. 107.

6   Marina Warner, *Alone of All Her Sex: The Myth and Cult of the Virgin Mary* (London: Picador, 1995) and Ann W. Astell, *The Song of Songs in the Middle Ages* (Ithaca: Cornell University Press, 1990), p. 46. For more on this popular trope, see B. H. Smith, *Traditional Images of Charity in Piers Plowman* (Mouton: The Hague, 1996), p. 26.
7   Astell, The Song of Songs in the Middle Ages, pp. 42–6.
8   Marina Warner, *Monuments and Maidens: The Allegory of the Female Form* (London: Picador, 1985), p. 194. C. W. Bynum, in *Jesus as Mother: Studies in the Spirituality of the Higher Middle Ages* (Berkeley: University of California Press, 1982), discusses thirteenth-century women mystics' development of the trope in her final chapter.
9   A. C. Cawley, ed., *Everyman and Medieval Miracle Plays* (London: Dent, 1990), pp. 35–49. The actors 'make signs of working with different tools' together and characters boast about their status in Chester, 'An axe I have, by my crown / As sharp as any in this town'.
10 Astell, *The Song of Songs in the Middle Ages*, p. 46.
11 Peter Happé, ed., *English Mystery Plays* (Harmondsworth: Penguin, 1985), p. 323, line 126. See also Matthew J. Kinservik, 'The Struggle over Mary's Body: Theological and Dramatic Resolution in the N-Town Assumption Play', *Journal of English and Germanic Philology* 95 (1996), 190–203 on Mary as '*mater mediatrix*, an active agent of the new law', p. 195.
12 In the A and B texts of the poem, her first word to Will (Passus I, l. 5) is 'Sone'. See A. V. C. Schmidt, ed., *William Langland: The Vision of Piers Plowman* (London: Dent, 1978) and Derek Pearsall, ed., *William Langland: Piers Plowman, The C Text* (Exeter: University of Exeter Press), 1994. Robertson and Huppé discuss this scene as a homiletic exposition of the apocalypse combining Christ, the church and the bride of the lamb. Robertson and Huppé, *Piers Plowman and the Scriptural Tradition* (New York: Octagon, 1969), p. 37 and M. Teresa Tavormina, *Kindly Similitude: Marriage and Family in Piers Plowman* (Cambridge: D. S. Brewer, 1995), p. 163. Anneke B. Mulder-Bakker sees the female teacher working as an exemplar. Anneke B. Mulder-Bakker, 'The Metamorphosis of Women: Transmission of Knowledge and the Problem of Gender', *Gender and History* 12:3 (2000).
13 This attack is clear in Passus II with the introduction of the antitype Lady Meed. Both editors discuss Langland's use of the convention (Schmidt, p. xxv, Pearsall, p. 42).
14 Cawley, *Everyman*, p. 108, l. 748.
15 Cawley, *Everyman*, esp. p. 122, ll. 350–60.
16 Happé, ed., *English Mystery Plays*, pp. 230–43.
17 Happé, ed., *English Mystery Plays*, p. 239, st. 39.
18 Happé, ed., *English Mystery Plays*, p. 239, st. 37.
19 Happé, ed., *English Mystery Plays*, p. 240, st. 40–1. Also see R. T. Davies, *The Corpus Christi Plays of the Middle Ages* (London: Faber, 1972), pp. 167–8.

The transformation of tradition 45

20 See Cawley, *Everyman*, pp. 167–9.
21 Joseph is silent in such representations, so that there is an exclusive focus upon the mother and child that engages with an iconographic tradition depicting the nursing of Christ. The familiar icon of the *Madonna lactans* was in a sense double-edged: it celebrated the power of the Father and the redundance of the man. See Davies, *The Corpus Christi Plays of the Middle Ages*, p. 166.
22 Warner, *Monuments and Maidens*, p. 202.
23 See Sarah Kay, 'Women's Body of Knowledge: Epistemology and Misogyny in the *Romance of the Rose*', in *Framing Medieval Bodies*, eds Sarah Kay and Miri Rubin (Manchester: Manchester University Press, 1994), pp. 211–35; p. 230.
24 Caroline Bynum, *Jesus as Mother: Studies in the Spirituality of the Higher Middle Ages* (Berkeley: University of California Press, 1982), pp. 129–30. Bynum shows that the link between Christ and maternity was complicated from the eleventh century by an 'increasing preference for analogies taken from human relationships'. She also describes 'a more accepting reaction to all natural things, including the physical body'.
25 Bynum, *Jesus as Mother*, pp. 129–30.
26 B. H. Smith describes the incarnation as a paradox: 'an event resulting in both the virgin-mother and the god-man' that informed an iconographic tradition which envisioned Christ the nurse androgynously as a bridegroom with breasts. See Bynum, *Jesus as Mother*, p. 115 and Smith, *Traditional Images of Charity in Piers Plowman*, p. 33.
27 St Anselm quoted from Bynum, *Jesus as Mother*, pp. 113–14. Bernard of Clairvaux describes Christ the nurse and, indeed, himself as Abbot, in terms of unfailing love and nurture (pp. 115–22).
28 Julian of Norwich, *Revelations of Divine Love*, ch. 60, p. 169. Bynum quotes St Anselm's description of Jesus 'as a hen gathering her chicks under her wing' and shows how he 'suggests that mother Jesus revives the soul at her breast'. Bynum, *Jesus as Mother*, p. 113. See the introduction to *Revelations of Divine Love*, p. 34, for the influence of Anselm and Bernard upon Julian of Norwich.
29 Julian of Norwich, *Revelations of Divine Love*, ch. 60, p. 171.
30 Chaucer wittily incorporated this into his 'Prologue to the Wife of Bath's Tale', where her spirited attack upon clerical antifeminism – 'no womman of no clerk is preysed' – is part of her vigorous promotion of femininity in a spiritually satisfying life. Geoffrey Chaucer, *Canterbury Tales*, ed. A. C. Cawley (London: Dent, 1978), 'The Wife of Bath's Prologue', p. 176, l. 706.
31 Margery Kempe, *The Book of Margery Kempe*, trans. B. A. Windeatt (Harmondsworth: Penguin, 1985), p. 52.
32 Sarah Beckwith, *Christ's Body: Identity, Culture and Society in Late Medieval Writings* (London: Routledge, 1993), pp. 83–8.
33 Kempe, *The Book of Margery Kempe*, pp. 73 and 84.

34 Michel Foucault, *The History of Sexuality* (Harmondsworth: Penguin, 1976), pp. 61–3.
35 Kempe, *The Book of Margery Kempe*, ch. 81, p. 236. Gail McMurray Gibson, *The Theatre of Devotion: East Anglian Drama and Society in the Late Middle Ages* (Chicago: University of Chicago Press, 1989), p. 51.
36 Gibson, *The Theatre of Devotion*, p. 51. Also see Kempe, *The Book of Margery Kempe*, ch. 30, p. 113.
37 Gibson, *The Theatre of Devotion*, pp. 63 and 105. Gibson discovers this in the Digby 'Killing of the Children' where suffering is juxtaposed with 'slapstick comedy', suggesting that the mothers in the play operate as 'a defining ritual that reveals the local, social "play" to be an integral part of salvation history' (p. 44).
38 Marion Jones, 'Early Moral Plays and the Earliest Secular Drama', in *The Revels History of Drama in English*, vol. I, ed. Lois Potter (London: Methuen, 1983), p. 215.
39 Jones, 'Early Moral Plays', p. 215.
40 Clifford Davidson discusses the closeness of the sexual and the spiritual in this allegory: 'the secular equivalent of divine love and attraction is human arousal to sexual stimulation'. See Clifford Davidson, *Visualising the Moral Life* (New York: AMS Press, 1989), p. 90. Also Peter Happé, *English Drama before Shakespeare* (London: Longman, 1999), p. 83.
41 Pamela King draws attention to the play's debt to St Augustine's *De Trinitate*, which refers to John 1:4, 'The word became flesh and dwelt among us'. See Pamela M. King, 'Morality Plays', in Richard Beadle, ed., *The Cambridge Companion to Medieval English Theatre* (Cambridge: Cambridge University Press, 1994), p. 252.
42 Lois Potter, 'The Plays and Playwrights', in Lois Potter, ed., *The Revels History of Drama in English*, vol. 2, 1500–1570 (London: Methuen, 1980), p. 149. Also W. A. Davenport, *Fifteenth-century English Drama* (Cambridge: D. S. Brewer, 1984), pp. 79–80.
43 Davidson, *Visualising the Moral Life*, p. 105. Darryll Grantley discusses the correspondence between the Digby *Mary Magdelane* and plays of the assumption of the Virgin and the likely common geographical origin of both plays. Darryll Grantley, 'Saints Plays', in Beadle, ed., *The Cambridge Companion to Medieval English Theatre*, p. 280.
44 Bevington, *From Mankind to Marlowe*, pp. 124–7.
45 Happé, *English Drama*, p. 85.
46 Alan H. Nelson, ed., *The Plays of Henry Medwall* (Cambridge: D. S. Brewer, 1980).
47 Farnham links this to St Thomas Aquinas's analysis of the link between God and nature in creating humanity. See W. Farnham, *The Medieval Heritage of Elizabethan Tragedy* (Oxford: Basil Blackwell, 1970), p. 199. For Peter Happé, the Catholicism in the play makes it a likely product of 'the political/religious controversy surrounding Henry VIII's divorce'. Happé, *English Drama*, p. 111.

48 Warner, *Monuments and Maidens*, p. 318.
49 Seymour Baker House, 'Literature, Drama and Politics', in *The Reign of Henry VIII: Politics, Policy and Piety*, ed. Diarmaid MacCulloch (London: Macmillan, 1995), p. 181. Baker House sees this as 'an appeal to the non-literate majority of the population', p. 186.
50 Gail McMurray Gibson, *The Theatre of Devotion: East Anglian Drama and Society in the Late Middle Ages* (Chicago: University of Chicago Press, 1989), pp. 166–8. Peter Happé speculates that the Townley version was torn from the original manuscript 'as an act of Reformation zeal'. Happé, *English Mystery Plays*, p. 625. Halliwell, who edited the N-town plays in the nineteenth century, suggests that a performance of the N-town 'Death, Funeral, Assumption and Coronation of the Virgin' sparked a riot in the Midlands at the time of Henry's rejection of Queen Katharine of Aragon, though subsequent scholarship has made this argument less persuasive. See J. O. Halliwell, ed., *Ludus Coventriea: a collection of Mysteries, formerly represented at Coventry on the feast of Corpus Christi* (London: The Shakespeare Society, 1841), p. 385.
51 Kinservik, 'The Struggle over Mary's Body', p. 194.
52 Stephen Spector, ed., *The N-Town Play*, vols 1 and 2, Early English Texts Society (Oxford: Oxford University Press, 1991), vol. 1 p. 389, l. 71. Spector sees the play as 'an interpolation – not mentioned in the Proclamation and different in prosody, style and orthography', vol. 2, p. 527.
53 Spector, *The N-Town Play*, vol. 2, p. 390, l. 81. Also Halliwell, *Ludus Coventriea*, p. 385.
54 Biblical allegory was popular with Katharine's sympathisers. See Bevington's discussion of *Godly Queen Hester*. David Bevington, *Tudor Drama and Politics* (Cambridge: Harvard University Press, 1968), pp. 88–94.
55 Kinservik discusses 'The Assumption' as 'the logical end of historical time in the salvation story', 'The Struggle over Mary's Body', p. 190. See H. C. Gardiner, *Mysteries' End: An Investigation into the Last Days of the Medieval Religious Stage* (Hamden, CT: Archon Books, 1967), p. 54, and Bevington, *Tudor Drama and Politics*, p. 95.
56 Jacqueline A. Vanhoutte, 'Engendering England: The Restructuring of Allegiance in the Writings of Richard Morison and John Bale', in *Renaissance and Reformation* 20:1 (1996), 49–77.
57 Vanhoutte, 'Engendering England', p. 57. Vanhoutte quotes Morison: 'Nature teacheth brute beasts to love them that gave them life, that nourished them'.
58 Christopher Haigh, English Reformations: Religion, Politics and Society under the Tudors (Oxford: Clarendon Press, 1993), p. 222.
59 This, alongside the closely related concept of mother church, was appropriated by English reformers and enjoined to the Protestant cause by John Foxe, who used the figure in his later play *Christus*

Triumphans (pub. 1556). Foxe depicts the persecution of his heroine, Ecclesia, by the Roman emperors and later by the pope. She triumphs as the Bride of Christ, in an appropriation of the Catholic trope. In Foxe's opening scene, two maternal archetypes, Eve and the Virgin Mary, lament together over their lost children. See Lois Potter, ed., *The Revels History in Drama in English*, vol. 2, p. 183.

60 Bevington, *Tudor Drama and Politics*, p. 98, suggests this. All references to *Kyng Johan* are taken from Peter Happé, ed., *The Complete Plays of John Bale*, vol. 1 (Cambridge: D. S. Brewer, 1985).

61 Bale's interest in the old structures of popular religious drama is evident in his Protestant play cycle, *God's Promises*, a performance of which he organised 'to the small contentacion of the Prestes and other Papistes' in the audience. Quoted in E. K. Chambers, *The Medieaval Stage* (London: Oxford University Press, 1903), vol. 2, p. 374. See G. Wickham, *Early English Stages*, vol. 2, 1576–1600, part 1 (London: Routledge, 1963), p. 36, for Bale's interest in miracle plays.

62 See Vanhoutte, *Engendering England*, p. 51. By associating the Catholic church with bestiality Bale reworks the conventions of anti-Catholic propaganda that had entered eastern England since the start of the Reformation. Bale had been a Carmelite monk in East Anglia, and would know the polemic, which is scatological and anticlerical. It was a technique he embraced with enthusiasm, earning the nickname 'Bilious Bale' from his detractors.

63 *Kyng Johan*, p. 32, l. 109.

64 See Vanhoutte, *Engendering England*, p. 55.

65 See D. Andrew Penny, 'Family Matters and Foxe's Acts and Monuments', *Historical Journal* 39:3 (1996), 602–3.

66 Penny, 'Family Matters', p. 603.

67 Foxe is quoted by John R. Knott, in 'John Foxe and the Joy of Suffering: Characterising Protestant Martyrs and their Experience in *Acts and Monuments*', *Sixteenth Century Journal* 27:3 (1996), 730. The need for mastery of the flesh by the spirit, a staple of Catholic sermons dramatised in the moral play *Mankynd*, was thus appropriated and reworked by Protestant polemicists.

68 *Kyng Johan*, p. 31, l. 42. This reworks the convention of non-recognition deployed by Langland, whose narrator cannot recognise Lady Holy Church when she first approaches him. Holy Church reprimands Will, 'thou oughtest me to know'. See the C text, ed. Pearsall, p. 45.

69 *Kyng Johan*, p. 31, ll. 68–70.

70 The affective tenor of such discourse remained at the heart of state propaganda during Elizabeth's reign, in such homilies as *Against Wilful Rebellion*, which makes an emotional plea for the loyalty of the subject to a loving monarch closely allied to loyalty to God (*Against Wilful Rebellion*, Church of England, 1562, p. 616): 'let us as the children of obedience, fear the dreadful execution of God and live in quiet obedience to be the children of everlasting salvation'. This assumes

that the laws of God and the state are the same. Bale reworked his play, developing this theme, in Elizabeth's reign.
71 *Kyng Johan*, p. 71, ll. 1610–11.
72 Vanhoutte, *Engendering England*, p. 55, quoting Morison, *A Lamentation in Which is Showed what Ruin and Destruction Cometh of Seditious Rebellion* (1536) from David Sindler Berkowitz, *Humanist Scholarship and Public Order: Two Tracts Against the Pilgrimage of Grace by Sir Richard Morison* (Washington: Folger Shakespeare Library, 1984), p. 88.
73 Vanhoutte, *Engendering England*, p. 50.
74 Quoted in J. G. Ridley, *The Life and Times of Mary Tudor* (London: Weidenfeld and Nicholson, 1973), p. 146. Versions of Mary's oration were also recorded by Henry Machyn, *The Diary of Henry Machyn of London 1550 to 1563*, ed. John Gough Nichols (London: Camden Society, 1848), p. 53, and by the Catholic propagandist (and according to Robert Tittler, a government propagandist) Procter, in his 'History of Wyatt's Rebellion'. See Robert Tittler, *The Reign of Mary I* (London: Longman, 1983), p. 19.
75 The importance of Mary's marriage to her realm was developed in the rhetoric deployed to counter the rebellion. Ann Weikel says that an earlier message had been sent to Wyatt insisting that 'the Queen would hear his petition if he believed that the marriage implied a divorce between her and her first Spouse: the Crown of England'. Ann Weikel, 'The Marian Council Revisited', in *The Mid-Tudor Polity c.1540–1560*, eds J. Loach and R. Tittler (London: Macmillan, 1980), p. 62.
76 David Loades, *The Reign of Mary Tudor* (London: Longman, 1991), p. 214. Weikel, 'The Marian Council Revisited', suggests that 'the court prevailed upon the Queen to make her famous speech'. Weikel cites the *Calender of State Papers, Spanish, xi–xii*, ed. Royal Tyler (London, 1916).
77 J. G. Ridley, *The Life and Times of Mary Tudor*, pp. 161–2. W. Schenk tells how, on hearing of Mary's accession to the throne, Pole had written to tell her that she 'could now like the Blessed Virgin, sing the *Magnificat*, and particularly the verse: "He has put down the mighty from their seat and has exalted the humble"'. W. Schenk, *Reginald Pole: Cardinal of England* (London: Longman, 1950), p. 124.
78 Bevington, *Tudor Drama and Politics*, p. 119. Loades, *The Reign of Mary Tudor*, p. 336, discusses this, also David Loades, *Mary Tudor: A Life* (Oxford: Basil Blackwell, 1989), p. 327.
79 Anne Rudloff Stanton, 'From Eve to Bathsheba and Beyond: Motherhood in the *Queen Mary Psalter*', in *Women and the Book: Assessing the Visual Evidence*, eds Lesley Smith and Jane H. M. Taylor, (Toronto: University of Toronto Press, 1996), p. 172.
80 John N. King, *Tudor Royal Iconography* (Princeton: Princeton University Press, 1989), p. 185. King notes that the book was a personal possession of the queen.

81 Stanton, 'From Eve to Bathsheba and Beyond', p. 184. Becket's life is illustrated in twenty-two scenes, including his birth. Stanton shows that the life of Becket's mother is typologically linked to the Old Testament story of Ruth.
82 Stanton, 'From Eve to Bathsheba and Beyond', p. 185. Stanton suggests this psalter was originally a gift to Isabella, wife of Edward II, to encourage her 'drastic action in the interests of her son'. 'From Eve to Bathsheba and Beyond', p. 186.
83 Udall's authorship is thought likely by Bevington, Boas and others. Boas posits a personal connection between Udall and Mary, showing that the writer delivered the Christmas revels in 1554. David Bevington, *From Mankynd to Marlowe* (Cambridge, MA: Harvard University Press, 1962), pp. 27–8, and F. S. Boas, *An Introduction to Tudor Drama* (Oxford: Clarendon Press, 1933), p. 27.
84 The play is listed in Chambers, *Medieval Stage*, p. 460 as a sixteenth-century manuscript entitled 'A Merye enterlude entitled *Respublica*, made in the year of our Lorde, 1553'. There are two twentieth-century editions. One is that of J. S. Farmer for the Early English Drama Society, originally produced in 1907, prefaced 'A Drama of Real Life in the Early Days of Queen Mary' and reprinted in *Recently Recovered 'Lost' Tudor Plays, With Some Others* (Guildford: Charles Traylen, 1966). The edition used for this discussion is *Respublica*, ed. W. W. Greg (London: Early English Texts Society, 1952). Quotation from lines 18–22.
85 Wickham, *Shakespeare's Dramatic Heritage: Collected Studies in Mediaeval, Tudor and Shakespearean Drama* (London: Routledge and Kegan Paul, 1969), p. 36.
86 Bevington, *Tudor Drama and Politics*, p. 115.
87 This emphasis upon her vulnerability echoes the martyrologists, who stress the economic, social and spiritual danger that afflicted the families of those executed.
88 Bevington, *Tudor Drama and Politics*, p.119.
89 King, *Tudor Royal Iconography*, p. 218.
90 Marie Axton, *The Queen's Two Bodies: Drama and the Elizabethan Succession* (London: Royal Historical Society, 1977), p. 17.
91 Axton, *The Queen's Two Bodies*, p. 12.
92 Haigh, *English Reformations*, p. 222.
93 Loades, *The Reign of Mary Tudor*, p. 165.
94 Cardinal Pole, as rendered by Foxe, quoted in Judith M. Richards, '"To Promote a Woman to Beare Rule": Talking of queens in Mid-Tudor England', *Sixteenth Century Journal* 28 (1997), 114.
95 King, *Tudor Royal Iconography*, p. 218.
96 Loades, *The Reign of Mary Tudor*, p. 164. Loades suggests not all Mary's subjects welcomed the news. See pp. 164–5.
97 Loades, *The Reign of Mary Tudor*, pp. 165–6.
98 Loades, *The Reign of Mary Tudor*, p. 332.

99 Tittler, *The Reign of Mary I*, p. 19.
100 This adjustment of propaganda is explored by Marcia Lee Metzger, in 'Controversy and "Correctness": English Chronicles and the Chroniclers, 1553–1568', in *Sixteenth Century Journal* 27 (1996), 437–51.
101 The definitive study of Elizabeth's association with the Virgin is Helen Hackett, *Virgin Mother, Maiden Queen: Elizabeth I and the Cult of the Virgin Mary* (London: Macmillan, 1995).
102 Allison Heisch, 'Queen Elizabeth and the Persistence of Patriarchy', *Feminist Review* 4 (1980), 46.
103 Heisch, 'Queen Elizabeth and the Persistence of Patriarchy', p. 50.
104 *Church of England Homilies* (London: Society for Promoting Christian Knowledge, 1908), p. 611.
105 Both quoted in Axton, *The Queen's Two Bodies*, pp. 38 and 39.
106 J. E. Neale, *Elizabeth I and her Parliaments 1559–1601*, vol 1 (London: J. Cape, 1953), p. 109.
107 From the Church of England collection, *Private Prayers put forth by Authority during the Time of Queen Elizabeth* (Cambridge: Cambridge University Press, 1851), pp. 461 and 480.
108 Hackett, *Virgin Mother, Maiden Queen*, p. 4.
109 Hackett, *Virgin Mother, Maiden Queen*, p. 4.
110 Hackett, *Virgin Mother, Maiden Queen*, pp. 49–50.
111 From Aylmer's reply to Knox, *An Harborowe for faithfull and trewe subiecte*, quoted in Hackett, *Virgin Mother, Maiden Queen*, p. 50.
112 Aylmer, quoted by Hackett, *Virgin Mother, Maiden Queen*, p. 51.
113 Aylmer, quoted in Hackett, *Virgin Mother, Maiden Queen*, p. 51. This distinction, while convenient for Elizabeth, was from Calvinist readings of Isaiah 49.23 that distinguish, says Hackett, between the 'nursing queen and the private woman'. See Hackett, *Virgin Mother, Maiden Queen*, p. 40.
114 Charlotte Kohler, quoted by Betty Travitsky in *The Paradise of Women: Writings by Englishwomen of the Renaissance* (New York: Columbia University Press, 1989), p. 169.
115 Anthropological studies link the experience of emotion with the incentive to action. See Paul Heelas, 'Emotion Talk across Cultures' in Rom Harré and W. Gerrod Parrott, eds, *The Emotions: Social, Cultural and Biological Dimensions* (London: Sage, 1996), pp. 171–99. Heelas cites Lutz: 'emotions are culturally constructed concepts which point to clusters of situations typically calling for some kind of action'.

2

Motherhood and the classical tradition

Seing my fleshe and bloude,
Against itselfe[1]
Gascoigne, *Jocasta*

University plays and politics

In the second half of the sixteenth century, a renewed interest in classical drama stimulated the development of new options for dramatising motherhood. Figures such as Medea, Agave and Jocasta offered novel, if alarming, models for mothers in dramatic narratives and extended the range of potential meanings that the mother figure could offer. This range was well suited to the political drama that developed as a response to anxieties about the Elizabethan succession. Classical narratives, which so often detailed the collapse of royal families and the wreck of dynasties, offered useful models for persuading the queen of the need for a secure future.

The successful accommodation of pagan myth within the framework of mainstream Christian culture had, of course, been facilitated over centuries.[2] But subjects considered suitable for dramatisation became increasingly diverse as the grammar schools taught rhetoric through the study of ancient drama, and a variety of potential source materials became available as cheap printing technologies advanced.[3] In 1581 a collected works of Seneca in translation was published, reflecting the interest in ancient drama which was already evident from the many performances in the universities and making classical narratives available to a wider readership, including those with 'small Latin and less Greek'.[4] Writing in the Senecan mode, so highly commended by critics such as Philip Sidney, meant not only imitating Latin rhetoric – 'stately speeches and well-sounding phrases, climbing to the height of

Seneca's style' – but also using drama for purposes of pleasurable moral instruction.⁵ Commentators like Sidney appreciated what they perceived to be the didacticism and morality inscribed in the narrative of these pagan plays that seemed to lend themselves, by a familiar pattern of exegesis, to an exposition of contemporary political preoccupations.⁶

Any direct attempt by Elizabeth's parliament to cut through her carefully constructed metaphor of the body politic and place the dynastic potential of her body natural on the agenda was doomed to fail. In 1563 Lord Rich wrote to the queen of his hope for 'heirs of your most royal body' and was not answered until the closing of parliament when Elizabeth offered to address the issues of marriage and succession – 'of which two', she said, 'I think best the last to be touched, and of the other a silent thought may serve'.⁷ It is unsurprising, therefore, that those who believed that a peaceful succession depended upon the queen producing children turned to marginally less direct ways of putting pressure upon her. As Marie Axton has shown, the inns of court and to a lesser extent the universities were the settings for a number of dramatic presentations in the earlier part of Elizabeth's reign, which obliquely pressed the queen to consider the implications for the nation of her refusal to fulfil the maternal potential of her body natural.⁸ Significantly, these are plays in which the narrative is classical in its references and constructed around a central mother who figures the controversy. These 'succession plays', informed by the amateur status, the classical training and interests of their authors, owe much in their construction to the moral interlude. *Respublica* and *Kyng Johan*, discussed in the previous chapter, took the morality play as their model, adapting a genre that was traditionally utilised as a vehicle of religious and moral instruction and which routinely used allegory as a means of fulfilling those aims. Classical plays were understood to perform a similar allegorising function and were appropriately glossed, in order to accommodate the dynamics of pagan narratives within the conventions of Christian culture.

Sackville and Norton first presented *Gorboduc* at the inns of court at Christmas 1561 in a performance which seems to have been well received.⁹ The play was taken to court by Lord Robert Dudley as part of a series of entertainments which pressed the queen to marry, and drew attention to the earl's own suit to the queen. *Gorboduc* continues the theme, describing the disastrous consequences of an uncertain succession. The unsubtle implications of the play were apparently acknowledged by Elizabeth at a Whitehall performance.[10] Writing in the same spirit of political didacticism as the authors of *Kyng Johan* and *Respublica*, the playwrights, selected their subject from chronicled English history but re-wrote it as classical tragedy, so that the analogues available in ancient accounts, such as that of Thebes, were made obvious.

Gorboduc represents an attempt to structure the matter of the political morality play into what was perceived as classical form. This is notable in the representation of the protagonist's consort, the infanticidal queen, Videna, which is influenced by the play's evident debt to Seneca's *Medea*. This was a play that Elizabethans tended to gloss as political allegory, reading Jason's duplicity and subsequent fall as 'a mirrour' for princes. Translators such as Richard Studeley ensured that their versions of the text made clear the political implications of the tale, explicitly making changes in order to do so. In the final Act of Studeley's 1566 translation, for example, the Chorus 'altered by Translator' spells out the import of the play: 'All things are topsy turvy turnde, / and wasted cleane to nought. / To passing great calamity / our Kingdome State is brought' (5.1.1–4).[11]

Medea, Jason's wife and the mother and murderess of his children, is, of course, the agent of that fall, which is described above by reference to the vernacular and medieval polemical notion of the apocalyptic 'world turned upside down'. Seneca's play was read, therefore, in terms of an understanding of Medea's activities as the consequence of political uncertainty. The mother becomes the agent of chaos, as in other classical plays which depicted similarly frightening versions of the mother that were glossed as the cause of political and personal disorder. Such dramatic narratives offered Elizabethan writers a means by which the troubled, loving, moral national mother of *Respublica* and *king Johan* articulated with a fearful version of the mother as an agent and symptom of national chaos and, indeed, formalised the means by which those connections could be expressed. The constraints of their allegorical roles had rendered Widowe Englande and Respublica essentially passive figures whose dramatic purpose was one of response to the activities of other characters. The grief-induced passion that provoked Medea and Clytemnestra to act may have been read as primarily a reaction to the political activities of their men, but in narrative terms it precipitated these mothers into action, offering new dramatic possibilities for the early modern representation of the mother in drama.

Videna's role is prophetic and choric; from the start she is 'tormented', her condition associated visually and rhetorically with the constitutional instability which she describes and the disruption which she prophesies at the start of the play. Her foresight is clearly as significant politically to the Elizabethan audience as it is pertinent to the world of the play, foreseeing 'Jove's just judgement and deserved wrath [and] cruel and reproachful death' for those who 'transpose the course of governance'. The ultimate consequence is the end of dynasty because Jove will 'root their names and kindreds from the earth' (1.1.59–67).

Representing classical narratives with reference to exegetical practices which were alien to the culture in which the plays were originally produced creates tensions in *Gorboduc* that are associated with subordinating traditional morality matter, informed by a contemporary Christian ethic and typology, to the strictures of what was perceived as classical form. Ideas that succeed in debate can work against the dynamic of the drama in performance. Seneca's *Medea* (like his *Phaedra*) is, classically, constructed out of a series of rhetorical exchanges between the protagonist and her nurse or the protagonist and her husband. *Gorboduc* seeks, in imitation, to structure the play likewise. But Videna, the 'jealous' and wretched mother, is a chaotic, destabilising presence whose function is more emblematic than narrative.[12] Even the son whom she champions makes clear the limitations of her role when he demands, 'Madam, leave care and careful plaint for me' (1.1.40) When she appears, she is pathetic but also vicious: a mix of traditional type and antitype that suggests that the adaptation of the classical mother figure in this play is always in tension with a desire to retain the dynamics of moral drama.

The tensions associated with this synthesis are evident in the fourth act of the play. This opens ominously with a dumb show consisting of a procession of furies driving mythical figures who killed their children, providing a classical – and Italianate – context for Videna's ensuing lament for her murdered favourite son and her resolution to kill his brother in revenge. Wolfgang Clemen has shown how much her speech is devised with reference to a Renaissance reading of classical rhetoric. However, it exhibits an equal debt to the allegorical tradition that utilised a rupture of the relationship between mother and child to figure the breakdown of relations within the state.[13] Videna repudiates her child by reference to the convention used by Bale in *Kyng Johan*, where a mother depicts a deviant child as a monster of unnatural provenance:

> Never, O wretch, this womb conceived thee,
> Nor never bore I painful throes for thee.
> Changeling to me thou art, and not my child,
> Nor to no wight that spark of pity knew.
> Ruthless, unkind, monster of nature's work,
> Thou never sucked the milk of woman's breast
> But from thy birth, the cruel tiger's teats
> Have nursed thee; nor yet of flesh and blood
> Formed is thy heart, but of hard iron wrought
> And wild and desert woods bore thee to life. (4.1.71–80)

Sackville and Norton drew upon familiar typology to link the mother's body, the family and the state. Faced with warring children, Videna is forced to repudiate one of them and in doing so cuts herself loose from the ties that bind a mother into the patriarchal structures of family and state that usually contain her. The effect is chilling. Without the typological structure of a moral play, Videna becomes an isolated symbol, redolent of chaos. The dramatists emphasise the connection in the fifth act, where ancient Britain is addressed (in part to the Elizabethan audience) as 'the Mother of ye all' (5.2.135) and the audience is exhorted to 'withhold / The slaying knife from your own mother's throat' (5.2.150–1) by securing a lasting peace through an established succession. Videna's isolation and madness prefigure an apocalyptic future that will be realised if 'kings will not consent, / To grave advice, but follow willful will' (5.2.234–5). There is a sense (reinforced by the references to a classical 'past') that the story of Gorboduc and his family has macrocosmic implications, and certainly the extended fantasy of destruction that closes the play sounds like the medieval end of the world:

> Lo, guiltless blood shall thus everywhere be shed:
> Thus shall the wasted soil yield forth no fruit
> But derth and famine shall possess the Land.
> The Towns shall be consumed and burnt with fire (5.2.224–7)

Such an experiment with dramatic form is perhaps to be expected in a play which advertises both its didactic, nationalistic intention and its aspirations as a neoclassical piece. Evidently well received by those contemporaries who appreciated the dramatists' intentions, *Gorboduc*'s success probably lay in approval of its rhetoric by an audience already confident with a 'glossed' version of the classical drama, which was appreciated as a means of addressing contemporary preoccupations. In such a context it presumably seemed entirely appropriate that, despite her formal presentation as a classical figure, Queen Videna displays qualities which owed much to the traditions of native English drama and the Christian narratives from which it drew meaning.

On a similar theme but retelling a classical tale, *Jocasta* was written by George Gascoigne and his Gray's Inn colleague Francis Kinwelmarshe for presentation at court in 1566. The dramatists advertised the play as 'A Tragedie written in Greeke by Euripides, translated and digested into Acte', though in fact the play was closely based on an Italian version of Euripides's *Phoenissae* by Ludovico Dolce which already contained elaborations of and additions to the original.[14] Gascoigne also freely added to and adapted his source to emphasise the play's engagement with contemporary political concerns. Euripides may have been a canny choice for a royal show, given that Elizabeth's former tutor, Roger Ascham, believed that the Greek dramatists were superior to 'our Seneca' in tragedies, offering 'the goodliest argument of all . . . for the vse either of a learned preacher, or a civill Ientleman', and citing an ideal combination of 'the trewe touch of Aristotles precepts and Euripides examples'.[15]

The political point of the new play is reinforced by a dumb show preceding the 'argument' of each act, and further enhanced, at least for the reader, by the addition of marginal glosses alongside some of the lines. These frequently rephrase certain verses in terms of the sort of sententious remark that the Elizabethans seem to have enjoyed discovering in classical writing, but they also seek to 'explain' the text, offering an interpretation of the Greek original which is compatible with the preoccupations of early modern Christian culture and with the requirements of the conventional dramatic model. In this way, Gascoigne and Kinwelmarshe confirm that their play addresses the consequences of an unseemly overreaching for power (a familiar Elizabethan concern) in such 'glosses' as 'Ambition doth destroye al: equalytie doth maynteyne al things' in the second act, or 'A mirrour for Magistrates' alongside Oedipus's valedictory speech in the fifth.[16] The point is made dramatically (for such addenda would not be immediately available to an audience) by following Dolce in making the mother Jocasta the eponymous heroine of the piece, for like Videna, Jocasta is cast in terms of the grieving mother familiar from political moral plays but adapted to figure the tragedy of incest and fraternal war.[17]

Gascoigne and Kinwelmarshe develop a rhetoric that shifts from a focus upon the mother as an emblem of the state towards a reading of the mother as a material embodiment of the nation, her physical person a microcosmic version of the nation that is threatened. This is clear in the way that Jocasta associates herself, 'a queene but barely bearing name', with Thebes:

> Seyng this towne, seing my fleshe and bloude,
> Against itselfe to Levie threatning armes,
> (Whereof to talke my heart it renders in twaine) (1.1.7–10)

For Gascoigne's Jocasta the experience of watching her family divided against itself is also the literal experience of heartbreak. She figures the divided nation, and its analogue the divided family, through the emblem of her broken body, her heart cleft in two. Marie Axton has shown that despite the play's pretensions as a classical piece, 'Jocasta often speaks as the morality figure Lady Respublica' though her representation goes further.[18] Jocasta herself draws attention to her dual function as a narrator of brutal conflict 'whereof to talke', establishing her function as both an allegory of state and its material signifier: the incarnation of the strife she describes. Her broken heart is an emblem suggestive of a bittersweet mix of mother's love and mother's pain.

This function of the mother's suffering physical body as an expression of conflict that demands an emotional response is usefully read alongside the work of sociologists who argue for emotions 'as existentially *embodied* modes of being which involve an *active* engagement with the world and an intimate engagement with both culture and self'[original italics].[19] Gillian Bendelow and Simon J. Williams argue that the 'embodiment' of emotion, in their terms, does not refer only to material or conceptual representations of the body. Rather, they suggest that it 'lies ambiguously . . . across a series of fundamental dualisms such as mind/body; nature/ culture; public private'. Taking this analysis to a study of *Jocasta* allows a fuller appreciation of her dual function in the play, offering a reformulation of its subject in terms of personal suffering. In this, the mother operates, as Bendelow and Williams argue that emotion does, to 'provide the "missing link" between "personal troubles" and "public issues" of social structure'.[20]

Jocasta refers to division of her body, her family and her nation simultaneously, presenting her own condition as emblematic of that of the nation which she already represents as its queen.

Motherhood and the classical tradition 59

As the play develops, scenes between the wretched mother and her children alternate with choric commentaries which remind the audience that the pain she suffers originates from 'greedie lust of mans ambitious eye' (1.1). The old story thus acquired a contemporary significance in a Christian neoclassical version which makes Jocasta both the main narrator and the central emblem of a play in which her bodily sufferings, like those of Widow Englande, serve to demonstrate the consequences of the inappropriate aspirations of her warring children. Marie Axton notes that the adaptation also allows the protagonist to figure the queen's two bodies:

> The translators are concerned to show a 'blind' Elizabeth the dangers of her metaphorical marriage with the realm and by implication to urge a real marriage, producing her own children not unnatural heirs. In the union polemic of the early seventeenth century both Jocasta and Gorboduc's Queen Videna explicitly represent the strife-torn realm.[21]

The dangers of resorting to metaphor, then, are described with reference to the literal breaking up of the mother's body by her unnatural progeny, while a figurative analogy is retained between that maternal body and the state. Unlike the uneasy alliance of classical motif and moral tradition that characterises the representation of the mother in *Gorboduc*, however, *Jocasta* succeeds in making the two work fruitfully together. Despite the changes and additions which had been foisted upon the original play, Jocasta remains in spirit a translation, with Gascoigne, through Dolce, expressing a firm commitment to Euripides' original. This leads to productive structural tensions, in that while Jocasta operates as an emblematic figure in the tradition of the moral play, the Gascoigne and Kinwelmarshe version still retains enough of the dynamic of Euripides's original to suggest that, when acted, the intended implications of the glosses and addenda will be suppressed in favour of an emotional dynamic which focuses attention upon the play as family tragedy as much as political allegory, and so offers a complex and affective account of its implications for the Elizabethan state.

Seneca, violence and dramatic pleasure

Gascoigne and Kinwelmarshe had discovered in the work of an Italian dramatist, Dolce, an adaptation of Euripides that offered a maternal protagonist appropriate to their political needs. In creating an alliance between the utility of classical narrative, with its focus upon physical suffering and punishment, and the structures and religious traditions of earlier native drama they also opened up the potential of the dramatised mother's physical body to function as a site of both love and suffering. This alliance of violence and pathos that had always been present in the religious typology of traditional English drama gained resonance from the influences of Italian versions of classical works, themselves coloured by exegesis. These, in turn, influenced the more recent Italian plays that became important to English dramatists. Robert Ornstein has demonstrated the popularity of such sources, arguing for a 'robust Elizabethan fascination with Italianate decadence', and Richard Hillman discusses the range of potential material: 'the corpus of original works in Italy and, especially, France was already considerable. The Italian avatars, beginning with Cinthio's *Orbecce* 1544, are an obvious source of extravagant and sensationalistic horror'.[22] Jean Seznec goes so far as to argue that the English got their classical mythology mostly from Italian versions.[23] A combination of violence and motherhood frequently functioned in such plays to produce a particular kind of dramatic pleasure, in which the satisfaction of seeing a moral tale properly worked through is enhanced by (and perhaps even subordinate to) the 'delight', to use Sidney's term, induced by a complex affective response to the mother's plight.[24]

Katherine Park has written about representations of motherhood in Renaissance Italy, focusing particularly upon mythical mothers who, like Jocasta, became sacrificial. Park notes that according to contemporary Italian readings of these figures a sacrificial mother is linked to the engendering and nurture of heroes, and she sees these stories as highly influential, 'part of a mythologised Roman history that played an important role in shaping and transmitting . . . patrician culture and identity'. She points out that 'fifteenth-century Florentines used episodes of this history to illustrate the values they saw underpinning the order of family and state. They told and retold it in Latin histories and orations and in vernacular poetry and chronicles'.[25] These tales – Park cites in particular stories about the death of Caesar's mother – provoke both pity and admiration for the mother alongside a sense of gratification because by her sacrifice she ensures the perpetuation of a heroic culture that engenders and celebrates great men. In a different context Julia Kristeva writes of the death of the mother as necessary for the autonomy of the individual: 'the *sine qua non* of our individuation'.²⁶ Both writers suggest that the concept of maternal suffering and death, appropriately mediated, offers an experience that is pleasurable and stimulating – even as it acknowledges loss, it precipitates action.

Philip Sidney, whose appreciation of Seneca's plays is well documented in his *Poetics*, associates 'delight' with both the satisfactions of well-constructed rhetoric and the gratification of a properly worked-out moral, arguing that the pleasure engendered by these things endows instruction with the power to move emotion and thus to provoke action.²⁷ He reworks Aristotle's association of pleasure with both imitation and learning with a Christian gloss to show how 'stirring the affects of admiration and commiseration teacheth the uncertainties of this world'.²⁸ For Sidney, the violence in a play is to be read morally and such a moral reading will bring both instruction and pleasure, the one enhancing the other. The meanings inscribed in the mother figure, her capacity to provoke both affective and cognitive responses and thereby to incite both pity and pleasure, are likely to be profoundly aroused therefore by the specific association of the mother's body with violence. This association was recognised by dramatists of the late sixteenth century in plays which tested and explored its dramatic potential. Three of the four plays discussed in this section – Alabaster's *Roxana*, Shakespeare's *Titus Andronicus* and Kyd's *The Spanish Tragedy* – make clear their dues to Senecan drama.

William Alabaster's adaptation of Groto's *La Dalida*, the Latin play *Roxana*, was performed at Trinity College, Cambridge, in 1592.²⁹ The effectiveness of the performance in a play which the author asks 'to be delivered in a ranting manner' is recorded, perhaps with some irony intended, by Thomas Fuller:

[Alabaster's] tragedy of *Roxana* admirably acted in college, and so pathetically that a gentlewoman present thereat (Reader, I had it from an authour whose credit it is sin with me to suspect) at the hearing of the last words thereof, Sequar, Sequar, so hideously pronounced, fell distracted, and never after fully recovered her senses.³⁰

Fuller was perhaps quite aware of the need to be cautious about the veracity of such tales. The dramatist Giambattista Giraldi Cinthio had already told a version of the story of the fainting woman in his account of the first performance of his *Orbecce*.³¹

Whether or not the story is true, it suggests that the performance was a success, deemed admirable, pathetic and thrilling enough to cause collapse in its female audience. Certainly *Roxana* is a violent play. Its climax involves a messenger speech which describes the protracted torture of a mistress, Roxana, by her lover's wife. The messenger recounts at length and explicitly how the victim was bound and flogged before having a sword placed between her hands and being forced to kill her own children who are later served up alongside their mother's body as a meal to their errant father. The messenger's speech is punctuated by the appearance of the ghost of the primary avenger, the victim's father (killed by her lover), who exclaims with delight at what he is hearing.[32] The play, according to one of its most recent editors, tones down some of Groto's more unpleasant images: 'he mercifully omits to translate Groto's passage describing Queen Berenice, compared to an industrious anatomist, dissecting and mincing her victims', but nevertheless still retains 'a very liberal helping of *atrocitas*'.[33]

The mother in this play embodies a series of tensions and contradictions. Her physical suffering generates a response in which the revulsion that allegedly precipitated the gentlewoman's collapse in Fuller's anecdote competes with a fascination with the processes of torture: a dynamic which operates through a rhetorically constructed focus upon the abuse of the mother's body. This culminates in what amounts to an enforced repudiation of Roxana's motherhood, which is symbolically obliterated by the incorporation of her children's flesh into the body of the father from whom they originally came. The plot is set up in such a way that Roxana's body becomes the carrier of a series of irreconcilable positions: she cannot be a good daughter and the mistress of her father's murderer; she is a mistress outside the social and hierarchical structures which are the norms emphasised in the play and she is a mother who commits infanticide, compelled though that may be. She is placed at an intersection between incompatible narratives: the Italian revenge tale in which conflict between two men is figured horribly and deliciously through the persecution of one woman by another – Atossa, the avenging wife, boasts that she has outdone Medea in her crime – and the traditional moral narrative which insists that women who upset or threaten conventional hierarchy should rightly and properly be punished.[34] Though, as Sutton points out, 'there is no overt criticism or moral evaluation of Atossa's disproportionately savage revenge', Roxana not only embodies corruption but is subject to it; she deserves and does not deserve her punishment, is violated and to be pitied, a scapegoat whose fate spectators like Sidney would presumably have understood as instructive, morally and metaphorically, even as the violence provoked their horror and pity.[35]

For Lisa Jardine, *Roxana* offers a theatrical pleasure specifically to men:

> Off stage, the male member of the audience recognises the representation of perennially threatening women (perennial source of horror) ... and recognises equally its absurd excessiveness. No woman of *his* will ever get this out of hand, and hence the representation is equally a source of delight.[36]

It is possible to read this play in terms of anxieties about the status of women in marriage and paternity, or as Elizabeth Richmond-Garza suggests, an indictment of 'thorough English inflexibility and atavism on the matter of marriage', though neither reading seems adequate to the ferocity of the violence that is recounted.[37] Dana Sutton sees the play as 'a tool to probe the ethical and psychological nature of tyranny' and this analysis, which sees the play interrogating the relationship between tyrant and victims, is perhaps more satisfying.[38] *Roxana*'s intense and protracted focus upon the process of torturing a mother – complicated and sexualised by her other role as mistress – fetishises her as a source of both disgust and pleasure.[39] The contradictions inscribed on Roxana's tortured body signal maternity simultaneously emphasised and denied, both 'the symbol of something and its negation'.[40] Emily Apter shows that fetishism functions to simultaneously critique and implicate the very phenomena that it seeks to expose and *Roxana* treats the mother with both 'affection and hostility', demonstrating a repudiation of maternity and a celebration of good motherhood; abhorring the violence that it simultaneously offers in deliciously descriptive detail.[41] As Apter says, 'the fetishist does indeed refuse to look, but in refusing to look, he *stares*. It is a "not looking" sustained paradoxically through visual fixation'.[42] This dramatised mother's body functions metonymically to demonstrate the impossibility of reconciling the conflicting demands of social, moral, mythic and literary narratives and is obliterated both physically and figuratively.[43] As a play which is perhaps concerned with representing matters of state but clearly also with academic matters associated with the development and appropriation of a variety of literary and dramatic narratives, *Roxana* demonstrates the functionality of the mother as a figure whose complexities and contradictions offer a unique pleasure: a pleasure produced by the pathos located at the disjunction between the meanings which Roxana embodies. The potential for containing contradiction, always present in representations of maternity, is turned to dramatic advantage through a resort to fetishism, where the irreconcilability of the multiple meanings carried by the mother in this play produces simultaneous horror and pleasure.

Atossa tortures Roxana in a room decorated with illustrations of Medea's atrocities, and of Penteus being devoured by his mother, in a macabre reversal of the – already macabre – Italian practice of using images of sacrificial mothers, such as Caesar's mother, to decorate the insides of their houses (4.1.1041–2). Thus the decorations in Atossa's torture chamber had a direct and subversive relevance in their Italian original. Park observes of such representations of Julius Caesar's birth that his mother was celebrated in such a way because 'her opened uterus marked her acceptance of, and compliance with, his dynastic interests'.[44] And there is certainly a link between the exposure of the mother to violence and suffering and the demands of patriarchal inheritance in Elizabethan plays that refer back to their Senecan and/or Italian sources. In these plays, the literal and/or metaphorical tearing apart or opening out of the body of the mother appears to offer a figurative means by which the honour of a family can somehow be recuperated.

Lisa Jardine links Alabaster's Atossa to Tamora in Shakespeare's *Titus Andronicus*, seeing both as part of a tradition which 'is careless of verisimilitude in the interests of the *frisson* of horror to be derived from such representations of threatening womanhood'.[45] If this is so, then the threat extends further than that of any individual characterisation. Just as *Roxana* has been read as a play that explores the psyche of the tyrant by reference to the violence done by one woman to another, so Titus Andronicus has been discussed by many critics in terms of the ways in which motherhood figures in the play: in the character of Tamora (and to a lesser extent Lavinia) and as a metaphor for Rome. For Jonathan Bate, 'Shakespeare is interrogating Rome, asking what kind of an example it provides for Elizabethan England', citing Elizabethan anxieties about the failure of established law, particularly in view of an anticipated crisis of succession.[46] If this is so, then the concept of a maternal state has implications for the relationship between Elizabeth and her subjects, for at the core of

Rome in this play is a thirst for blood that brings the nation to the point of collapse; a thirst linked to – and emblematised by – a dangerous and pervasive maternity at its heart.

This is present from the first scene, which depicts the ritual burial of Titus's sons, killed in martial service to Rome. The funeral culminates in a speech from Titus which opens with a salutation to a personified, female state – 'Hail Rome, victorious in thy mourning weeds' – and ends with an address to a specific site, the family tomb:

> O sacred receptacle of my Joys,
> Sweet cell of virtue and nobility,
> How many sons hast thou of mine in store,
> That thou wilt never render to me more! (1.1.92–5)

Titus addresses the tomb as a wife, a lover, the container of his children. The symbolic implications of this have been explored most notably by David Willbern, who suggests that Saturninus's address to Rome at the beginning of the scene voices a similar address to a city which is overwhelmingly maternal: 'Rome, be as just and gracious unto me / As I am confident and kind to thee. / Open the gates and let me in' (1.1.60–3). In this reading, Saturninus's address 'implicitly voices a desire for maternal affection and acceptance'. Willbern continues: 'the wished-for opening of the gates is latently sexual and highly ambivalent: entry into the mother's body, in both genital and oral terms, is unconsciously as terrifying as it may be pleasurable'.[47] This resonates with Katherine Park's discussion of the dissection of mother's bodies in the cause of maintaining patriarchal norms: 'good wives and mothers ... opened themselves to scrutiny in the interests of their children and their husbands' families to whom those children by definition belonged'.[48] Park is writing about Renaissance Italy but the ideas that she argues influenced such practices are pertinent to Elizabethan plays like *Titus Andronicus* and *Roxana* that are so closely and self-consciously modelled upon Senecan and Italian sources.[49]

In this analysis, the open gates of Rome, like the gaping tomb of the Andronici, have the same function as the body of Roxana in Alabaster's play: as the point of intersection between discordant discourses. The mother generously opens herself to her children but is also their predator. A disturbing and threatening predominance of the maternal resonates ironically at moments where masculine, martial victory is most celebrated. The tomb works metonymically to suggest the monuments of the 'Capitol', emblematising the success of the martial state, but a state bound to its mother, Rome. It is at the same time a greedy maternal receptacle, a sweet 'cell' which is also an earthly grave, an image of civic statuary which combines with the fecund earth to receive the corpses of the hero's children. The established early modern understanding of the womb as mobile and greedy (originally from Plato) contributed to the effect of the metaphor.[50] In the face of such power, the patriarchal, martial state appears as fragile as fatherhood, and as inextricably dependent upon an incomprehensible maternity. In Park's analysis, 'The precarious nature of fatherhood, and thus of the family itself, centred on the uterus, the dark, inaccessible place where the child's tie with its father was created, its sex determined and its body shaped'.[51] For Willbern, 'the equation of womb and tomb is central to the unconscious action of *Titus Andronicus*'; Marion Wynne-Davies shows that the womb is 'one of the corporeal symbols of the play' and extends this idea to the image of the earth, which she calls the 'womb of the ultimate female body' in the play.[52] Wynne-Davies seeks to contrast a patriarchal, imperial Rome with 'the all-consuming mouth of the feminine earth', noting the 'unexpected similarities and contrasts' that such figures engender.[53] Rome and the tomb operate as ambivalent concepts, signifying both the personal sacrifice that is necessary to successful, masculine, martial and politic activities, and, simultaneously, denoting a subversive, earthy, greedy maternity that has reclaimed the bodies of twenty-one of Titus's offspring.[54] The demand from mother earth for blood is, as many critics have noted, made visually explicit not only in the spectacle of the tomb, but in the description of the hole in the ground into which Bassanius is later thrown before Lavinia is raped, so that both civic and pastoral Rome are shown in spectacle and rhetoric to be pervaded by a rapacious and devouring maternity.[55]

Bate emphasises a thematic opposition between Titus Andronicus and Tamora, something which he finds reproduced in Henry Peachum's well-known drawing of a scene from the play.[56] She is first presented as a pitiable mother who pleads for the life of her eldest son but later becomes a vengeful Medea-like figure bent upon terrible revenge. Despite the fact that she spends most of the play in the second role, Peachum, one of the play's earliest spectators, drew an apparently dignified and supplicant Tamora. As Marion Wynne-Davies has asked, 'why did Peacham choose to depict Tamora as royal and sympathetic?'[57] For Wynne-Davies the answer is in 'the play's rejection of the common stereotyping of women into virgins and whores'. She argues that, 'instead, it appears both to enact and to confuse these treatments of women: feminine power and female sexuality are inextricably linked, simultaneously provoking and repressed'.[58] This is not entirely a move away from the certainties of straightforward typology, relying as it does upon the familiar link between femininity, madness, and the disintegration of the state. Titus's refusal of clemency, despite Tamora's desperate resistance to the Roman rituals which require the life of her son, provokes the release of a furious maternity which is analogous to that signified by the tomb in its drive towards real degeneration and chaos. Tamora's plea to Titus to 'stain not thy tomb with blood' is also a kind of threat, imagining as it does the defacement of the Roman monument by the heathen blood of her son (*Titus* 1.1.119). Articulated by the frantic mother, this cry of and for blood associates that blood with maternity and the threatening potential of the maternal body. Taking Jardine's point about the pleasures offered by the depiction of violent women, it is clear that in *Titus Andronicus* these pleasures are provoked by the threat to the established order of things from an overabundant and aggressive maternity which becomes personified in Tamora.

Bate's point about the opposition of Tamora and Titus is significant. As Peacham draws it, the queen of the Goths kneels royal but supplicant. Her regal status demonstrates her potential power just as her physical position indicates her powerlessness. Behind her, her children and her foreign lover attest to the havoc that the uncontrollable forces of maternal revenge and female sexual desire will wreak upon the Roman and his conventionally dressed companions. The Peacham picture demonstrates a confrontation between the certainties of the civilised state and the unleashed threat emblematised by Queen Tamora and her train. The first scene of the play similarly sets up an opposition in which Titus, ostensibly in control, is in fact placed at the mercy of an abundant, consuming maternity that has begun the process of bringing about his destruction. The figure of Tamora offers a spectacular and sustained realisation of the excess of maternity that characterises the corruption of Rome. Maternity infects her role as Saturninus's wife, 'A loving nurse, a mother to his youth'; she produces a foreign bastard child instead of a Roman heir. (1.1.333) It inflects the language in which she expresses her sexual desires:

'hounds and horns and sweet melodious birds / Be unto us as is a nurse's song / Of lullaby to bring her babe asleep'. (3.2.27–9) It exists, moreover, outside the parameters of the dramatic action – Rome is already greedy for blood and Tamora is already a mother when the narrative begins – and so is beyond the control of the Romans who struggle against it. David Willbern situates Lavinia as the symbolic opposite to this, representing an alternative Rome, the 'pure and virtuous mother' who is under attack.[59] Certainly, it is Lavinia's potential as the locus of a non-threatening, controllable maternity (and thus a suitable vehicle for the continuation of patriarchy) that is set against Tamora's fearsome maternal status, a status forged in an unfamiliar time and place beyond the scope of the play. It is not femininity but maternity that infects Rome. Janet Adelman, who develops the link between motherhood and feeding in Shakespeare's later plays, also acknowledges 'the horrific devouring mother in *Titus Andronicus*' in whose presence 'all identity and all family bonds dissolve'.[60] It is thus appropriate that the emblem of this poisonous and hungry motherhood should be annihilated at the end of the play, which closes with the image of her body being thrown 'to beasts and birds to prey' (5.3.198) to be herself devoured.

In *Titus Andronicus*, it is the impossibility of containing the maternal that provides the primary dynamic of the play. In Kyd's *The Spanish Tragedy*, the potential for violence implicit in the maternal is instead turned upon itself in a world dominated by policy which is impervious to either the threats or the pleas of the mother. In this play it is the vulnerability of maternity which is emphasised, offering a pathetic testament to the immorality of the political machinations that constitute the main plot. Isabella, whose son is murdered, has no sustained narrative function but appears in three crucial scenes to emblematise the drive towards revenge which structures the play as she degenerates from grief to madness and suicide. She operates in this pseudo-Senecan drama as a familiar combination of fury and mother, articulating her desire for revenge while simultaneously eliciting pity and sympathy. Michael Hattaway has described the way in which this play operates as a series of scenes, 'a sequence of performed actions', and Isabella's part fits well with the analogy with opera that he offers. She makes three brief appearances which work like arias to offer an emotional and dramatic focus as well as to push the dynamic of the play forward towards its spectacular and bloody conclusion.[61]

Kate McLuskie has drawn attention to the importance of Isabella's role in 'making revenge an emotional as well as a plot necessity, adding to the play's dramatic power'.[62] Isabella's first appearance is to join her avenging husband, Hieronimo, in a lament before the hanging body of their murdered son.[63] Her function is not more than conventional, a kind of choric support for Hieronimo's calls for revenge, emblematising and articulating the grief which is essential to the revenge motif, but nevertheless her part is crucial. The evocative spectacle of the mourning mother looking up at her son's corpse clearly represents a conventional trope that associates motherhood with loss, as Michael Hattaway acknowledges: 'these images need no comment: they are the stuff of popular ballads but also of high art'.[64] The scene combines the pious sympathy elicited by visual reference to Christian iconography with the voyeurism more usually expressed in popular commercial literature where the intimate experience of personal grief becomes, for the observer, a source of prurient pleasure. The mother here is at once venerable and ridiculous, more so when she next appears, 'running lunatic' and, in a futile gesture, cutting down the arbour where her son was hanged. (3.8) Hattaway again draws attention to the importance of spectacle when he explains how 'Isabella's rich court robes would have been replaced by a loose and torn smock, her tied-up hair and headpiece replaced by a long flowing wig, the conventional stage symbol of distraction'.[65] The distracted mother, conventionally emblematic of public and private breakdown, is here part of a process of transformation which ends with Isabella's suicide. In a pathetic combination of the Christian icon of grief and a classical avenging fury, she opts for a Senecan death, calling for revenge and stabbing herself in 'the hapless breast that gave Horatio suck' (4.2.37).

There is a tension here between the classical idea of honourable suicide and the Christian sin of despair. This is both complicated and elucidated by the mother's reference to her own body which becomes the point of articulation between the two. The breast, a site of both shame and honour, emblem of both humankind's bestiality and idealised maternity, and her suicide, simultaneously courageous and cowardly, enable the revenge motif to refer both to Christian guilt and classical shame. Revenge in this narrative is desirable for the reputation of the public person and yet requires punishment for the good of the same person's spiritual self. Overburdened with meaning like Roxana, Isabella denotes both the political and personal implications of 'policy' while emblematising their irreconcilability. The focus upon the mother's body allows the interplay of concepts of private family and public dynasty, the two brought together by the bittersweet and contradictory pleasures induced by the spectacle of the victimised mother, first tortured by madness and then stabbed through her breast, dead upon the stage. And the effect of that spectacle is tantalisingly vague. Both Hattaway and Edwards refer to the problem of getting the body off the stage.[66] She has to be shifted somehow, and the practicalities of this have implications for the way an audience responds to her death. Unless the body is immediately removed (in which case the nature of her removal will create its own effect: comic, pathetic, tragic, or whatever) the audience, who will have been absorbed in watching the death enacted, will bear the responsibility of deciding when to break the link – when to look away from the body – and this ensures their continued emotional engagement with what is being enacted.[67]

The mother's body, both alive and dead, is similarly and spectacularly utilised by Christopher Marlowe in the first and second plays of *Tamburlaine*.[68] Though these are two of the most violent plays in the Elizabethan theatre, Marlowe wittily interrogates the conventional link between motherhood and violence that this chapter has discussed by creating a mother untouched by pain but whose very perfection makes her dangerous. Zenocrate, originally Tamburlaine's captive, transcends any association with violence; she is responsible for no deaths and herself dies of natural causes. In *Tamburlaine I* a contrast is drawn between Zabina, the wife of Bajazeth, Tamburlaine's enemy, and Zenocrate, then the hero's prospective bride. Before the battle in which Bajazeth will be defeated, both he and Tamburlaine offer eulogies to their women. Bajazeth celebrates Zabina as the mother of 'three brauer boies, / Than *Hercules*' – a breeder of fighters like their father:

> Their shoulders broad, for complet armour fit,
> Their lims more large and of a bigger size
> Than all the brats ysprong from *Typhons* loins:
> Who, when they come vnto their fathers age,
> Will batter Turrets with their manly fists.
> Sit here vpon this royal chaire of state,
> And on thy head weare my Emperiall crowne (*Tamb. I*, ll. 1201–11)

Bajazeth's rhetoric, coloured by references to classical mythology which emphasise the solidity of the dynasty he describes, enhances the visual power of his crowned and enthroned queen whose motherhood he makes central to her meaning. Zabina's personal success as a mother of warlike boys and her consequent political success as a queen make her an emblem of those established and apparently unassailable political structures that the upstart Tamburlaine repeatedly challenges. Tamburlaine's retort, called by Shepherd a 'fetishising' of Zenocrate's beauty and chastity, is to place his princess, 'adorned with my Crowne, / As if thou wert the Empresse of the world'[69] (ll. 1222–3). Zenocrate, in contrast to Zabina, has no sexual history. In this 'male competition' between the two warriors (as Simon Shepherd characterises it) it is Zenocrate's *potential* as a future wife, queen and mother that Tamburlaine celebrates.[70] Marlowe brings together two paradigms of femininity and allows a play of irony between them. The older mother and the inexperienced girl are compared as much to show up one another's deficiencies as to display positive examples of womanhood. The language contributes to this by drawing attention to the differences between them: after the men compete rhetorically over the importance of their women, the women bicker about the superiority of their men. This verbal competition tends to undermine the iconic value of the spectacle of the two female types, thereby setting up an ironic resonance between them. Zenocrate's peculiar status here, not quite wife, not yet mother, both indicates her implication in Tamburlaine's future success and foreshadows her detachment from it.

After Bajazeth's defeat and subsequent suicide, Zabina, like Isabella in Kyd's play, runs lunatic and kills herself. Her mad speech, in prose which stands out from the blank verse of the rest of the scene, contains an evocative cluster of images which creates a typological link between her particular circumstance as Tamburlaine's victim and conventions linked to maternal grief:

> O Baiazet, O Turk, O emperor, giue him his liquor? Not I, bring milk and fire, and my blood I bring him againe, teare me in peeces, give me the sworde with a ball of wildefire vpon it. Downe with him, downe with him. Goe to my child, away, away, away. Ah, saue that Infant, saue him, saue him. (ll. 2090–5)

The spectacle of the mad mother, together with the apocalyptic images in this speech, operate to dismantle the concept of successful maternity and queenliness that Bajazeth set up so thoroughly in his celebration of Zabina quoted above. Against the solidity of the classical mythology invoked by the emperor to celebrate his queen is set the chaotic and pathetic story of the massacre of the innocents. The milk and the blood of maternity are set against images of fire and sword and shown to be inadequate. Zabina's final cry before she dies, 'Hel, death, Tamburlain, Hell, make ready my Coch, my chaire, my iewels, I come, I come, I come', reinforces a sense of the futility of all that was celebrated by her husband, as neither her function as mother nor the trappings of wealth and royalty have any currency in the face of the new power structures that Tamburlaine is setting in place.[71]

Motherhood's function in maintaining patriarchy, articulated by Bajazeth and undermined by Tamburlaine's triumphs in the first play of the pair, recurs as a concern in *Tamburlaine II*. Like Zabina, Zenocrate has produced three sons, but, ironically, sons who are reproductions of their mother rather than their father. Marlowe plays upon conventional understandings of patriarchy that assert a physical resemblance between father and son as an affirmation of the dynastic line. The womanish appearance of the hero's children is a source of anxiety that is articulated by Tamburlaine as he arranges his family into what Judith Weil characterises as 'a portrait group' in the second play. The family arranged into a formal group should signify the dynastic success of its patriarch.[72] But Tamburlaine's words reveal a crucial instability at its heart. His sons are not like him:

> But yet me thinks their looks are amorous,
> Not martiall as the sons of *Tamburlaine*.
> Water and ayre being simbolisde in one
> Argue their want of courage and of wit,
> Their haire as white as milke and soft as Downe,
> Which should be like the quills of Porcupines,
> As black as Ieat, and hard as Iron or steel,
> Bewraies they are too dainty for the wars.
> Their fingers made to quauer on a Lute,
> Their armes to hang about a Ladies necke:
> Their legs to dance and caper in the aire:
> Would make me thinke them Bastards, not my sons,
> But that I know they issued from thy wombe,
> That neuer look'd on man but *Tamburlaine*. (*Tamb. II*, ll. 2590–603)

Patriarchy here has been struck where it is most vulnerable, at the incubation of the child within its mother's body, where a bastard might be sustained, or a monstrous prodigy might be nurtured before entering the world to upset the established order.[73] Marlowe uses this to set up an ironic reconsideration of his hero's achievements, so spectacular and yet ultimately so precarious. While Bajazeth's son, Calapine, exhibits his father's qualities in a daredevil escape from captivity, Tamburlaine's eldest boy, Calyphas, disdains his father's triumphs, preferring the company of his mother: 'But while my brothers follow armes my lord / Let me accompany my gratious mother' (*Tamb. II*, 2634–5).

Tamburlaine's speech depends upon its visual context for effect. The spectacular impact of son and mother, so physically alike, together on the stage creates a link between them which challenges the play's – and the hero's – construction of masculinity as martial, active and aggressive. The transmission to her sons of Zenocrate's womanishness problematises the dynastic ambitions that are implicit in martial endeavour, so that maternity, essential for the continuation of the patriarchal line, is shown to be also its greatest liability. After Zenocrate's death, the antipathy between father and son spills over into infanticide, when Tamburlaine kills Calyphas for staying in his tent during a battle and refusing to fight (3794). This is the point, says D. J. Palmer, where Tamburlaine 'has turned upon Nature'.[74] Nature nevertheless triumphs through the mediation of the body of the ostensibly powerless captive girl who mothered his offspring. Just as Zabina, in *Tamburlaine I*, died in a way that emphasised the futility of dynastic ambition, so the death of this son who is so like his mother demonstrates the limits of the hero's aspirations. Serene and supportive as a wife, beautiful beyond compare as a lover, Zenocrate is in the end the unwitting agent of public and private disaster on a grand scale – the collapse of both family and empire. Motherhood is as vicious for Tamburlaine as it was for Titus, Roxana and Isabella. Tamburlaine, who in the first play claimed power over even those universal concepts that are traditionally gendered feminine – 'I hold the Fates bound fast in yron chaines, / And with my hand turn Fortunes wheel about' (*Tamb. I*, ll. 369–70) – discovers the inadequacy of such claims in the second, an inadequacy which is emblematised by a pervasive and infectious femininity, transmitted through the conquered princess whose body bore, and left her mother's mark upon, his children.[75]

Zenocrate's preserved body continues to accompany her husband and children until his death. Her continued presence on stage – the stage direction at the start of Act 3 requires 'foure bearing the hearse of Zenocrate' – signals her continued influence upon the dynasty she was supposed to secure, and reinforces the fact of its ultimate failure. Doris Feldman draws attention to the way in which Tamburlaine makes 'the feminine function ... as an extension of the masculine principle', exercising control over Zenocrate's body 'by first taking it captive, then aestheticising and idealising and finally embalming it', but concludes that the enduring power is Zenocrate's.[76] Mary Stripling notes that in Tamburlaine's dying speech to his surviving sons he rediscovers them in his own image: 'My flesh divided in your precious shapes / Shall still retain my spirit though I die'. For Stripling this is 'a birthing of sorts, in which [Tamburlaine] produces children who are free of maternal influence' but the audience already knows too much and has already been shown the limitations of this family. At the end of the play Tamburlaine's son laments his parents' death in words that reconcile, at last, the maternal and paternal: 'earth hath spent the pride of all her fruit, / And heauen consum'd his choisest liuing fire' (ll. 4642–4).[77] Thus the final focus is upon exhausted powers and passions: the end of dynasty.

In each of the plays discussed in this chapter the reconsideration of traditional representations of maternity in the light of classical and Italian sources has contributed to the creation of narratives which relish their new usage of the mother figure to shock or to disturb, and thus to engage her audience in an active consideration of the substance of the drama. It is this potential to challenge, even as she signifies, matters of state that makes the typology of the mother so useful in the dramatic depiction of the nation, and it is to this that the discussion turns in, Chapter 3.

Notes

1 George Gascoigne and Francis Kinwelmarshe, *Jocasta*, in *The Complete Works of George Gascoigne*, vol. 1, ed. J. W. Cunliffe (Cambridge: Cambridge University Press, 1907), 1.1.8–9. All subsequent references to this play are taken from this edition.
2 Jean Seznec, *The Survival of the Pagan Gods* (New York: Pantheon Books, 1953), p. 84.
3 For the implications of print culture see Michael D. Bristol and Arthur F. Marotti, eds, *Print, Manuscript, Performance: The Changing Relations of the Media in Early Modern England* (Columbus: Ohio State University Press, 2000), pp. 1–32. Bristol and Marotti argue that the social significance of new theatres is 'fully understood only against the background of printing', p. 11. Also Elizabeth Eisenstein,

Motherhood and the classical tradition 75

     The Printing Press as an Agent of Change (Cambridge: Cambridge University Press, 1979). Eisenstein emphasises continuities, as does Tessa Watt in *Cheap Print and Popular Piety 1550–1640* (Cambridge: Cambridge University Press, 1991).
4 Thomas Newton, ed., *The Tenne Tragedies of Seneca* (New York: The Spenser Society, 1887 and 1967). See also A. Harbage, ed., *Annals of English Drama 975–1700* (London: Methuen, 1964) and T. W. Baldwin, *Shakespeare's Small Latin and Less Greek* (Urbana: University of Illinois Press, 1944), vol. 2.
5 Philip Sidney, *A Defence of Poetry*, ed. J. A. Van Dorsten (Oxford: Oxford University Press, 1966), p. 65.
6 Marie Axton, *The Queen's Two Bodies* (London: Royal Historical Society, 1977).
7 John Ernest Neale, *Elizabeth I and Her Parliaments* (London: Cape, 1953), pp. 110 and 128.
8 Axton, *The Queen's Two Bodies*, pp. 38–60.
9 I. B. Cauthen, ed., *'Gorboduc' by Thomas Sackville and Thomas Norton* (London: Arnold, 1970), p. xii.
10 See Axton, *The Queen's Two Bodies*, p. 40.
11 See Richard Studeley, 'Medea', in Newton (ed.), *The Tenne Tragedies of Seneca*, p. 248. Subsequent quotations are from this edition of the play.
12 See Studeley, *Medea*, 1.1.35–9, where Videna's sacrifices to the gods in the interests of her favourite son anticipate Lady Macbeth's much later exhortations to a malign supernatural power.
13 Wolfgang Clemen, *English Tragedy before Shakespeare* (London: Methuen, 1967), Ch. 2.
14 Gascoigne, *Jocasta*, p. 244.
15 See W. Aldis Wright, ed., *English Works of Roger Ascham* (Cambridge: Cambridge University Press, 1970), pp. 276 and 284.
16 Gascoigne, *Jocasta*, pp. 272 and 324.
17 C. T. Prouty, *George Gascoigne: Elizabethan Courtier, Soldier and Poet* (New York: Blom, 1942), pp. 154–5.
18 Axton, *The Queen's Two Bodies*, p. 54.
19 Gillian Bendelow and Simon J. Williams, ed., *Emotions in Social Life: Critical Themes and Contemporary Issues* (London: Routledge, 1998), pp. xvi and xvii.
20 See Bendelow and Williams, *Emotions in Social Life*, pp. xvi and xvii.
21 Axton, *The Queen's Two Bodies*, p. 54.
22 Richard Hillman, 'Out of Their Classical Depth: From Pathos to Bathos in Early English Tragedy, or, The Comedy of Terrors', in *Thêta 7: Théâtre Tudor* (Feb. 2007), pp. 17–38.
23 Jean Seznec, *The Survival of the Pagan Gods* (Princeton: Princeton University Press, 1953), p. 312. See also Robert Ornstein, *The Moral Vision of Jacobean Tragedy* (Wisconsin: University of Wisconsin Press, 1960), p. 61.

24 See Stephen Halliwell, *The Poetics of Aristotle: Translation and Commentary* (London: Duckworth, 1987), and K. McLeish, *Aristotle's Poetics* (London: Duckworth, 1998). Aristotle's *Poetics* (which informed Sidney's analysis), describes the cathartic effect of the fear and pity, translated by Halliwell as 'pleasure' and by McLeish as 'satisfaction'.
25 Katherine Park, *Secrets of Women: Gender, Generation and the Origins of Human Dissection* (New York: Zone Books, 2006), p. 156.
26 Julia Kristeva, *Black Sun: Depression and Melancholia*, trans. Leon S. Roudiez (New York: Columbia University Press, 1989), pp. 27–8.
27 See Paul Heelas, 'Emotion Talk across Cultures', in *The Emotions: Social, Cultural and Biological Dimensions*, eds Rom Harré and W. Gerrod Parrott (London: Sage, 1996), pp. 171–99. For an elucidation of Sidney's discussion, see the introduction to Stephen Halliwell's edition of the *Poetics*, p. 46. For a discussion of traditional and modern readings of catharsis see Timothy J. Wiles, *The Theatre Event: Modern Theories of Performance* (Chicago: University of Chicago Press, 1980), pp. 4–5 and 126. See also K. McLeish, *Aristotle's Poetics* (London: Nick Hern, 1999), p. 18.
28 *A Defence of Poetry*, ed. Van Dorsten, p. 65. Relatively recent and controversial readings of Aristotle, for example in *Poetics*, trans. Leon Golden (New York: Prentice Hall, 1968), argue for catharsis as meaning 'clarification of incident', so referring to the point or place at which things fearful and pitiful are justified.
29 Dana F. Sutton, ed., *Roxana*, hypertext critical edition, 1998. www.philological.bham.ac.uk/alabaster.
30 Thomas Fuller, in *Worthies of England*, quoted by J. W. Binns in C. D. N. Costa, ed., *Seneca* (London: Routledge and Kegan Paul, 1974), p. 211.
31 See Elizabeth Richmond-Garza, ' "She Never Recovered Her Senses": Roxana and Dramatic Representations of Women at Oxbridge in the Elizabethan Age', in *Sex and Gender in Medieval and Renaissance Texts: The Latin Tradition*, eds Barbara K. Gold, Paul Allen Miller and Charles Platter (Albany: State University of New York Press, 1997), p. 242. Heywood deploys a version of the tale in his *Apology for Actors*; see K. Sturgess, *Three Elizabethan Domestic Tragedies* (Harmondsworth: Penguin, 1969), p. 15.
32 J. W. Binns, 'Seneca and Neo-Latin Tragedy in England', in *Seneca*, ed. Costa, p. 208.
33 Dana F. Sutton, ed., *Roxana*, introduction, points 20 and 24.
34 Binns, 'Seneca and Neo-Latin Tragedy in England', p. 218.
35 Dana F. Sutton, ed., *Roxana*, point 20.
36 Lisa Jardine, *Still Harping on Daughters: Women and Drama in the Age of Shakespeare* (Brighton: Harvester, 1983), p. 97.
37 Jardine, *Still Harping on Daughters*, p. 96. Richmond-Garza, ' "She Never Recovered Her Senses" ', p. 240.
38 Sutton, ed., *Roxana*, point 24.

39 Emily Apter, *Feminising the Fetish: Psychoanalysis and Narrative Obsession in Turn-of-the-Century France* (Ithaca: Cornell University Press, 1991), p. 2.
40 Giorgio Agamben, *Stanzas: Word and Phantasm in Western Culture*, trans. Ronald L. Martinez (Minneapolis: University of Minnesota Press, 1993), p. 34.
41 Juliet Mitchell, *Psychoanalysis and Feminism* (Harmondsworth: Penguin, 1990), p. 85.
42 Apter, *Feminising the Fetish*, p. xiii.
43 See Agamben, *Stanzas*, p. 32, for a discussion of connections between fetish and metonymy.
44 Park, *Secrets of Women*, p. 156.
45 Jardine, *Still Harping on Daughters*, p. 36.
46 William Shakespeare, *Titus Andronicus*, ed. Jonathan Bate (London: Routledge, 1995), pp. 17 and 27.
47 David Willbern, 'Rape and Revenge in Titus Andronicus', in *English Literary Renaissance* 8 (1978), 161.
48 Park, *Secrets of Women*, p. 129.
49 Park, *Secrets of Women*, p. 24.
50 Audrey Eccles, *Obstetrics and Gynaecology in Tudor and Stuart England* (London: Croom Helm, 1982), pp. 82–3.
51 Park, *Secrets of Women*, p. 25.
52 Willbern, 'Rape and Revenge in Titus Andronicus', p. 162.
53 Marion Wynne-Davies, '"The Swallowing Womb": Consumed and Consuming Women in Titus Andronicus', in Valerie Wayne, ed., *The Matter of Difference: Materialist Feminist Criticism of Shakespeare* (Hemel Hempstead: Harvester Wheatsheaf, 1991), pp. 135–9.
54 Wynne-Davies, '"The Swallowing Womb"', pp. 135–9.
55 See Shakespeare, *Titus Andronicus*, 1.3. 198–200.
56 Bate contends that 'The opposed gestures of Titus and Tamora are also the central gestures of the play: Authoritative command against supplication on knees with hands in a gesture of pleading', p. 42.
57 Wynne-Davies, '"The Swallowing Womb"', p. 34.
58 Wynne-Davies, '"The Swallowing Womb"', p. 34.
59 See Willbern, 'Rape and Revenge in Titus Andronicus', p. 164.
60 Adelman, *Suffocating Mothers*, p. 9.
61 Michael Hattaway, *Elizabethan Popular Theatre* (London: Routledge, 1982), p. 106.
62 Kathleen McLuskie, *Renaissance Dramatists* (Hemel Hempstead: Harvester Wheatsheaf, 1989), pp. 131–2.
63 All references to the play are from Philip Edwards's edition of *The Spanish Tragedy*, Revels Plays series (Manchester: Manchester University Press, 1977).
64 Hattaway, *Elizabethan Popular Theatre*, p. 122.
65 Hattaway, *Elizabethan Popular Theatre*, p. 124.
66 Hattaway, *Elizabethan Popular Theatre*, p. 126.

67 In depictions of the crucifixion in the mystery plays Christ insists that the audience 'take tent' of the processes and significance of his death. At the close of the play there is a pause in which the audience must decide whether to keep looking and when it is appropriate to look away. See A. C. Cawley, ed., *Everyman and Medieval Miracle Plays* (London: Dent, 1990).
68 All references to the play are from *Tamburlaine the Great*, in *The Works of Christopher Marlowe*, ed. C. F. Tucker Brooke (Oxford: Clarendon Press, 1910).
69 Simon Shepherd, *Amazons and Warrior Women: Varieties of Feminism in Seventeenth-century Drama* (Brighton: Harvester, 1981), p. 183.
70 Shepherd, *Amazons and Warrior Women*, p. 183.
71 It is well known that blood and milk were associated through contemporary medical theories. See G. K. Paster, *The Body Embarrassed: Drama and the Disciplines of Shame in Early Modern England* (Ithaca: Cornell University Press, 1993), ch. 2.
72 Judith Weil, *Christopher Marlowe, Merlin's Prophet* (Cambridge: Cambridge University Press, 1977), p. 134.
73 This idea is significant, for example, in Shakespeare's *Richard III* and is set out in the soliloquy which opens that play.
74 D. J. Palmer, 'Marlowe's Naturalism' in Brian Morris, ed., *Christopher Marlowe*, Mermaid Critical Commentaries series (London: Ernest Benn, 1968), p. 77.
75 See Douglas Cole, *Suffering and Evil in the Plays of Christopher Marlowe* (New Jersey: Princeton University Press, 1962), pp. 118–19.
76 Doris Feldman, 'Gendered Bodies in Marlowe's Plays', in *The Body in Late Medieval and Early Modern Culture*, eds Darryll Grantley and Nina Taunton (Aldershot: Ashgate, 2000), p. 27.
77 Mary Stripling, 'Tamburlaine's Domestic Threat', in Kathryn E. McPherson and Kathryn M. Moncrief, eds, *Performing Maternity in Early Modern England* (Aldershot: Ashgate), p. 223.

3

Motherhood and history

> This our noble island, in the bowels whereof, as in the womb of my
> mother, I was both bred and bor[1]
>
> Philip Stubbes

Narrating history

Jean Howard and Phyllis Rackin, who have worked so extensively on Shakespeare's history plays, note that they contain 'relatively few and often sketchy' images of women and their comment is applicable to Elizabethan history plays in general.[2] Those who are represented in such plays, and, indeed, their sources, referred to by A. P. Rossiter as 'that long line of women broken in the course of great events', are mostly mothers.[3] The typological link between mother and state discussed in previous chapters meant that motherhood developed importance as a trope by which the dramatisation of political conflict acquired validity and complexity. In historical narratives the mother tended to operate, like Jocasta, to divert dramatic focus towards the condition of the nation and away from the subjectivity of the individual monarch. Her role in the construction of dramatic narrative developed to inform the dynamics involved in representing national history: complicating familiar stories about politics and war by figuring alternative histories and other perspectives and inviting an audience to reconsider history and its meaning for the present.

In her argument that Shakespeare's history plays display a politically risky perspectivism, Paola Pugliatti suggests that the creation of invented characters (or characters 'invented' in the sense that their dramatic representation bears little relation to their description in the source material) enabled Shakespeare to create narrative flexibility and complexity:

The inclusion of invented characters in historical plots allows the conflation of heterogeneous components and points of view; and the orchestration of diversity in discourses, genres, conventions and languages, highlights discrepancies and conflicts of interest, introducing differences ... thus foregrounding the concurring systems of a multiplicity of histories.[4]

Dramatised mothers contribute to this complexity. This is evident in *Kyng Johan*, where although Bale subordinates the presentation of chronicle history to the demands of religious propaganda, Widow Englande's polemical power is achieved through a fusion of moral play and history which allowed the mother to signify religious and political principles and ideas purportedly greater and more permanent than the deeds and lives of men and their rulers.[5]

The effectiveness of the mother figure in history plays gained from the ways in which motherhood was presented in other discourses, including chronicles. The period saw a shift of emphasis in drama from theology to teleology, impelled in part by the changing preoccupations of an audience no longer so exercised by religious conflict (except in so far as it affected issues related to the succession), and in part by the reliance of dramatists like Peele, Marlowe and Shakespeare upon Holinshed and Hall as sources for their history. Religious concerns had not disappeared from chronicles but they were inscribed within a Protestant reading of the past which brought together 'God's Law and the king's' and tended to discover elements of Catholicism in political subversion.[6] Such readings depended for effect upon a teleological, causal construction of history that directed its aims towards the celebration of a better present. The chronicles necessarily promoted a dynastic reading of history and have been read as an 'exercise of conformist political ethics' which favoured the Tudor cause.[7] Annabel Patterson, though, reads Holinshed's *Chronicles* as demonstrating a deliberate multivocality; a resistance on the part of the editors of both editions to the idea of a grand narrative, in favour of the recording of diverse discourses which offer a complex version of events where accounts are frequently in competition or conflict. Patterson cites Holinshed's 'Preface to the Reader' to support her contention:

> I have collected out of manie and sundrie authors, in whom what contrarietie, negligence, and rashnesse sometimes is found in their

reports; I leave to the discretion of those who have perused their works: for my part, I have in things doubtful rather chosen to shew the diversitie of their writings, than by over-ruling them, and using a preremptorie censure, to frame them to agree to my liking: leaving it neverthelesse to each mans judgement, to controll them as he seeth cause.[8]

Pugliatti rightly points out that such a preamble probably had much to do with nervousness in the face of the operation of censorship, which she says exerted a double pressure upon the chroniclers: 'What the authorities feared, in particular . . . was the way in which historians connected past events with the present, although they considered that the establishing of such connections was one of the obligations of historians'.[9] The inclusion of detailed stories about mothers in the chronicles had an effect upon the history plays for which they were the major sources. The dramatisation of the chronicle mother accommodated her as the emblematic focus for a voice that often operates in counterpoint to the martial and political impulses that constitute the plot. This allows for a representation of chronicle history in which the stories themselves, and the way they are told, can be tested against other discourses and other perspectives.

History, in the period, was the subject of serious study and some revision. There was an appreciation of a need for objective, dispassionate academic study, although John Bale's insistence upon the importance of recording events 'al affections set a part' is a reminder, in view of his extreme partiality, that the idea of 'indifference' which he was keen to promote was itself a highly qualified notion.[10] However, the popular practice of representing past events as propaganda, implying the value of the past as a mirror for the present, was well established in drama. History, in such versions, remained open-ended, allowing ideas about the past to bleed into the interpretation of the present and so to contribute to perceptions of the future. Hayden White shows that this is what distinguishes the chronicle as a kind of history that 'is marked by a failure to achieve narrative closure',[11] so that the story breaks off 'in medias res, in the chronicler's own present; it leaves things unresolved'.[12]

The mother figure offers an alternative to the relentless teleology of the chronicle. She functions as an anachronism, working in the narrative against a chronology of martial and political incidents to allow for the imagination of a number of histories, only one of which is the sequential and episodic reiteration of key political or military moments which are plotted to give the play its story.

Mothers, queens and the shaping of national identity

Richardus Tertius, written by Thomas Legge in the mid 1570s, uses a classical model to account for recent English political history. Adapting chronicle history to a Senecan model and performed in Latin to an elite audience, the play centres upon the situation of the widowed Queen Elizabeth (mother of the princes eventually murdered in the Tower) and her efforts to protect her family from the machinations of the eponymous king.[13] Richard's reign had become mythologised as a tyranny by the time the play was written and the play reworks Hall's account of the conflict between Elizabeth and Richard's men, who want to remove her younger son to join his brother under the king's 'protection' in the Tower.[14] Legge reconfigures this with reference to Seneca's *Troades*, a play organised as a debate between Andromache, who fights for the life of her child, and Ulysses, who, for reasons of policy, must kill it. The significance of this trope for Renaissance literature has been explored by Eric Auerbach, who shows how a mother's pain in such conflicts is typically articulated in terms of detail: the sleepless nights; the mundane habits peculiar to grief. He shows how this lends such tales a kind of 'realism' and sees it as an important shift in the Renaissance reworking of the classics.[15] Motherhood, Auerbach shows, implies the personal and the instinctive, and a sense that the meanings of events mediated through the mother figure have some anchor in an appreciation of the experience of what is 'real' in the sense of an emotional engagement that is 'creatural' (Auerbach's term as translated by Trask from the German). The mothers of the Innocents in earlier cycle plays, whose pain is articulated through the details of their physical fight to defend their children – 'Out on thee I cry / have at thy groin / An othere!' – offer their audience an upsetting and literal depiction of maternal grief whilst simultaneously figuring the mothers' typological function, for example.[16] Legge's play owes as much to such conventions of typology as to the Senecan conflict of the *Troades*. It could be argued that what he depicts in *Richardus Tertius* is an English history version of *Jocasta*, a psychomachia of state, which is adumbrated through the conventional figure of a distracted mother queen. This is further complicated by the audience's awareness that the events represented by the play are grounded in the real past and therefore what is depicted has implications for the present. The play thus invites engagement beyond the level of intellectual debate, hinting at realism in its intimations of personal feeling and thereby provoking an emotional response to the historical Elizabeth's plight. Her personal fears mirror public anxiety and political uncertainty:

> Even though the happy sceptre of my son
> urges me, his mother, to rejoice, yet my
> ardent mind does not dare to hope for itself
> the promised joy; it fears a good when obtained,
> and fear once born breeds fear, and hence
> my anxious heart burns with many cares.[17]

The stylised language of the play (more so in the Latin) promotes Elizabeth as a generic type as well as a specific historical character: 'I, a mother, enriched the home of the King with a double heir'.[18] She embodies the irreconcilable personal and political demands of her maternity; its abundant love and its innate vulnerability: tensions which resonate back through Christian history and literary tradition and simultaneously forward to the Tudor political future. Specific and generic meanings exist together, lending the mother queen poignancy in the tension between her historic individuality and her generic significance. Legge enriches Hall's narrative by adapting the chronicle's use of Elizabeth as a locus of pathos so that she is given an enhanced political, as well as emotionally provocative, dramatic function.

The play therefore offers meaning from several temporal perspectives. Syntagmatically the drama depicts a linear chronology of incidents that are invested by the plot with political and moral meanings that will be resolved at the end of the play. Simultaneously motherhood endows the play with significance in a way that Paul Ricoeur has called '*trans*historical', using the term to describe types that run 'through history in a cumulative rather than just an additive manner' so that what is played out in the drama resonates beyond the boundaries of the play's chronology.[19] Elizabeth figures the point where an episode located at a particular historical moment (and performed at another such moment) carries meaning for both.[20]

What brings these meanings into proximity with one another in *Richardus Tertius* is that together they construct an idea of nationality which is formed out of an emotional engagement with history: the historic mother queen becomes, when dramatised, an emblem of the well-being of England *now*.[21] This gives an extra resonance to the link between Elizabeth's individual situation and its association with the public mood by her enemies and their agents: 'why do you turn cares about in your anxious heart and weigh down the public joy with your sorrow?' They are unable to appreciate the significance of the relationship between queen and nation that they unwittingly describe and thus seem out of touch (and therefore wrong).[22] When Richard's cardinal fails to see the significance of Elizabeth's fear, her ironic response – 'may you remain ignorant of anything more miserable than my sorrows' – relies for its effect upon her dual function as parent and figure of state, and engenders a response to both the mother's predicament and the national disaster that is inscribed within it.[23]

Legge exploits the traditions discussed in the previous chapters. Elizabeth prophesies civil war in language that associates conflict with personal physical trauma and emblematises the war-torn nation through the physical manifestations of her distraction. A messenger describes her 'uncertain breathing' and unconventional costume – 'her sense of decorum made her put away her regal clothing' – amplifying the meaning of her distracted appearance when she appears.[24] Richard's forced 'unnatural' separation of mother from child is associated with the start of civil war; where his followers insist that the conflict between the interests of the mother and those of the nation is inevitable, the emotional dynamic of the play ensures that such assertions can only be understood ironically. Legge amplifies his sources so that Richard's agent Howard demonstrates a brief and significant moment of remorse in a monologic aside – 'Why have you disturbed the dear heart of the mother so?' – in response to the spectacle of Elizabeth's tearful and protracted farewell to her second son.[25] In the person of the mother, *Richardus Tertius* uses emotional, maternal responses to personally traumatic circumstances to foreground political instability. It simultaneously contemplates a potential subversiveness in the mother who is prepared to defy the state. Chronicle history, re-presented as drama, works to dramatise the telling of the story as well as the story itself and to thicken the texture of the history it offers, inviting a reconsideration of its function and its significance.

George Peele's *Edward I* was registered in 1593, and there are records of performances of a play called *Longshanks*, which may be the same play, in Henslowe's diaries in 1595.[26] The gap between the dates of publication and recorded performance perhaps accounts for some of the peculiarities of a script that has challenged its editors; possibly this is a text which had been considerably reworked during the early 1590s. Written in Peele's eclectic style, the play presents major problems of narrative consistency. Motherhood is integral to the construction of the plot, and the play's peculiar disjunctions in fact reveal a working out of mother queen's dramatic function which offers a useful measure to bring to the reading of more familiar history plays.

There are two royal mothers in this play. The first, the queen mother, appears only once at the beginning of the play, to celebrate her son's return from the crusades.[27] The play begins with her entry on stage, the only female figure, surrounded by powerful men: '*Enter* Gilbart de Clare *Earle of Glocester, with the Earle of Sussex, Mortimer the Earle of March,* David Lluellens *brother, waiting on* Helinor *the queene mother*'. The spectacular effect of this entrance – the sole woman waited on by several men – is compounded by Helinor's control of the scene: she speaks first, announcing her son's return and dispatching her nobles to meet him. She assumes authority both in the world of the play and as a kind of omniscient narrator, placing the events that the play describes in the context of a long view of English history through a formal monologue that eulogises England and identifies her son's place in it. She compares England to Troy as an 'ancient seat of kings' who rule a 'warlike nation' and links this to the return of her own son, the king 'louely Eduard':

> *Longshanke* your king, your glory and our sonne,
> With troops of conquering Lords and warlike knights,
> Like bloudy crested Mars orelookes his hoste,
> Higher than all his armie by the head,
> Martching along as bright as *Phoebus* eyes,
> And we his mother shall beholde our sonne,
> And Englands Peeres shall see their Soueraigne. (ll. 16–45)

Her speech is striking in its similarity to Gaunt's celebration of England in Shakespeare's *Richard II*, and has a similar narrative function, eulogising the nation at a time when, as we are to discover in Peele's play, it is under threat.[28] Peele and Shakespeare both utilise the tradition that links nation and mother but whereas Shakespeare often confines his use of the trope to rhetoric, 'This nurse, this teeming womb of royal kings', Peele, in giving the mother of the monarch a spectacular set piece, makes her emblematic of the nation that she so joyfully celebrates.[29] Helinor moves from the articulation of a personal desire to see her child – 'Vntil his mother see hir princely sonne' – to an expression of their reunion as a public, political moment in the final couplet. This is indicated by her move to the plural pronoun 'we, his mother' and her linking of maternal satisfaction at seeing Edward with public celebration of the return of the king.

Helinor asserts her mythic function as genitor of a monarch who is equivalent to the Trojan heroes, a king like 'bloudy crested Mars'. As in Legge's play, the connection between the historically placed queen mother and the mother myth offers an alternative long view of English history. In a development of Bale's appropriation of the mother for political purposes, Peele evokes through Helinor a sense of national ease and celebration. Unlike the beleaguered figure of Legge's Elizabeth, caught in an irreconcilable conflict between what she instinctively knows and desires and what is politically demanded of her, Helinor coalesces both maternal pride and national celebration: her roles as mother and as queen are in harmony at a moment of political and personal triumph for the monarch. Howard and Rackin argue that Shakespeare's Gaunt in *Richard II* is nostalgically hankering after a masculinised England, constructing an antithesis between 'a warlike, masculine historical world and a degenerate, effeminate present' that is 'projected in opposition to the present realities of female power and authority'. There is a difference between effeminacy and femininity and in Peele's play this is clear. The queen mother is capable of representing and articulating the triumph of the martially successful nation and also the abundance of emotion generated by her son's return.[30]

Vulnerability is as important to this celebration of successful maternity as it is elsewhere. Here, it adumbrates the proper relation of monarch to the state and reminds an audience of the fragility of that relation, shown in Helinor's response to her son's arrival. She greets the king and his brother with what sounds like spontaneous intimacy, 'O my sweete sonnes', and then falls fainting, overcome by 'mothers loue'. Her physical collapse in the face of ceremonial formality provokes a nice tension between a display of private emotion and the meanings engendered by public ritual. One spills into the other, apparently unbearably. Helinor's collapsed body – no longer speaking, no longer in control – is emblematic of that mythic motherhood which exists outside the chronology of the play, but which is always present in the text. The effect is to promote what was present, though less theatrically asserted, in Legge's play: that nationality is a personal, emotional experience as well as a public and political identity, an effect intended perhaps to engender a sense of national pride in an audience moved by the spectacularly overwhelmed feelings of the king's mother. Her involuntary faint works as a moment of realism intruding into the formalised rhetoric and ceremonial spectacle of the play so far but it is also symbolic: the queen mother, figuring both personal love and the affection of the nation, falling before her king.[31]

This symbolic role is reinforced towards the end of the scene, where Peele, who was meticulous in his attention to spectacle, demonstrates the importance of the female figure to the visual success of his play: *'The queene Mother being set on the one side, and queene Elinor* [Edward's wife] *on the other, the king sitteth in the middest mounted highest, and at his feete the Ensigne underneath him'* (116–19).[32] This set piece operates allegorically to signify a perfect, triumphant moment in the nation's history as the all-conquering monarch is framed by royal mothers: emblems of both the past and the future of the English body politic. Martha Hester Fleische has pointed out that the tableau refers to the conventional image of Christ in Majesty, adding a Christian gloss to the celebration of a moment of military success in English history.[33] The triumphalism and oddness of this 'monumental and stationery' presentation are compounded by the fact that the queen mother, her specific, emblematic work done, does not appear again after this.[34]

Edward's wife (confusingly called Elinor) becomes a major figure in the rest of the play. She is remarkable for having two distinctive dramatic personae which appear to conflict absolutely, so that it is difficult to ascertain quite how Peele intended her to be played, or how far this is the consequence of a particularly corrupt text.[35] Elinor is, in one role, beloved Nell, the wife to whom the king is devoted, who has followed him loyally throughout his campaigns, who expresses great pride in and love for her husband and her children and who professes herself an enthusiastic promoter of English interests. But she is also a vicious creature full of 'Spanish pride', who rejects much of what England has to offer, who physically attacks the king more than once, who murders another woman and is an adulteress. This odd combination of characteristics seems to have little to do with the chronicle material that was available to Peele; indeed the historical Elinor is rather a shadowy figure.[36]

A clue to the purpose of this duality comes towards the end of the first scene of the play, where Elinor not only controls her husband – 'you will allow what I do, will you not?' – but describes herself, worryingly, as 'the king of Englandes wife, and the king of Spaines daughter'. Peele structures the scene to end as it began, with a stage controlled by women, but this time Queen Elinor and her daughter Joan (ll. 188–200). In contrast to the certainties that opened the scene there is a subversive tenor to the closing exchanges that hints at political instability. Elinor reveals an alarming penchant for ostentatious dress, informed by a desire to promote Spanish interests: 'That Spaine reaping renowne by Elinor / And Elinor adding renowne to Spaine / Britaine may her magnificence admire' (ll. 257–60). This sets up an opposition that seems central to the play, characterised by David Bevington as 'a patriotic and exaggerated study in contrasts between English "familiar majesty" and a foreign tyranny in which political problematics are articulated, indeed metaphorised, through a merging of the relations between the personal and the public'.[37] Joan (whose generic name implies Englishness, despite the nationality of her mother) remonstrates with the queen in a speech which highlights the consequences of personal behaviour for political success: 'Let not your honour make your manners change' (l. 271). The power relations – the daughter advising the mother – are clearly unusual here, undermining Elinor's status both as mother and queen.

The scene is remarkable for the fact that it is presented as a private exchange between mother and daughter. Such a pairing on the stage would conventionally signify privacy and domesticity but here they address matters of state. The collision of political and personal that worked to celebrate England and the English king at the beginning of the scene becomes dangerous here. Joan's advice to her mother that Englishwomen '[lay] their lives at princes' feet', recalls and reinforces the symbolic value of the queen mother's collapse at the start of the play (l. 274). Her concern is that Elinor is confusing private desires with public duties and bringing into conflict those personal and political aspects of wifehood and maternity that were demonstrated in such harmony in Helinor. Elinor's response to Joan – 'Indeed we count them headstrong Englishmen / But we shall hold them in a Spanish yoake / And make them know their Lord and soveraigne' – confirms Joan's fears and reveals the problematic nature of Elinor's status as a Spanish woman on an English throne and her potentially dangerous presence at the English court. This unhistorical emphasis upon Elinor's Spanish connections is perplexing. Certainly there is a manifestation of anti-Spanish, anti-Catholic sentiment, perhaps tapping into popular feeling following the Spanish threat and the defeat of the armada alongside anxieties associated with the political turmoil of the 1590s, especially frightening at this late stage in Elizabeth's reign.[38] David Home accuses Peele of an 'unhistorical and unjustified libel on Edward's Spanish Queen' that can be fully accounted for 'only by assuming that he was pandering to popular taste', while Marie Axton, like Bevington, sees the play as having a more subtle political strategy.[39] For Axton, the play 'face[s] squarely the English nightmare: a Spanish Infanta seated upon the throne of England' by setting up a version of history which illegitimises any Spanish claims to England by inventing a genealogy and a pattern of events which work, she argues, as metaphor, rather than as restatement of fact.[40] Peele's apparent sources for most of the narrative material which vilifies the queen are two contemporary ballads: 'The lamentable Fall of Queen Elinor' and 'Queen Eleanor's Confessions', which tell different stories about the evil machinations of (different) English queens of the same foreign name upon the English throne.[41] Whatever the figurative sophistication of Peele's play, there is a sense that history is being rewritten for real both in the play and the popular ballads which all present the political failures of the past as the consequence of foreign, female duplicity.[42]

This refashioning of the past works because Peele's use of dramatic typology coerces his preposterous storylines into a familiar set of structures. The synthesis of classical and popular dramatic forms brings together the potential of the politically seditious mothers of classical drama and the Christian tradition of representing duplicitous maternity by reference to typology. Elinor's fecundity is consistently emphasised in the play; she is visibly pregnant or in childbed for much of it. Her expectant belly works as a comic signifier of the sins of Eve, a reminder of the conventional fallibilities of women – vanity, garrulousness, lasciviousness, deceit – and of the conventional punishments for them – the discomforts of pregnancy – as corporeal signifiers of the threat of damnation.[43] Elinor's is a body made doubly grotesque, first because of the way in which her pregnancy is represented (she complains of her bulk and the sweat that drips from her), and secondly because hers is a body shown to be luxuriating in spectacular material excess. Her arrival 'great with child' in Wales is an exhibition of exotic luxury that, if set against Joan's earlier account of the 'milde' temperament of Englishwomen, is clearly gratuitous indulgence:

> The trumpets sound, Queene Elinor in her litter borne by foure Negro Mores, Ione of Acon with her, attended on by the Earle of Gloucester, and her foure footemen, one having set a ladder to the side of the litter. She discended, and her daughter followeth. (ll. 1100–4)

The spectacle of the pregnant queen, complaining of the heat and her sweat, clambering down from her litter as if out of the ark, operates like that of the old Noah plays as both comic and, by dint of typological association, redolent of the threat of evil, understood in this play as political subversion. Elinor is disgruntled with the king for making her travel and their argument descends into violence as she hits him (as Noah's wife hits her husband), boasting that mighty England has felt her fist. Peele's fascination with earlier popular drama seems to be responsible for these earthy scenes in which Elinor and her husband engage in the kind of husband and wife banter familiar, as Axton notes, from depictions of Adam and Eve, and of Noah and his wife, whose representation reaches back through the cycle plays to fertility rituals and community games.[44] Her appeal at these moments has to do with the recognition of familiar comic types: the scold and the irascible pregnant woman, both of which signify danger and disruption to a patriarchally structured and politically driven world. The on-stage fisticuffs are like those between Noah and his wife in which the woman always deals the last and most successful blow. Edward, exactly like Noah, turns to his audience to give a rueful warning: 'Learne lords gainst you be maried men to bow to womens yoke: / And sturdy though you be you may not stur for every stroke' (ll. 1248–9). Hook sees this scene as promoting Elinor as a sympathetic figure, though if this is true then her subsequent behaviour would dissipate any remaining sympathies:

> Nell's actions are as earthy as her speech. Arriving in Wales, she climbs from her litter gasping for breath and dripping perspiration in the humid Welsh summer. She is beset by an uncontrollable desire

to box Ned's royal ear ... In speech and action this Nell is more
woman than Queen, but that very quality lends her sympathetic
appeal.[45]

The figure of Elinor in the play as it now exists is perhaps the
result of a collision, rather than a synthesis, of diverse narrative
sources and structures, resulting in a mother-queen resonant with
conflicting typologies. Rather than seeking some kind of coherence
of narrative, it is useful to consider motherhood working in this
play in terms of a series of interruptions to the chronological story:
events that cut across the teleological drive which organises the
dominant narrative.[46] Pierre Nora has characterised 'events' as
'vehicles for a whole collection of emotions, habits, realities, of
inherited representations of the past which suddenly show on the
surface of society', and this might offer an analogy for the operation
of motherhood in Peele's play as a complex of meanings which
erupts at intervals through the story of Edward's campaign to
create or to presage misrule, and its sinister obverse, sedition.[47]
Peele's play sets up spectacular celebrations in between representing Edward's military exploits – folk play, church ritual and
civic ceremony – only to have Elinor thrust into their midst to
subvert and undermine them.[48] The effect is weirdly surreal, as
the usual boundaries between genres blur. This is evident in a scene
where Edward visits Elinor 'lying in' after the birth of his son. The
stage directions require a special tent for the queen on stage, large
enough to hold several actors, so that there is a visual sense of an
enclosed world, dominated by the figure of the queen 'discovered
in her bed'. In a fascinating piece of theatrical spectacle, Edward
and his male companions enter the stage and then 'the Queen's
tent opens' to discover a hitherto concealed place occupied only
by women. The relatively rare (and usually comic) dramatic
depictions of 'lying in' in Elizabethan theatre tend to emphasise
female control of the ritual and to joke about the emasculation of
male visitors at these occasions. The ceremony as theatrical
spectacle acquires a double edge, offering the potential for a joke
about emasculated men and powerful women while creating a
visual arrangement not unlike that of a nativity scene. In *Edward
I*, the curtains draw back to reveal the queen 'dandling' the baby
which she presents to its father, the king who is, for Elizabethan
Protestants, God's representative as head of the Church of England.
This is a complex dramatic moment, celebrating the birth of an
English heir by reference to Christian iconography whilst teetering,

in its display of luxury and comic, sinful womanhood, very close to travesty.[49] Elinor's successful motherhood has done the nation a service, and as the mother of a future monarch she is blessed. But simultaneously she is comic, dandling the child in bed, talking too much, making outrageous demands, becoming simultaneously mad and dangerous in her demand that all Englishmen should shave and all women have their right breasts cut off, something Bevington says is 'intended to be a test of absolute royal supremacy over the personal lives of subjects'.[50] An Elizabethan audience knew that this prince was the future Edward II and this might also colour their reading of this scene. If, as Katherine Park has noted, the absence of the mother at birth was traditionally linked to the engendering of heroes, then the intense focus in this scene upon the feminine – the enclosed chamber, the maternal 'dandling' and nursing of the new prince by women – reminds the audience that there is a thin line between benign and malign motherhood. Another Eleanor refers to Queen Margaret's emasculating influence in Shakespeare's *Henry VI*: 'she'll hamper thee and dandle thee like a baby' (1.3.145–7).[51] Dod and Cleaver's household manual, written 'for the ordering of private families', warns of the prospects for a child 'cockhered and made wanton by the mother' who will be more intractable 'when the father shall seek to bend him to good'.[52]

Type and antitype are deployed in tension in this scene. The queen figures both: confusingly, but perhaps deliberately. There is a sense in which the oppositions combined in Elinor resemble the psychomachia of state addressed through the deployment of idealised motherhood in Legge's play. In Elinor's frowardness and pride, displayed alongside her affection for and loyalty to the king and her service to the nation, it is possible to see a figure that expresses the demands, compromises and conflicts inherent in the *realpolitik* which is the subject of much of the political content of the play: the tension between the religious and political pressures of domestic and international negotiation and the need to consolidate a sense of national integrity at home.

The birth of Prince Edward marks the point where Peele turns to the ballad material. From here, Elinor is an incarnation of malevolence. Diana Purkiss has noted that women lying in were thought to be particularly vulnerable to the influences of witchcraft and perhaps this also influences the play.[53] The ballad describes an unhistorical incident where the mayoress of London is churched after the birth of her long-awaited son and insists upon the poignancy of the mayoress's long wait being rewarded in her husband's term of office.[54] Elinor, offended by what she perceives as an affront to her own ritual pre-eminence, takes revenge in a bizarre scene where she and her Spanish maid tie the mayoress to a chair and force her to suckle an adder until she dies.

The incorporation of this incident into the play perhaps attests to the contemporary popularity of the ballad: certainly it signals the dramatic transformation of the queen into a kind of witch who attacks a good, and importantly, English wife and mother. Like Lady Macbeth, Elinor transforms herself into the devil's agent. Deborah Willis has shown how a commonplace of early modern thinking was that witches represented a version of 'mothers "gone bad"' and Elinor's torture of the mayoress through a perverted parody of maternal suckling appears to tap into this.[55] The shock of the tale is that it brings together jarring places and stories: the snakes of Eden infest the city of London through the agency of a Spanish witch. The mayoress with snakes at her breast also reminds onlookers of the witch who suckles her familiars; the loving wife and mother is transformed, through her torture, into a grotesque version of the malevolent witch who is her murderer. This terrifying scene of infiltration mirrors the transformation of Elinor the queen into Elinor the witch: neither city nor state is safe. Willis refers to John Jewel's 1563 sermon to Elizabeth I which refers to a 'marvellous increase' in witches and sorcerors, which is, 'of course due to the Catholic rule of Mary I'.[56] Purkiss notes a contemporary 'opposition between the queen and witches' in that 'Witches, acting on behalf of the devil (or Spain, or the Pope) were assumed to be interested in removing her'.[57]

The odd story in the ballad and the play that the queen sank into the ground at Charing Cross and rose up again at Potters Hithe is in keeping with her new witchlike identity. Purkiss describes a contemporary understanding of women's bodies in terms of 'a formlessness that engulfs all forms, a disorder that threatens all order'. The witch has a protean ability to transform and to infiltrate not only the bodies of others but also their households, cities and states.[58] Marina Warner shows that a propensity to such metamorphosis 'often serves to distinguish good from evil ... in the Christian heaven nothing is mutable, whereas in hell everything combines and recombines'.[59] Queen Elinor may or may not be conscious of her terrifying other self, for hellish possession might mean a foreign (in all senses of the word in this case) body 'taking possession of you and masquerading as you inside your own person'. This may have happened, says Warner, 'without your knowing it'.[60] This mutability of evil is behind the practice of placing figures of those wished harm in dunghills, where they would melt in the heat. In 1578 three such figures, one apparently representing the queen, were found, according to Reginald Scot, to 'the terror & astonishment of manie thousands' fraught, as Purkiss notes, with terror of Spanish invasion.[61] For Scot, who was debunking the idea of witchery, the true threat was the treasonous intent behind the figures: 'therein is manifested a traitorous heart to the queene and a presumption against God'.[62] In a version of this, the evil Elinor melts into the ground and arises in a different spot, once more changed, close to death and ready to make confession. Editors of the ballad agree that the story has much to do with anti-Spanish feeling, but are undecided as to its specific target. William Dicey, an early eighteenth-century printer of the song, sees it as already old by the 1590s and expressing a generalised anti-Catholic sentiment: 'a Satyr, written in the days of Queen *Mary* the First'.[63] Dicey reads the ballad, as Axton and Bevington read the play, as figurative: the subversive machinations of an invented mad mother queen function, in both accounts, to denote the unpredictability and danger of foreign alliance. However, the incident with the mayoress may have specific meaning. The circumstances of the birth of her son in the year of his father's office and the pageantry of the churching ceremony in which she first appears link her to a tightening of the play's nationalism to focus upon London itself. The foreign queen is shown attacking the nation literally at its very heart (and where the play's audience physically is); her adders suck blood from English breasts that should produce sustaining milk.[64] The spectre of such malevolence (however metaphorical) on the stage, so close to home, is very disturbing, working like a morality play to demonstrate the power of evil in the midst of what is most familiar.[65] Bevington suggests that Peele deliberately localises the queen's tyranny: 'Peele overtly appeals not only to Londoners' fear of Catholic takeover, but to their insistence on citizens' prerogatives and a consequent restraint of monarchical authority ... Most of all, the English monarchy must respect the privileges of the city of London'.[66]

Elinor dies 'in childbed' confessing to the king, who is disguised as a friar, that Princess Joan is the illegitimate daughter of a 'lusty friar' (l. 2679). In extracting this confession, Edward is able to regain and claim authority over Elinor because as Deborah Willis shows, the limits of a witch's power are always discovered in the face of the legitimate, sanctioned authority of God and monarch.[67]

Throughout the play, Edward does not reject the queen, but contains and counters her excesses. His pragmatic but firm approach to the dangers of 'Spanish pride' offers a version of monarchy that is neither aggressive nor defensive, but that confidently contains foreign and Catholic threats.[68] Bevington notes that 'this portrait obviously bears little personal resemblance to Elizabeth, even less to the historical Edward I. It is London's sentimentalised projection of a king created in her own image'.[69] It is also a reworking of English history in which the concept of royal motherhood is central both in celebrating the nation and in undermining it. Using opposing typologies of motherhood to tear through the main narrative at symbolically significant moments in the play, Peele offers a version of the past in which motherhood supplies a schema by which Elizabethan audiences were able to reappraise their own relation to recent, and not so recent, history, and to contemporary political circumstance.

Civil war

As is clear from *Richardus Tertius*, the chronicles, which provided such useful source material for so many historical dramas of the 1590s, exhibited a tendency to embellish their source materials, notably by importing conventional narratives and ideas about motherhood in order to give their work clear emotional (and political) direction. For example, here is Hall relating the moment of separation between Queen Elizabeth and her son, who will be murdered by Richard III, and milking the incident with enthusiasm:

> And therewith all she saied to the child, fare well mine owne swete sonne, God send you good kepyng, let me once kisse you or you go, for God knoweth when we shal kisse together again & therewith she kissed hym & blessed hym, and turned her backe and wepte, goyng her waie, leaving the poore innocent chylde wepyng as faste as the mother.[70]

For Howard and Rackin, the chronicle is essentially a masculine genre which takes a patriarchal view, representing the nation as repeatedly challenged by subversive women.[71] In their analysis such women often represent foreign threats: 'foreign worlds are typically characterized as women'.[72] And yet, as is suggested in the above discussion of Peele's play, such a narrative strategy can be shown to have a more complex intention. The contradictory meanings embodied in the figures of women who are also mothers allow for an intricate and multifaceted telling of a constantly shifting story. As Lawrence Danson recognises in his discussion of the first tetralogy, 'the shape of history in the three parts of Henry VI is forever changing – an incessant forming and re-forming and betrayal of alliances and also curiously repetitive in its endless battles for power'.[73] The mutable alliances, values and strategies in two of Shakespeare's stories of the Wars of the Roses (*Henry VI Parts 2 and 3*) have their complexities and contradictions mirrored in a narrative structure which operates through a depiction of the career of the admired and despised figure of Queen Margaret. In this character, the ambivalence and contradiction so schematically drawn by Peele are reconfigured and integrated.

Hall's chronicles describe the alarming manliness of Margaret's character, which, set alongside the gentleness of her husband, has informed so much critical appreciation of the plays: 'This woman excelled all other, as well as in beautie and favor, as in wit and pollicie, and was of stomack and corage, more like to a man, then a woman'.[74] Such grudging admiration ('This manly woman, this courageous Quene') is always tempered in Hall's narrative by the implicit threat, thoroughly discussed by Rackin and Howard, that a woman who embodies so many manly qualities is, by her very nature, subversive. It has been generally noted that Margaret, like Elinor in Peele's play, is reminiscent of the unruly woman or the manly woman of the world-turned-upside-down that is the prequel to apocalypse in so many traditional narratives.[75] Willis links this to the witch: 'a masculine-feminine hybrid, a beautiful erotic hybrid with masculine traits'.[76]

In Shakespeare's reworking of the chronicles, which follows Hall, Margaret, the English royal wife and mother, uses all her power, albeit ineffectually in the end, to promote the interests of her husband and child. Her courage and political daring are celebrated despite the cruelty that characterises some of her efforts. It is possible to account for this apparently paradoxical representation by referring to Hall's assertion of both Margaret and her husband as victims of a kind of cruel fate. However, the mother's capacity to embody and indeed to figure contradiction allows the dramatist to create a narrative that is capable of articulating the tensions and conflicts that are peculiar to civil war.[77]

It is notable that in the chronicles that provide the bases for Shakespeare's plays on Henry VI and Richard III, Queen Margaret is characterised with a complexity that is reminiscent of the puzzling, inconsistent Elinor in Peele's play:

> the Quene . . . was a woman of a greate witte, and yet of no greater witte, then of haute stomacke, desirous of glory, and covetous of honor, and of reason, policye, councaill, and other giftes and talentes of nature belonging to a man, full and flowynge . . . but yet she had one point of a very woman: for often tyme, when she was vehement and fully bente in a matter, she was sodainly like a wethercocke, mutable and turning.[78]

Margaret is here contrasted with the king, who is described as one who 'studied onely for the health of his soule'. Hall's admiration, horror and anxiety find expression in the use of metaphors which, again, are familiar from Peele's queen, as he laments that she was often 'perswaded, incensed and exhorted' by 'venomous serpents, and malicious Tygers'. Like Elinor, Margaret is a force for good as much as evil. Whatever these women may be in terms of their original nationality or their unbecoming masculinity, they are also the wives of English kings and the mothers of English princes, and because of this they are celebrated as much as, and often at the same time as, they are condemned.

Shakespeare's representation of Margaret as an adulteress in *2 Henry VI* appears to place her on the bad side in terms of morality, in a familiar reworking of the conventional type so well drawn upon by Peele in his play. Margaret boxes Henry's ears, as Peele's Elinor had boxed her Edward's ears, and Margaret is shown to attack and humiliate Eleanor of Gloucester, as Elinor attacked the mayor's wife in *Edward I*.[79] Margaret's more spectacular perversion of her potential maternity, clasping her dead lover's detached head to her bosom – 'here may his head lie on my throbbing breast' (4.4.19) – can be read as true to type, the bad woman whose sexual and maternal tendencies are misdirected in the service of her own desires. Adelman reads this as a lesson on the dangers of the mother's body; it 'suggests what happens to men who succumb to its allure'.[80]

And yet the characterisation of Margaret is complicated. The passion between Suffolk and Margaret, and her pain at his death, are depicted sympathetically, and her assertion of control in the English court is not so much the dangerous ambition of a dominant and malevolent woman but the inevitable consequence of the masculine weakness that surrounds her. Suffolk had imagined himself dying at her breast, turning his lover into a comforting mother in a fantasy that her later behaviour recalls: 'Here could I breathe my soul into the air, / As mild and gentle as the cradle-babe / Dying with mother's dug between its lips' (3.2.312–14). Such a discomfiting confusion of roles serves, it might be argued, to infantilise Suffolk rather than to vilify Margaret. She is dangerous because she can provoke such confusion, and Howard and Rackin see this scene as evidence of female sexuality as 'dangerous to men and the good order of the kingdom'.[81]

But the scene reveals the dangers of masculine weakness too. Willis points out that 'disorder is invited into the world of the tetralogy by the male order itself' and Margaret turns to Suffolk for the kind of manliness she cannot discover in Henry:

> I tell thee, Pole, when in the city Tours
> Thou ran'st a-tilt in honour of my love
> And stol'st away the ladies' hearts of France,
> I thought King Henry had resembled thee
> In courage, courtship and proportion;
> But all his mind is bent to holiness (1.3.50–5).[82]

This retreat by men from the usual order is evident when Henry does not rescue Gloucester from danger but reacts as an emasculated victim. Howard and Rackin see the king here as 'the author of his own disempowerment'.[83] Just as Suffolk turned himself into an infant before Margaret in the scene discussed above, Henry describes himself to her 'as the dam runs lowing up and down / . . . and can do naught': not man but beast, not man but mother (3.1.214–15). This goes against convention. For example, Bale's *Kyng Johan* made clear that the king's role is to defend his country, not to take on her identity. The typological relation between king and nation is breached by Henry, revealing his unkingliness as well as his unmanliness in the image he chooses.[84] The presence of the hapless Margaret on the stage in both these exchanges is telling: repeatedly the addressee of such abjurations from masculine authority, her necessary response (and dramatic function) is to fill the gap. The scene where Margaret clasps Suffolk's severed head to her breast is therefore pathetic: the head is all she has left of the protector and support to whom she turned. The visual effect is that there is one body where there should be two, and it emphasises Margaret's isolation and the consequent necessity of assuming a public and political role.

The play repeatedly shows retreats by men from proper masculine martial conduct. The accusations of bastardy that fly between Warwick and Suffolk appear as almost plaintive attempts to place the responsibility for present conflict upon past mothers (3.2.210–23). Willis comments that 'Shakespeare makes any certainty about the mother's culpability problematic' and it does appear that Shakespeare is aiming to dramatise the complexity of narrative, circumstance and character that he discovered in Hall.[85] Alongside the familiar tropes is a more subtle portrait of a woman who is in fact the product of a civil war – her behaviour a consequence, rather than a cause, of masculine failure.

Hall's chronicle draws attention to the coexistence of Margaret's commendable talents and feminine weaknesses and it should not be taken as a given that her historical reputation was that of an evil woman any more than it should be assumed that Shakespeare's plays necessarily portray her as one. As Cox and Rasmussen point out, her place in early modern historical narratives varied: 'Thomas Heywood, Shakespeare's contemporary ... identified [Margaret] as one of the nine female worthies of England, despite what he knew about her from Shakespeare's early history plays'. However, they disappointingly retreat from reading any of this complexity in Shakespeare's portrayal of her: 'in short, Margaret is a type and Bevington's "domineering female" identified her type as well as any label has'.[86]

Rackin writes that women in the early histories, including Margaret, are defined as 'opponents and subverters of the historical and historiographical enterprise, in short, as anti-historians'.[87] Margaret is anti-historical partly because the meaning generated by her motherhood operates as a corollary to her characterisation, giving her an emblematic function at crucial moments in the narrative which works transhistorically and against the teleology of the play. In *3 Henry VI* she is always in the service of a masculine, dynastic enterprise, accruing power to herself only for her husband and, especially, her son. Shakespeare follows Hall in emphasising the close relationship, personal and political, between Margaret and her son. The prince and his mother are always together on stage, creating a visual statement about her support for him and his attachment to her.[88] They make their first entrance after Henry has disinherited his son and Margaret is again forced to take control after her husband refuses to do so:

Exeter:	Here comes the Queen, whose looks bewray her anger.
	I'll steal away.
King Henry:	Exeter, so will I.
Queen Margaret:	Nay, go not from me; I will follow thee.
King Henry:	Be patient, gentle Queen, and I will stay.
Queen Margaret:	Who can be patient in such extremes? (1.1.211–15)

Faced with a stageful of fleeing men, Margaret has no choice but to take control and to condemn her husband, setting up her pain and sacrifice as a mother against Henry's lack of effort to support his child:

Hadst thou but loved him half as well as I,
Or felt that pain which I did for him once,
Or nourished him as I did with my blood,
Thou wouldst have left they dearest heart-blood there,
Rather than have made that savage Duke thine heir
And disinherited thine only son. (1.1.221–26)

Margaret speaks of the bond of motherhood in terms of blood and pain to draw an analogy with battle and to link her roles as mother and warrior. She uses the contemporary understanding that mother's milk is blood transformed to compare her nourishing blood with Henry's bloodlessness and to make motherhood her reason to fight.[89] Throughout the scene her determination in the face of Henry's passivity enhances an image of her as the warrior mother, enraged because she must protect her young. This is reinforced by her son's polite refusal to remain with his ineffectual father while political times are tough: 'When I return with victory from the field / I'll see your grace; till then, I'll follow her.' (1.1.261–3) Indeed, Margaret's assumption of warrior status is not only acknowledged as perfectly reasonable, but positively welcomed by her husband:

Poor Queen, how love to me and to her son
Hath made her break out into terms of rage.
Revenged may she be on that hateful Duke,
Whose haughty spirit, winged with desire,
Will coast my crown and, like an empty eagle,
Tire on the flesh of me and of my son. (1.1.264–9)

Henry willingly abdicates his paternal and kingly role of defender of both himself and his son here and Margaret is forced to assume the dominant role, not because she is a tyrant or unwomanly, but because she has no choice as a wife and mother except to fill the gap left by Henry's abdication. Coppelia Kahn's argument that in Shakespeare's early history plays 'liaisons with women are invariably disastrous because they subvert or destroy more valued alliances between men' might, in this analysis, be mistaking the symptom for the cause. The warlike Margaret is the product of the breakdown of masculine relations, rather than its source.[90]

It is the infamous scene of the mocking of York that has confirmed for many critics Margaret's reputation as an unnatural monster. Certainly the execution of York is a turning point in terms of Margaret's fate in the play, as it is in Hall, but it is as much a turning point in terms of the history of England.[91] The dramatic continuity of the story, though, makes sense of Margaret's behaviour. York is guilty of treason, and she metes out to him the humiliation that traitors deserve:

What, was it you that would be England's king?
Was't you that revelled in our Parliament
And made a preachment of your high descent?
Where are your mess of sons to back you now? (1.4.70–3)

The impact of this scene is created visually as much as rhetorically. Margaret is accompanied by her son, the prince, and his silent presence attests to his dynastic claim, and thus to York's treason: she is the mother of York's victim. When Margaret mocks York by reference to his sons, and most cruelly with the blood of his youngest child, she is enacting revenge for the treasonous hurts that he has inflicted upon her son. And yet her behaviour is excessive. She seems to answer to Hall's description of her disposition as 'mutable and turnyng'; there is a sense that her nature takes her too far and she becomes cruel without restraint. This combination of furious mother and warrior is a terrifying spectacle because the mother takes the warrior way beyond the boundaries of political or martial protocol. The images that are famously used to describe Margaret – the tigress (in Hall and Shakespeare) and the she-wolf – refer not only to the reputation of unrestrained ferocity that these beasts held, but also to their equally celebrated qualities as mothers and nurses in popular mythology. York's famous attack, 'O, tiger's heart wrapped in a woman's hide', says something about the terrifying lengths to which the mother might go to protect – and to nurture – her own. Margaret attacks York through his sons because her child has been attacked, but her revenge becomes unbearably cruel.[92] It is a revenge all the more pathetic and terrible because it brings Margaret's ally Northumberland, as well as York, to tears. Men may weep but with her son beside her, Margaret is mindful of the past and present political danger:

> What, weeping-ripe my Lord Northumberland?
> Think but upon the wrong he did us all,
> And that will quickly dry thy melting tears. (1.4.172–5)

Margaret stabs York, with an ironic salute to her inept husband: 'And here's to right our gentle-hearted King!'(1.4.176). Her frustration with 'gentle-hearted' men at a time when they should be made of stronger stuff is wryly acknowledged here.

In terms of narrative, though, this extended cruelty breaks through the story of the politics, fighting and intrigue to force contemplation of the bloody actuality of the wars that the plays depict. After the previous thrills of argument and battle, the sudden drop in pace of this anguishingly slow scene creates a narrative jolt. Margaret as signifier breaks through the story here, the meanings generated by her motherhood overarching the dramatic action even as she determines its course. She becomes an emblem of civil war and its implications: the decimation of dynasties, the killing of children, the breakdown of protocol and social and political boundaries. Willis characterises her as 'an exemplary clan-centred mother, fighting valiantly for her son's rights, but ... also a monstrous *national* mother, malevolently turning upon England's children'.[93] This is a shocking scene because Margaret forces the spectator to confront the implications of what it shows: what becomes of people in the extreme of civil war – beyond the bounds of the story; beyond the limits of a particular historical moment – and it is all the more upsetting for that.

The death of Prince Edward offers another such moment. It is not often noted that Margaret is constructed as a dutiful queen and loving mother in this play, whatever she has also been. Her frustrations with Henry do not seem to affect his respect for her; in fact, he follows her lead, whether in taking up her suggestion that he confers a knighthood on their son (quick thinking by Margaret, seeking a gesture which will rally their disheartened troops) or leaving the battlefield with his family in the face of defeat.[94] Henry worries about her as 'a poor soul' whose grief would tame tigers rather than make her tigerish: 'a woman to be pitied much' (3.1.36–53). The prince, always at her side, is protective of her, demanding that she is addressed as 'Queen' (3.3.78). Her determination on behalf of her family and the concern with which they recognise her efforts undercuts a straightforward understanding of her as simply 'domineering' or even subversive and offers a version of her as loyal, loved and determined: a glimpse of the qualities admired by Heywood, perhaps. That she has these qualities is what makes her collapse at Edward's death so pathetic, her plea for annihilation, 'O kill me too!', and her physical collapse making her the locus of pity and simultaneously a dramatic emblem that signifies the end of the political struggle, the capitulation of the nation to the Yorkists.

As Cox and Ramussen show, Margaret's lament over the body of her dead son endows her with a value which transcends the story in which it is situated. Pointing out that 'the stage configuration is a pietà' they argue that 'Margaret's lament for her son is another example of Shakespeare's secularising stage tradition by using an element from the dramatic history of salvation for its emotional effect while displacing it literally from its narrative and moral context'.[95] Shakespeare creates a moment which evokes dramatic and iconographical tradition but Margaret's plight demands of its audience a wider consideration: not only of the personal implications of the political, but also of the implications of history and the structuring of the narratives which re-present it.

The eruption of motherhood with all its meanings into the teleological narrative of war forces a long view: a view of history which embraces what has been and what is to come, as the mother embodies both the causes and consequences of civil disruption. By incorporating narratives of motherhood and it meanings into the telling of an historical story, dramatists are able to present a more anguished and complicated analysis of civil war from the perspective of the suffering state. It would be wrong to assume that because motherhood at its most protective is also dangerous, violent, frightening and 'mutable', it is not also admirable. Where mothers appear in history plays their role, however integrated into the stories in which they are situated, also operates outside the plot to emblematise the wider significance of the activities in which they are embroiled. The meanings of the mother figure, determined by the traditions of English culture and coloured by an appropriation of classical tropes, are manifest in emblematic 'events' where meaning pushes against chronology. She functions as a point of intersection between theatricality and chronicle narrative, mythology and ideology, nurture and danger, past and future history: an emblem that turns narrative focus away from preoccupations of dynasty, monarchy or the order of a particular political moment and towards the nation.

Notes

1 Philip Stubbes, *A Motive to Good Workes. Or Rather, to True Christianitie Indeede* (1593), quoted in Patrick Collinson, 'The Elizabethan Church and the New Religion', in *The Reign of Elizabeth I*, ed. Christopher Haigh (London: Macmillan, 1987), p. 169.
2 Jean Howard and Phillis Rackin, *Engendering a Nation: A Feminist Reading of Shakespeare's English Histories* (London and New York: Routledge, 1997), p. 20.
3 A. P. Rossiter, *Angel with Horns and Other Shakespeare Lectures*, ed. Graham Storey (London: Longmans, 1961), p. 41.
4 Paola Pugliatti, *Shakespeare the Historian* (Basingstoke: Macmillan, 1996), p. 72.
5 See the introduction to Susana Onega and Jose Angel Garcia Landa, *Narratology: An Introduction* (Harlow: Longman, 1996), 'a *story* is the signified of a narrative text', p. 6.
6 Prologue to *Nice Wanton*, in R. Dodsley and W. C. Hazlitt, eds, *A Selection of Old English Plays* (London: Reeves and Turner, 1876).
7 Pugliatti, *Shakespeare the Historian*, p. 31. For more on this see Peter Saccio, *Shakespeare's English Kings* (Oxford: Oxford University Press, 1977), p. 115.
8 In Annabel Patterson, *Reading Holinshead's Chronicles* (Chicago: University of Chicago Press, 1994), p. 15.
9 Pugliatti, *Shakespeare the Historian*, p. 33.
10 Quoted in Patterson, *Reading Holinshead's Chronicles*, preface, p. viii.
11 Hayden White, 'Three Forms of the Historical Representation of Reality, Annals: Chronicle: Historical Narrative', in Onega, and Garcia Landa, *Narratology: An Introduction*, p. 277.
12 White, 'Three Forms of the Historical Representation of Reality', p. 277.
13 Thomas Legge, *Richardus Tertius*, ed. R. J. Lordi (London: Garland, 1979), p. v. All subsequent references are to this version of the text. The play is an occasional piece, intended for playing on consecutive days. The only recorded performance was at St John's College, Cambridge, in March 1579 or 1580. Francis Meres placed Legge in the company of Marlowe, Peele, Shakespeare, Kyd, Drayton, Chapman, Dekker and Johnson in his list of '"our beste for Tragedie"'. Lordi

also mentiones the approbation of Heywood, Fuller and Harington for Legge's work (Lordi, p. iv). Chambers quotes Harington's praise of *Richardus Tertius* as having the power to '"moue even tyrants"', as well as Meres. (E. K. Chambers, *The Elizabethan* Stage, vol. 4 (Oxford: Clarendon Press, 1974, p. 238.) Legge's continuing celebrity is evident in a passing mention of his work in Nashe's play *Have with You to Saffron Walden*. See Chambers, *The Elizabethan* Stage, vol. 3, p. 408.

14 This shift is noted by G. Bullough, who irritably observes that Legge 'took every advantage afforded by the chronicles to introduce scenes with female participants'. G. Bullough, *Narrative and Dramatic Sources of Shakespeare*, vol. 3, (London: Routledge and Kegan Paul, 1960). Bullough notes that Hall's narrative 'added pathos wherever possible', pp. 226 and 235.

15 Erich Auerbach, *Mimesis*, trans. Ronald Trask (Princeton: Princeton University Press, 1953), ch. 10, p. 203. Auerbach's analysis is challenged by Paul Ricoeur in *Time and Narrative*, vol. 1, trans. Kathleen McLaughlin and David Pellauer (Chicago: University of Chicago Press, 1984) in scattered references, for e.g., p. 245.

16 A. C. Cawley, *Everyman and Medieval Miracle Plays*, 'The Wakefield Pageant of Herod the Great, (London: Dent, 1990), 381–2.

17 Legge, *Richardus Tertius*, pp. 26–7.

18 Legge, *Richardus Tertius*, pp. 26–7.

19 See Ricoeur, *Time and Narrative*, vol. 2, p. 15.

20 As Howard and Rackin show, both chronicle history and chorography offered coexisting models of national identity in the late sixteenth century. Howard and Rackin, *Engendering a Nation*, p. 49.

21 Michael Bath writes that religious emblems are 'intent on discovering the meanings already inscribed in the books of scriptures and nature'. See Bath, *Speaking Pictures: English Emblem Books and Renaissance Culture* (London and New York: Longman), p. 3.

22 Legge, *Richardus Tertius*, p. 268.

23 Legge, *Richardus Tertius*, p. 268.

24 Legge, *Richardus Tertius*, pp. 269 and 286–7.

25 Legge, *Richardus Tertius*, p. 315.

26 See *King Edward the First by George Peele 1593*, Malone Society (London: Oxford University Press, 1911), p. vi. All subsequent references to the play come from this edition. See Chambers in *The Elizabethan Stage*, vol. 3, p. 461, and Roslyn L. Knutson, in 'Play Identifications: *The Wise Men of Chester and John a Kent and John a Cumber; Longshanks* and *Edward I*', *HLQ* 47 (1984), 1–11.

27 To avoid a tangle of terminology, reigning queens who are also mothers in history plays are referred to as 'the mother queen'. 'Queen mother' retains its modern meaning as the mother of a reigning monarch.

28 See William Shakespeare, *Richard II*, ed. Peter Ure, The Arden Shakespeare (London: Methuen, 1964), 2.1.40–60. Subsequent references

come from this edition. Appendix III quotes from John Eliot's *Ortho-Epia Gallica* (1593) where France is described as 'The nurse of many learned wits', and Appendix IV quotes Sylvester's Du Bartas, from *Divine Weekes and Workes*, published in 1605, where 'Albion' is hailed as a 'Thrice-happy Mother, which aye bringest-forth / Such Chiualry as daunteth all the Earth'. Both pieces are typical in that they contain references to other lands, to the sea and to nature, all of which were typically gendered female and specified as maternal in contemporary allegory. In his edition of *Edward I*, Frank S. Hook suggests that Peele is borrowing from Marlowe's *Tamburlaine I*, but while Peele appears to aspire to a similar rhetorical style to Marlowe, parallels of imagery are too commonplace to make a definite connection. See Frank S. Hook, ed., *The Dramatic Works of George Peele* (New Haven and London: Yale University Press, 1961), p. 24, p. 50.

29 Shakespeare, *Richard II*, 2.1.51.
30 See Howard and Rackin, *Engendering a Nation*, pp. 147–8.
31 See Edwin Davenport, 'The Representation of Robin Hood in Elizabethan Drama: *George a Greene* and *Edward I*', in *Playing Robin Hood: The Legend in Performance*, ed. Lois Potter (London: Associated University Presses, 1998), p. 55, where he discusses the play in terms of 'national struggles metonymised into personal relationships'.
32 Inga-Stina Ewbank, acknowledging the textual problems the play poses, says that 'if . . . we try to glimpse the original and unrevised structure of the play, we find it to be . . . a primarily visual one. The action moves through a series of pageants and shows that even in passages of formal rhetoric, there is an emphasis upon the way things look'. Inga-Stina Ewbank, 'George Peele and the Importance of Spectacle', in E. G. Hubbard, ed., *The Elizabethan Theatre V* (London: Macmillan, 1975), p. 145.
33 Martha Hester Fleische, *Iconography of the English History Play* (Salzburg: Universität Salzburg, Institut für Englische Sprache and Literatur, 1974), p. 55.
34 John Cox has discussed this tendency to represent power in 'tableau-like scenes in which theatrical images tend to be monumental and stationery rather then fluid and mimetic'. John D. Cox, *Shakespeare and the Dramaturgy of Power* (Princeton: Princeton University Press, 1989).
35 Noting that *Edward I* is 'an unusually corrupt text', Frank S. Hook acknowledges that it is impossible to try to make sense of the play in terms of consistency. See Hook, ed., *The Dramatic Works of George Peele*, pp. 19 and 37.
36 See Michael Prestwich, *Edward I* (London: Methuen, 1988), pp. 123–8; and *The Thirteenth Century 1216–1307*, ed. Sir Maurice Powicke (Oxford: Clarendon Press, 1962), p. 408. For a discussion of chronicle support for Peele's version of Elinor, see David H. Home, *The Life and Minor Works of George Peele* (New Haven: Yale University Press, 1952), p. 107.

37 See David Bevington, *Tudor Drama and Politics* (Cambridge, MA: Harvard University Press, 1968), p. 206.
38 The anti-Catholic sentiment implicit in Peele's play finds fuller expression in the anonymous *Troublesome Raigne of John, King of England* published in 1591. Like *Kyng Johan*, this play deploys a version of history to emphasise the dangers of Catholic intervention. As in *Edward I* the monarch's mother opens with a speech which links her motherhood with the continuing health of the nation and offers her body (her 'wombe') as the source and symbol of safe government, the material means by which continuity and national stability prevail.
39 Home, *The Life and Minor Works of George Peele*, p. 107. Also, Marie Axton, *The Queen's Two Bodies: Drama and the English Succession* (London: Royal Historical Society, 1977), pp. 101–4.
40 Axton, *The Queen's Two Bodies*, pp. 101–2.
41 The first is printed in Hook, ed., *The Dramatic Works of George Peele*, pp. 210–11 as 'The lamentable Fall of Queene Elinor, who for her pride and wickednesse, by Gods Judgement sunke into the ground at Charing crosse and rose up againe at queene hive. To the tune of, Gentle and curteous'. The second, which attacks Eleanor of Aquitane, wife to Henry II, is titled 'Queen Elinor's Confession, shewing how king Henry with the Earl Martial in Fryars Habits, came to her instead of two Fryars from France which she sent for'. This provides the narrative for the last scene of Peele's play.
42 See also Howard and Rackin, *Engendering a Nation*, esp. on Joan of Arc and Margaret of Anjou in the first two Henry VI plays, p. 49.
43 Typological antecedents of this kind of mother include Gill, the wife of the trickster in the Wakefield Second Shepherd's play.
44 Axton, *The Queen's Two Bodies*, p. 101.
45 Hook, ed., *The Dramatic Works of George Peele*, p. 24.
46 See Paul Ricoeur: 'A story is made out of events to the extent that plot makes events into a story'. This is important because 'the plot, therefore, places us at the crossing point of temporality and narrativity'. See Paul Ricoeur, 'Narrative Time', in *On Narrative*, ed. W. J. T. Mitchell (Chicago: University of Chicago Press, 1981), p. 167. See also Roland Barthes: 'to understand a narrative is not merely to follow the unfolding of the story, it is also to recognise its construction in "storeys", to project the horizontal concatenations of the narrative "thread" on to an implicitly vertical axis; to read (to listen to) a narrative is not merely to move from one word to the next, it is also to move from one level to the next'. Roland Barthes, *Image, Music, Text*, trans. Stephen Heath (London: Flamingo, 1984), p. 87.
47 Pierre Nora, 'Le Retour de l'événement', in Jacques le Goff and Pierre Nora, eds, *Faire de l'histoire*, vol. 1: *Nouveaux problèmes* (Paris: Gallimard, 1974), pp. 210–28: 'événements véhiculent tout un matériel d'émotions, d'habitudes, de routines, de représentations héritées du passe qui affleurent soudain à la surface de la société ... une

événement est... une dechirure du tissu sociale', p. 224. Nora characterises events as essentially spectacular and theatrical, and always tragic or prescient of tragedy: 'Il n'y a pas d'événements heureux, ce sont toujours des catastrophes', p. 220.

48 Bevington and Axton both argue that these celebrations engage with the realities of Elizabethan national politics.
49 Elinor will not have been 'churched' and so is polluted following childbirth. Fleische sees this moment as a 'profane nativity'. See Fleische, *Iconography of the English History Play*, p. 92.
50 Bevington, *Tudor Drama and Politics*, p. 206.
51 Park, *Secrets of Women*, p. 154.
52 John Dod and Robert Cleaver, A Godlie Forme of Houeholde Government: For the ordering of private families according to the direction of God's word (London, 1561), p. 53.
53 Diane Purkiss, *The Witch in History* (London and New York: Routledge, 1996), p. 102.
54 This is a structural opposite to Elinor's lying-in scene; the mayoress has been cleansed of all pollution.
55 Deborah Willis, *Malevolent Nurture: Witch-hunting and Maternal Power in Early Modern England* (Ithaca: Cornell University Press, 1995), p. ix.
56 Willis, *Malevolent Nurture*, p. 84. Willis also talks about the period as 'experiencing an unprecedented number of women in positions of power' and links anxiety about powerful women, especially powerful catholic women, to this, p. 120.
57 Purkiss, *The Witch in History*, p. 185.
58 Purkiss, *The Witch in History*, pp. 120–2.
59 Marina Warner, *Fantastic Metamorphosis, Other Worlds* (Oxford: Oxford University Press, 2002), p. 35.
60 Warner, *Fantastic Metamorphosis*, p. 164.
61 Reginald Scot in *Witchcraft in England 1558–1618*, ed. Barbara Rosen (Amherst, MA: University of Massachussetts Press, 1991), p. 90. See also Louis A. Montrose, 'Idols of the Queen: Policy, Gender, and the Picturing of Elizabeth I', *Representations*, 68. (Autumn 1999), 108–61, 112. Purkiss, *The Witch in History*, p. 185.
62 In Montrose, 'Idols of the Queen: Policy, Gender, and the Picturing of Elizabeth I', p. 112.
63 Quoted in Hook, *The Dramatic Works of George Peele*, p. 211. Bullen believes that the ballad stems from the strong anti-Spanish feeling at the time of the Armada. See Hook, *The Dramatic Works of George Peele*, p. 20.
64 Michael Prestwich says that the king's minister Pecham 'wrote in very direct terms to Elinor, telling her that the king's harshness [to London] was attributed to her influence'. Michael Prestwich, *Edward I* (London: Methuen, 1988), p. 125.
65 Peele's father was clerk of Christ's Hospital, administered by the City of London. See George Peele, *The Old Wife's Tale*, ed. Charles

Whitworth, New Mermaid ed (London: A. and C. Black, 1996), p. xiv.
66 David Bevington, *Tudor Drama and Politics*, pp. 206–7. The ballad is reproduced in Hook, *The Dramatic Works of George Peele*, p. 204.
67 Willis, *Malevolent Nurture*, p.64.
68 James I later displayed similar pragmatism in permitting Middleton's anti-Spanish satire, *A Game at Chess*, to play briefly before closing it down. This demonstrates both how pertinent and how popular plays displaying such sentiment were from 1590. See Annabel Patterson in *Censorship and Interpretation: The Conditions of Reading and Writing in Early Modern England* (Madison, WI: University of Wisconsin Press, 1984), p. 17.
69 Bevington, *Tudor Drama and Politics*, p. 207.
70 Quoted in Bullough, *Narrative and Dramatic Sources of Shakespeare*, p. 261. Howard and Rackin cite Nashe's celebration of the history play which 'imagines an audience of men inspired by the representation of a heroic, masculine world, to emulate the manly virtue of the forefathers'. Howard and Rackin, *Engendering a Nation*, p. 104.
71 Howard and Rackin, *Engendering a Nation*, p. 61.
72 Howard and Rackin, *Engendering a Nation*, p. 51.
73 Lawrence Danson, *Shakespeare's Dramatic Genres*, Oxford Shakespeare Topics Series (Oxford: Oxford University Press, 2000), p. 92.
74 Geoffrey Bullough, *Narrative and Dramatic Sources of Shakespeare*, vol. 3: *Early English History Plays* (London: Routledge and Kegan Paul, 1960), p. 102. See the introduction to *King Henry VI Part 2*, ed. Ronald Knowles, The Arden Shakespeare (Walton-on-Thames: Thomas Nelson and Sons Ltd., 1999), p. 37.
75 Bullough, *Narrative and Dramatic Sources of Shakespeare*, p. 106; Rackin, *Stages of History*; Howard and Rackin, *Engendering a Nation*, and Knowles in his introduction to the Arden edition of the play.
76 Willis, *Malevolent Nurture*, p. 182.
77 See Bullough, *Narrative and Dramatic Sources*, p. 103, where he quotes Hall: 'Suche is worldly unstableness, and so wavereying is false flattering fortune'. Knowles, however, reads Hall as showing 'a distinctly sceptical attitude towards any claim to discern the divine at work in history, for example in his remark concerning "man's fantasies" rather than "divine revelation"'. Knowles, ed., *King Henry VI Part II*, p. 53.
78 Bullough, *Narrative and Dramatic Sources*, pp. 105–6.
79 The boxing of Henry's ears (which Howard and Rackin link with the foreignness of the queen, something which could equally be applied to Peele's Spanish Elinor) occurs in 1.3.135–40. The humiliation of the Duchess of Gloucester is in Act 2, Scene 3.
80 Janet Adelman, *Suffocating Mothers: Fantasies of Maternal Origin in Shakespeare's Plays* (London: Routledge, 1992), p. 3.
81 Howard and Rackin, *Engendering a Nation*, p. 73.

82 See Willis, *Malevolent Nurture*, p. 172.
83 Howard and Rackin, *Engendering a Nation*, p. 71.
84 See also Shakespeare's *Richard II*, 3.2.4–26, where the king flings himself upon England's earth on his return from Ireland, to the consternation of his companions.
85 Willis, *Malevolent Nurture*, p. 169. Quotation from Howard and Rackin, *Engendering a Nation*, p. 172.
86 Howard and Rackin, *Engendering a Nation*, pp. 141–2, quoting David Bevington in 'The Domineering Female in *I Henry IV*', *Shakespeare Studies* 2 (1966), 51. Also William Shakespeare, *Henry VI Part 3*, eds John D. Cox and Eric Rasmussen, The Arden Shakespeare (London: Thompson Learning, 2001), p. 148. All subseqent references to the play are from this edition.
87 Phyllis Rackin, *Stages of History: Shakespeares's English Chronicles* (London: Routledge, 1991), p. 148.
88 In Hall, as in Shakespeare's *3 Henry VI*, Margaret is always described in the company of her son, 'the Quene her selfe, and her sonne'. See Bullough, *Narrative and Dramatic Sources of Shakespeare*, p. 178.
89 See Audrey Eccles, *Obstetrics and Gynaecology in Tudor and Stuart England* (London: Croom Helm, 1982), pp. 51–2, and Cox and Rasmussen, *Henry VI Part 3*, p. 201. When Lady Macbeth is discussing her husband's lack of masculine ambition she equates him with a lactating mother full of the 'milk of human kindness' in a reversal of what Margaret is doing here.
90 Coppelia Kahn, 'The Absent Mother in King Lear', *King Lear*, ed. Kiernan Ryan, New Casebook Series (London: Macmillan, 1993), p. 55.
91 Hall describes how 'many laughed then, that sore lamented after, as the Quene her selfe, and her sonne'. Bullough, *Narrative and Dramatic Sources*, p. 178.
92 Adelman observes that Margaret's behaviour recalls Medea, whose action is likewise complex: part of a pattern of revenge initiated by Jason. Adelman, *Suffocating Mothers*, p. 3.
93 Willis, *Malevolent Nurture*, p. 190.
94 Margaret finds ways to rally her husband's faltering troops more than once in this play. Her suggestion that her son is knighted follows from her observation that the soldiers will lose heart if they glimpse the king's own misgivings in 2.2.56–8. She exhorts the troops before her final battle in a long speech which draws approval of her 'valiant spirit' from her son. See 5.4.1–38. Henry follows Margaret and Edward off the battlefield at the end of 2.5.
95 Cox and Ramussen, *Henry VI Part 3*, p. 146.

4

'Pleasing punishment': motherhood and comic narrative

the pleasing punishment that women bear[1]
        Shakespeare, *The Comedy of Errors*

Bodies and meanings

Previous chapters have focused upon the mother figure as a signifier of spiritual, personal and political concerns that is often mediated through an association of the mother's body with suffering and violence as well as boundless love and nurture. This chapter considers the material signifiers of maternity that were so thoroughly exploited by Peele in *Edward I* and that routinely colour the construction of the dramatised mother figure. The mother's body implies, and invites consideration of, the conditions of gestation and lactation and in doing so evokes a response where moral, spiritual and political meanings are complicated by the pleasures and anxieties generated by contemplating the mother's physical body. This complexity is of particular value in the development of narratives that depict family disruption and endangerment from which to work to a comic resolution, or, as is the case with *Romeo and Juliet*, the final play discussed in this chapter, swerve away from comic structures to produce a tragic conclusion.

As he describes the tragedy which has befallen his family, Aegeon, the father whose tale of bereavement opens Shakespeare's *The Comedy of Errors*, links his wife's labour to the shipwreck which caused the breaking up of his family: her pregnant body figures both the boat that breaks and the family that is dispersed. Aegeon speaks of mothering as 'pleasing punishment', referring to the physical pain of parturition, the discomfort and pleasure of breastfeeding; the suffering that comes with love; the painful separation of mother and child that is the inevitable consequence of a loving act of conception; and the endowment of death that is explicit in the act of giving birth. Aegeon speaks of his wife 'almost at fainting' in her pregnancy, emphasising the physical processes and demands of motherhood as a means of expressing the value of what has been lost (and what is to be found) in the play.

Whereas motherhood as an idea can be accommodated into a generalised patriarchal view of political, religious and social relations, as a practice this is more problematic. In terms of early modern social conventions, the physical processes of maternity tended to remove the heavily pregnant or lactating mother from the social and economic world of her husband. The processes of childbirth and lactation were almost always managed by women for women so that the father and husband had no distinct practical function.[2] The practicalities and the social conventions associated with early modern maternity thus demonstrated a potential tension between the practices of being a wife (in the sense of 'helpmeet') and those of being a mother. As Puritan ideas about the family slid into mainstream Protestant ideology and practice, such tensions became increasingly visible in dramatic and other discourses.

Chapter 1 of this book addressed the emphasis, in pre-Reformation drama, upon the significance of Mary's maternity rather than her experience of it, setting the miraculous birth against the mundanities of everyday experience, inviting spectators to consider conflicting accounts of the truth. The Virgin's unpolluted body signifies God's mercy and providence, as does the only physical sign of parturition on her body: the milk-filled breasts of the *Madonna lactans*.[3] Many depictions of the nursing Virgin show her baby already dead, which is significant for her own story and also a reminder that, as John Donne later warned, 'wee have a winding sheete in our Mothers wombe, which growes with us from our conception'.[4] The function of the image of the mother's breast in organising the emotional dynamic of dramatic narratives was therefore well established by the sixteenth century. Often the mother's capacity for nurture is cited at moments when her ability to fulfil that potential, or to benefit from it, is under threat. Mystery plays included references to redundant breasts and bodies in the laments of the bereaved mothers of the innocents, where the mothers' grief is linked to the pains of labour:

Me lytyll chylde lyth all lame
That lullyd on me pappys.
My fourty wekys gronynge
Hath sent me sefne yere sorwynge.[5]

In an analogous classical trope in the *Oresteia*, Clytemnestra's appeal to the significance of her proffered breast fails to modify the murderous intentions of her vengeful son: 'Wait, my son – no respect for this, my child? / The breast you held, drowsing away the hours / Soft gums tugging the milk that made you grow?'[6] In such instances, the potential power of the mother as signified by her breast is circumscribed by the assertion of a greater power which is operated through apparently fixed mechanisms such as law, justice and authority, whose agents are inevitably male (Orestes, Herod, God). In early drama, therefore, the breast functions rhetorically as an image of pathos; it signifies the power of maternity at the moment when such power is in abeyance. Marina Warner links images of the *Madonna lactans* to the 'exemplary humility' of the Virgin which, she argues, depended upon 'social practices that made breast-feeding an act of humiliation'. But as Warner points out, 'the prejudices themselves were bound up with Christian teaching. Womankind had been especially punished for Eve's sins by the sufferings of childbearing in all its biological aspects, from menstruation to lactation'.[7] For all its potential as a symbol of emotional abundance and spiritual triumph, lactation paradoxically indicated humility: the humble mother's body always at odds with the marvellous but involuntary processes by which it operates and from which maternity derives meaning. Janet Adelman reads this tension psychoanalytically in relation to the early modern practice of putting children to nurse, suggesting that it generated an ambivalent response in the adult: 'many would have experienced a long period of infantile dependency, during which they were subject to pleasures and dangers especially associated with nursing and the maternal body'.[8]

From this perspective contemporary practices generated a desire to control the processes of the mother's body, to render them safe. Gail Kern Paster shows that, 'even within the hermetic enclosures of the womb, the birthing chamber, and the nursing dyad, patriarchy continued to deploy the disciplinary mechanisms of shame' in early modern culture, making it possible to 'manage the female bodiliness so visible in the symptomatology of pregnancy and lactation'.[9] The representation of such 'management' in drama continued to resonate in post-Reformation plays, appropriated from and as part of a developing Protestant discourse around the idea of family. The control that Paster discusses is evident in the promotion of a link between the biological advantages of maternal nursing and the importance of maternal breastfeeding as good Christian practice. According to the later Puritan William Gouge, 'Many strong arguments there be to presse it upon the consciences of mothers, and to shew that (so farre as they are able) they are bound to give sucke to their owne children. Some are taken from the light of Gods word and some from the light of nature'.[10]

This concern with the 'natural', biological, aspects of motherhood, and their relation to morality, is paralleled, in the later sixteenth and early seventeenth centuries, by an increasing interest in the obstetric control of women's bodies. This is evident, for example, in the publication of books about the management of pregnancy, childbirth and lactation, usually written, translated and published by men.[11] *The Byrth of Mankynde*, for example, first appeared as a translation by Richard Jonas of a German text, Rösslin's *De Partu Hominis*, and was reworked by Thomas Raynalde for publication in 1545, running to several editions in the next fifty years.[12] These texts aimed to provide practical support to mothers and those who helped them as they proceeded from pregnancy to parturition and lactation. Their continued revision and publication attests to their commercial success and to a readiness on the part of the buying public to engage imaginatively and practically with the processes and challenges of maternity. Inevitably, such texts find themselves addressing the practical ramifications of family politics. Later versions of Raynalde's text refer to breastfeeding as a potential area of conflict, or at least an issue of authority, between husband and wife:

> I am of the opinion that it is for every Mother to nurse her own Child, because her milk which is nothing but the blood whitened, which nourished the child in the womb and of which the child was conceived, and formed, is fittest and more naturall to the Child, then the milk of a stranger ... but in case the Mother be sick or weak; or hath no milk, or that her Husband will not let her nurse her Child, then it is necessary to look out a nurse, but most men doe know how hard it is to get a good one.[13]

The same text appears in the 1610 translation of Guillemeau's *The Happy Deliverie of Women*: 'yet since they may be hindered by sickness; or for that they are too weake and tender, or else because their Husbands will not suffer them, therefore I say, it will be very necessary to seeke out another Nurse: and every one knowes how hard a thing it is, to finde a good one'.[14] The issue had been the subject of discussion and disagreement since classical times and had more recently been discussed by Erasmus and More, among others.[15] From the second half of the sixteenth century it was increasingly addressed in Protestant teaching on the family which might attest to changes in wider social practice. Elisabeth Badinter cites the French example a woman married in 1532 who nursed her children; her daughters made occasional use of wet nurses, and her granddaughters routinely did so. If this pattern mirrored English practices, as the exhortations in sermons and obstetric books seem to suggest, there was clearly a significant change in a relatively short time.[16] Anxieties appeared in printed texts at the beginning of the seventeenth century, when clerics like Gouge strove to promote maternal breastfeeding, stressing its advantages from a practical and spiritual point of view, and implying, in their energetic promotion of it, that there was considerable resistance among their congregations. Janet Adelman suggests that sending babies out to nurse was 'sometimes tantamount to murder' and though this assessment might be extreme, it is clear that it could be a dangerous practice.[17] Elizabeth Clinton, in a text inspired by the deaths of two of her own babies, wrote to promote breast-feeding, explaining that she had not breastfed her children 'not for want of Will in myself, but partly I was over-ruled by another's Authority, and partly deceived by some ill Counsel'.[18] She expresses a resigned recognition that the duties of the mother are inevitably circumscribed by those of a wife:

> Wives must use all the reasons they can by themselves or others to persuade their husbands to let them perform it ... They may not make themselves accessory to their husbands fault by providing a nurse and sending the children away themselves: if their husbands will stand upon their authority, and be persuaded by no means to the contrary, they must be meere patients in suffering the child to be taken away.[19]

Certainly the decision whether or not to breastfeed was not left to mothers alone. Sir William Knollys wrote to his goddaughter Ann Fitton that he would not like it 'that you play the nurse, if you were my wife', adding that though 'it argueth great love', it 'breedeth much trouble to yourself'. Her father wrote likewise, 'I am sorry that you yourself will needs nurse her'. Patricia Crawford suggests that reasons might vary with social class and the need for wealthier families to produce heirs so that 'wealthy women could theoretically have a new pregnancy every year or so'. For the rest, she suggests: 'husbands did not want the inconvenience of having small babies in the home ... In many families, particularly those of merchants and other traders, women had an important role to play in running a household business so that it was cheaper for the husband to employ a wet nurse for his child than to find a replacement for his wife while she suckled'.[20] Gouge admitted that patriarchal authority ultimately counted. Answering the question whether a wife should yield even to a wicked husband, he concluded that, 'yes, because in his office he is in Christ's stead'.[21]

Anxiety about the cultural significance of breastfeeding is evident, too, in contemporary popular discourse. At a time when commentators (only half jokingly, according to Keith Thomas) still debated whether women were closer to beasts than to men, the significance of suckling was problematic, commendably fulfilling natural law (or God's will) and simultaneously debasing the practitioner. The relationship between woman and beast was not merely analogous; lactating women and nanny goats were both used to suckle sick human adults, and a woman seeking to relieve engorged breasts might send for a puppy to take her milk. The language of childbirth was peppered with the imagery of the stalls; pregnant women were often likened to farrowing sows; the period of lying-in after childbirth was referred to as being 'in the straw'. Like the mess and pain of birth itself, the involuntary nature of lactation affirmed woman's ambiguous affinity with the natural world.[22] Despite his evident enthusiasm, William Gouge may not have been doing his cause much of a favour when he preached that 'unreasonable creatures, and among them the most savage wild beasts, such as tigers and dragons, yea sea-monsters give suck to their young ones'.[23] From this perspective nursing could either be construed as occupying a dangerous and uncivilised place where maternity was threatening and monstrous, or understood as evidence of God's benevolence through the operation of natural instinct.

Grissil's bereft breasts

After the Reformation the ideal, breastfeeding mother was refigured to operate as a moral type that emphasised the emotional bond that the practice created. This is evident in two plays which rework, very differently, the familiar story of Patient Griselda, in which motherhood is rhetorically and emblematically central to the emotional dynamic of the drama. By the sixteenth century several poetic versions of the story were available. It is the last tale of Boccaccio's *Decameron* and tells of a poor girl chosen by a rich man for his wife. He subjects her to cruelty and humiliation to test her constancy, removing her children, making her dress in her peasant rags and sending her home to her father. Griselda is at last rewarded for her endurance and humility by her reinstatement. In all versions of the tale, the heroine's body is made emblematic of her changing status. In the *Decameron* she is stripped naked at her wedding, as her rags are exchanged for the fine clothes she will wear as a ruler's wife; at her banishment the courtly clothes are once again removed, to be replaced by a shift for which Griselda pleads 'in exchange for my virginity', which 'I brought here and cannot carry away'. What she wears not only alludes to her material prosperity and sexual status, but also emblematises her virtue.[24]

Versions of the story available to sixteenth-century readers are clear in their anxieties concerning its implications. In Boccaccio's version, the narrator refers to the husband's 'silly brutality' before even beginning his story.[25] In *The Canterbury Tales*, Chaucer's Clerk chooses to retell the tale as a parable and distances himself from a too literal appreciation of the narrative by emphasising the general moral point that he insists lies at the heart of his version:

> This story is seyd, nat for that wyves shoulde
> Folwen Grisilde as in humylitee,
> For it were inportable though they woulde;
> But that for every wight, in his degree,
> Sholde be constant in adversitee
> As was Grisilde[26]

Here, the cruelty described in the tale is contextualised by a moral framework devised and controlled by a storyteller whose authority is crucial in structuring the pleasures that the story offers its audience. As Cristelle Baskins has observed, such control operates through a sequence of patriarchal interventions. Male characters exert absolute control over the woman in the story, though they agonise over doing so; fictional narrators condemn the way she is abused, but tell the story anyway; writers express concern that the cruelty detailed in their work should not be taken as a literal recommendation concerning the treatment of wives by their husbands, but nevertheless reproduce the tale.[27] There is thus a consistent awareness of tension between the pleasures engendered by this story and its ostensible function as moral edification.

The tale was dramatised twice for audiences in Elizabethan England, first by a Protestant balladeer and polemicist, John Phillip, whose play was published in 1565, and then later by the commercial dramatists Dekker, Chettle and Haughton, performed in about 1599.[28] Both versions retain a focus upon the body of the heroine and both shift the visual emphasis from the image of the bride stripped bare which is the emblematic focus of the earlier stories, to the body of Grissil (as she is called in both plays) as a mother. The main crisis in both versions is focused upon the mother's body in distressing scenes when Grissil, a new and lactating mother, has her babies forcibly removed from her before the audience.

Dramatisation inevitably alters the dynamic of a moral narrative; it makes available the often disturbing and complicating pleasure of what an audience sees. This can undermine a reading of the tale as morally edifying, as narrative and spectacle make competing demands upon their audience. In her discussion of pictorial representations of Griselda, Baskins alerts us to the dangers of theorising the story only as literary allegory, or of reading it as historical evidence. She argues that the tale as realised in painting is complicated by a tension between the dominant meanings of the story as narrative and its effect when climactic moments from it are visually depicted.[29] 'Seeing' the girl's naked body as she is stripped in preparation for her transformation from maid to wife, or the woman's exposed breasts as she later pleads for the lives of her children, sets up a complex tension between titillation and moral meaning in which the woman's body becomes dominant in structuring the response of the spectator.[30] Baskins' warning is important as a corrective when reading the text in terms of social preoccupations as Linda Woodbridge does: 'The patient Grissil figure in literature was ... a male wish-fulfilment fantasy appropriate to historical periods when few living wives behaved like Patient Grissil. When women began swaggering the streets in male attire and weaponry, male authors provided male readers and playgoers with a comforting fantasy into which they could retreat.'[31] This reading is important both in its attention to the importance of fantasy and in its placing of comedy in the context of social change.

But to say that this story offers collective male wish-fulfilment, or to suggest that it represents an ideology which promotes the control and restriction of women, is perhaps only part of an analysis that must consider the meanings that the mother carries.

John Phillip wrote his play during the second wave of Protestantism in England. It is probably written for schoolboys and is typical of 'youth plays' of the period in its appropriation of a morality structure to support a Protestant homiletic argument. The moral framework of the play is made explicit in a preface which exhorts the audience to learn with Grissil 'in weale and woe the Lord our God to praise', explaining that this tale is to be read as a parable (Aii, 20). Before the Reformation there had been a clerical tradition of reading the story of Griselda as an allegory that described the relationship between mankind and God with reference to the mediating figure of Mary, so that Phillip offers a Protestant appropriation of an older exegetical tradition for new polemical purposes.[32] The heroine, in one of the many songs which separate episodes of the action, sings, 'God to me hath given such charge / as in his lawe is seen at large', clearly explaining her function as an exemplum and inviting a moral reading of the action to follow (Bii, 239–40).

The heroine's story is emblematised as a series of paradigm states through which Grissil progresses to the play's triumphant resolution, each marked by a song underscoring the heroine's change in status from daughter to wife, to mother, to banishment and reinstatement. Songs are a conventional way of separating out narrative stages in this genre, but here, sung by a heroine who advertises herself as emblematic, they draw attention to her generic significance while paradoxically asserting a selfhood, a personal integrity, which individualises her and offers a complication of the familiar typology. This assertion of self as separate would be associated by a sympathetic, private audience for whom it is most likely to have been written, with a Protestant emphasis upon individual spiritual and social responsibility and a concomitant promotion of the family unit as the place where an individual sense of duty to the common weal is promoted.[33]

If Grissil functions as a combination of morality type and mimetic self, her husband, Gautier, is conventionally placed as a man led astray, freed from guilt by being recast as a victim. A Vice figure called Politic Persuasion organises and sets up the ensuing plot and tempts Gautier into his ill treatment of Grissil.[34] Thus the play becomes a kind of psychomachia, with the battle between good and evil fought over the material body of the heroine. Her physical condition first as maid (visually symbolised by her demure dress and the water pot she carries), then as mother, first pregnant, then lactating, emblematises both her virtue and her vulnerability, the visual signals offered by her clothes adding meaning to what we know about her body. The Vice, whose business it is to undermine the authority of Grissil's virtue, imagines her transformation from daughter to wife, from girl to mother, into a thing of physical repugnance: 'The pretie foole is puft up, her belly is bigge, / I conjecture the trull will bringe forth some proper Pigge' (ll. 901–2). In contrast, Gautier's later order to separate Grissil from her child constructs an ideal picture of maternal nursing that is shockingly disrupted by an image of violent enforced separation:

> Thou knowest Grissil, my Ladie and wife,
> With whom in Love and Feare I have led my life:
> Farther, thou knowest my daughter, which shee doth nourish,
> And with the mylke of her breastes foster and cherishe,
> I will that make semblant, at my commaundiment,
> With thy swerde in sonder, to devide that Innocent. (ll. 1020–5)

Marriage and motherhood are differentiated here. In the first two lines it is the relationship between Gautier and Grissil which is described; in the second two, Grissil and her daughter. The commons, says Politick Persuasion, do not relish Gautier's heir being the child of a commoner. The Vice's temptation of the husband is thus centred upon the dual identity of Grissil as wife and mother: at this point in the play her status as wife is acceptable but that of mother is dangerous.

In this play, Grissil the mother represents the powers of goodness which the Vice threatens to overthrow, and as embodying a threat which must be contained as part of the working out of the moral of the play. This is played out through tension between the demands of duty and desire, configured as a conflict between the demands of wifehood and those of maternity. While it is always clear that maternal desire must be subordinated in order to achieve the important moral resolution of the play and to establish Grissil's exemplary status, her grief is crucial in figuring the psychomachia, articulating the despair and the resistance to it which are important to the organisation of a moral play. She acquiesces to Gautier's demands without question, before turning to the other women on stage (and perhaps in the audience) to appeal for support, not in challenging her husband's intentions, but in sympathising with her state: 'Ye matrons milde deplore my case, take fountaines to your eyes / Oh let your clamours penitrat the hawtie clowded skyes' (2000–1).

Sacrifice is inscribed in the Protestant idealisation of maternity as an aspect of wifehood. An ideal mother will give up her life for her child, but an ideal wife must subordinate her maternal feelings in deference to her husband's interests, and indeed in practice may have to do so, as Elizabeth Clinton made clear. Megan Matchinske has shown that in recusant ideology, too, such submission became the ideal: the role of wife is paralleled with that of an obedient servant of God, going so far as to construct martyrdom in terms of wifely sacrifice. Writing on the Catholic martyr Margaret Clitherow, who died in 1586, Matchinske discusses the ideal of the 'domestic saint/martyr' for whom silence and separation become 'a *topos* of ideal female behaviour'. Clitherow's final act before being pressed to death was to send her husband her hat as a final gesture of her submission to him.[35]

In the dramatisation of such ideals in Grissil's story there is a danger of a complicating clash between ideal maternity and ideal wifehood. To sustain the value of Grissil's wifely sacrifice, the moral and ethical implications of her acquiescence and its consequence – the removal of the babies from their mother's breast to apparent death – are expressed not by Grissil but by the nurse who accompanies her on the stage.

The version of the nurse deployed here is familiar from classical drama, where the character is often used to assert the voice of reason, as in Seneca's *Medea*.[36] There is a link, too, with the nurse figure in Roman comedy, whose comic role is associated with a natural, instinctive world. The nurse in Phillip's play pleads for the lives of Grissil's children first by reference to Christian precepts, quoting the commandment against murder, then by an appeal to what is 'natural' behaviour by reference to wild animals: tigers, lions and bears, which instinctively protect and nurture their young. She even offers herself as a version of the foraging, protecting creature-mother that she has described:

> I will fead and nourishe hir and take hir as mine owne
> These brestes shall bringe hir up these handes shall fynd hir food
> I will not cease but carefull be to fend hyr guiltles blood. (ll. 1170–3)

The nurse is able to plead for the child and to challenge Grissil's husband in a way that the exemplary heroine, bound to obey her husband, cannot do. She functions to reassert a relationship between mothering and 'natural' behaviour, and thus evokes sympathy for her mistress, who must suppress instinct in the interests of duty. She contributes to a tightening of the moral argument, which is important for the allegorical significance of what is happening on stage. She deflects acknowledgement of natural instincts associated with maternity away from Grissil, who as a now silent presence emblematises the spiritual qualities of sacrifice.

The nurse's speech has emotional power as an acknowledgement of the familiar version of the maternal instinct as something life-preserving and innate in the female creature, but its dramatic effect is circumscribed by the fact that Phillip's audience is already aware that Gautier has in fact ensured his child's safety. There is always a sense in which the nurse's plea is redundant. The relationship that she asserts between natural behaviour and human wisdom is appreciated by the audience in rather different terms from those in which she expresses it because the audience has access to Gautier's 'wisdom' and recognises that it necessarily places him in control of the natural state of affairs which she describes. What he has done is to provide his daughter with an alternative mother who, as he assures his companions, will undertake those activities of sustenance and protection (in a controlled and civilised environment) which the nurse so eloquently describes. Motherhood is split between Grissil, the nurse and the stepmother; not to segregate good and evil notions of maternity in the conventional sense, but rather, to create three complementary versions of positive motherhood. Rather than create an unthreatening locus for anger, as does Bruno Bettelheim's model of the mother 'split' into good and evil, this arrangement diffuses that anger: the children are still comfortably mothered because the father attends to their best interests. It is the wife alone who is tested.[37]

In this scene motherhood is fragmented, atomised and thus rendered unthreatening. Phillip creates three mother figures, each with a distinct dramatic and discursive purpose. The child's new guardian is shown to be an enthusiastic substitute mother: 'my hart revyves and skipes for joy', demonstrating concern for its physical well-being, 'Come on to give it foode' (ll. 1274 and 1291). This reassures the audience that Grissil's child is provided with the environment and instruction that the nurse, who is of inferior social status, could not provide. The stepmother fulfils that function of the mother which Grissil celebrated in an earlier lament for her own mother's death – 'my mother was ... my joy and best instructress' – as well as providing an audience with reassurance by her presence upon the stage (l. 487). This fragmentation of the mother establishes maternal care as the province of women who possess an innate and common knowledge of its processes. This is reinforced by the heroine's desperate appeals to the women around her, on stage and beyond, for support in her distress. Splitting the mothering of his children into wife, nurse and stepmother puts Gautier in control (and able, ultimately, to vanquish the Vice), and leaves the dramatist able to keep tight rein upon the potentially destabilising stage presence of the complete mother whose multiplicity of meanings is always in danger of complicating the moral framework of the play. Grissil is left free to enact an emblematic role, allowing the audience to enjoy the moral satisfactions of her sacrifice.

At the close of the separation scene Grissil bursts into a lament in which her lack of power and the pathos of her condition serve only to heighten the moral significance of her grief. It is a complex speech which absolves her husband ('how is my Lord abused'), invokes the image of her daughter torn from her lactating breast ('My daughter reft from tender paps, alas my wofull paine') before turning to the women in the audience for support:

> Help spoused Dames help Grissil now, hir fate with teares to
>   plore
> Gush forth your Brinie streames let trickling teares abound
> The earth and fyrmament above fyll with your mournfull sownd
> My child alas in swadling clouts, bereft and slaine with sword.
> Lord help, Lord ayd, my wofull plight on me take some remord
> Albeit such dirfull hap hath chauncst, graunt pacience to my
>   paine
> That I may seme this crosse of thine, with ioye for to sustaine.
>   (ll. 1195–201)[38]

Grissil's direct appeal to the audience creates a tension between an emotional sympathetic reaction to her plight and collusion with the onlooking Vice, with whom the audience shares the spectacle of this surrender and outpouring of grief. The audience experiences vicariously the pleasures of the power that operates against Grissil.

But Grissil's humility and willingness to bear her cross offer another sort of collusion, ensuring that pleasure and power are controlled and contextualised by the morality framework that ensures that both husband and wife are understood as victims of a wider conflict between good and evil, orchestrated by the Vice. Despite this being a Protestant play, the tropes of the old Catholic religious drama, particularly the massacre of the innocents, clearly resonate here. Both the select audience who would have seen this play, and the children acting, knew how they were supposed to interpret both the narrative and the pathos: it was wrong of the Vice to arrange for Grissil's torture, but it was right for her to submit to it. The pleasures offered by both the spectacle and rhetoric of tormented motherhood made safe are subsumed into a reading of the play as edification. The threat that maternity, with its visceral, emotional, overwhelming aspects always in tension with its idealisation and potential as pleasure, might erupt to destroy what is right, is thwarted. The audience does not see Grissil as a mother again until the end of the play, reinstated when her children are themselves old enough to be married and no longer have claims upon her body. As his mother is at last reinstated as an exemplary wife, Grissil's adult son places her physical maternity as a safe memory – her sacrifice can be safely celebrated and venerated:

> Ah dear mother, in whose wombe I was nourished,
> And therein by devine essence, fortie weekes cherished,
> Hast thou suffred for mee, such anguishing tribulacion,
> God graunt I may requite the, with condinge venerasion.
>   (ll. 1963–6)[39]

Phillip's play was written during a period of religious consolidation, when the autonomy of the individual began to be dramatised and when the family was reasserted as a Protestant ideal. As family relations were recoded, the conflicting demands of wifehood and maternity were expressed in the drama as a source of anxiety. Phillip's play can, then, be read as seeking to affirm a consolidating Protestant moral order to an audience which appreciates the point. Caught at the intersection between religious, ideological, dramaturgical and social transformation, the breastfeeding mother is potentially a site of destabilisation, emblematising anxieties which might be explained in part through the historical context of the play. At a time when a young Protestant queen was carefully using the ideological implications of motherhood to promote a sense of political stability after the uncertainties of the Marian years, a play which celebrates the ideals implicit in the notion of maternity, but renders them stable and controlled, can be read as engaging with and affirming contemporary political preoccupations through its promotion of safe, fragmented motherhood, celebrated in the exemplary figure of Patient Grissil.

By the time Dekker, Chettle and Haughton collaborated to dramatise their version of the story, first performed in about 1599, the public theatre for which it was written had an established, paying audience for whom theatregoing constituted recreation rather than edification. Theirs is essentially a wife-taming play which celebrates the heroine's exemplary submissive conduct (which is set against that of a domineering female Welsh relation) while suppressing the allegorical significance of its subject. Where Phillip offers the satisfaction of the working out of a moral tale, the Dekker version offers the pleasures of an exercise in control.[40]

In this version, the husband, Gwalter, is a trickster; he admits to having previously wooed Grissil in disguise, and at his first official meeting with her he asks her to choose between himself and his two courtiers who is 'the properest man' in a parody of the tempting of Paris made grotesque by the imbalance of power between court and poor subject demonstrated on the stage.[41] Grissil, still emblematically clutching her filled pitcher, is here given phoney power over her master, despite her clear subjection to him. Her inequality is demonstrated in terms not only of social class but of gender: she is surrounded by male characters for most of the play (the Phillip play, by contrast, has a large number of female roles).[42] Grissil's subordination, signified by her simple clothes, hints at the kind of pleasure with which the play seduces its audience, for this is a cruel play where the paying audience finds itself deliciously and safely placed as voyeur.[43] The spectators become complicit, like Gwalter's male companions who watch and occasionally join in with his game when he expresses his plan to torture his wife in terms which hint at sexual pleasures: 'Yet is my bosom burnt up with desires / To try my Grissil's patience'(2.2, p. 28). He anticipates with relish the exotic confusion of sensation that such a scheme will produce: 'My tongue shall jar, my heart be musical' (2.2, p. 28). The images of violent sexual manipulation which colour his plan – 'when that hand lifts up to strike / It shall fly open and embrace my love' (2.2, p. 28) – are asserted as part of a general recommendation to the men watching the play: 'men men trie your wives / Love that abides sharp tempests, sweeteley thrives'(2.2, p. 28).[44] His cruelty is visually reinforced when, as part of her humiliation, Grissil is forced to stoop to pick up the deliberately dropped glove of his companion, and then made to kneel before the same character to tie his shoelaces (2.2, p. 30).

Something horrible happens to the story of Grissil in the forty or so years since Phillip tapped into anxieties about the maternal to render it safe for Protestant family values in his moral tale. Without the morality framework which in Phillip's play allowed Grissil's suffering to be understood in relation to contemporary religious and social preoccupations, the story as developed by Dekker enjoins an audience to share in the pleasures of patriarchal control. Kate McLuskie makes the point that Grissil's frequent assertions of her own personal integrity in the play, which counter her husband's demands, though she still obeys his orders, change the 'feel' of the testing scenes, so that rather than offering the satisfactions of the spectacle of maternal sacrifice, the play offers the pleasurable story of an individual 'who can flout the turns of fortune'.[45] But at the emotional climax of the play, part of the pleasure of the testing game for an audience is to see how far it is possible to inflict pain, or to resist, before something cracks. Gwalter swings dizzily from eulogising his tormented wife – 'Oh, strange! Oh, admirable patience! / I fear when Grissil's bones sleep in her grave, / The world a second Grissil ne'er will have' (2.2, p. 30) – to accusing her of torturing him: 'And must thou, therefore, come to torture me?'(2.2, p. 31). This is echoed in the dramatic structure of the play, where the scenes of Grissil's humiliation are juxtaposed with comic episodes which feature the domineering Welsh widow and a henpecked knight.

The fourth act of the play begins unusually, with the marquis and his companion carrying a child that they admit to having taken from Grissil while she slept. The theft of the baby is underscored in dialogue in which the husband seems to wish to eradicate Grissil's maternity entirely:

Marquis: Furio, behold it well; to whom is't like?
Furio: You: there's your nose and black eyebrows. (4.1, p. 50)

Another courtier is asked his opinion: 'view this child; doth not his lips, his nose, his forehead, / And every other part, resemble mine?'(4.1, p. 50). Gwalter self-consciously dandles his infant, appropriating a conventionally maternal gesture: 'A great Romaine Lord / Taught his yong sonne to hobby-horse / Then why should I think scorne to dandle mine?' (4.1, p. 50). Gwalter appropriates the maternal role alongside the paternal, eradicating Grissil as mother even as he celebrates her as a wife. Her patience is continually remarked upon by exchanges between her ever-watching husband and his companions which provide a continual commentary upon her extraordinary steadfastness. Gwalter's refusal to acknowledge Grissil as a mother – 'You are but nurse to them, they are not thine' (4.1, p. 50) – is repeatedly linked with an insistence upon her duty as his wife:

> *Marquis:* If they [the babies] could speak, what think you they would say?
> *Grissil:* That I in all things will your will obey.
> *Marquis:* Obey it then in silence. Shall I not
> Bestow what is mine own as likes me best? (4.1, p. 51)

In instructing a courtier to steal the second baby, again the marquis sets up a voyeuristic image of the wife/mother asleep and vulnerable, in language which expresses both tenderness and cruelty: 'Her white hand is the pillow to those cares / Which I ungently lodge within her head' (4.1, p. 50).

The sweetness of this image of the vulnerable sleeping girl with her baby adds a terrible poignancy to the ensuing violent scene in which she tries unsuccessfully to assert her motherhood and keep her children. The conflict between her desire for her babies and obedience to Gwalter at which the marquis expresses delight – 'sweet sound this discord makes' (4.1, p. 54) – reaches its climax in a sequence where the separation of mother and children takes place. Grissil is first refused permission to hold her babes, then permission to feed them, and finally endures their removal from her and from the stage.

The bittersweet pleasures of this spectacle are derived once again from juxtaposing the image of the nursing mother with the violent intervention of the husband's agents; the babies are passed between the father and his male companions while she stands helpless on the stage. As the torture persists, Grissil literally overflows with grief as tears and milk pour from her:

> ... see heer's a fountain
> Which heaven into these Alabaster bowles,
> Onstiled to nourish them: man theyle crie,
> and blame thee that this ronnes so lavishly
> [...]
> I pray thee let them suck, I am most meet

To play their Nurse: theyle smile and say tis sweet,
Which streames from hence, if thou dost bear them hence
My angrie breasts will swell, and as mine eyes
Let fall salt drops, with these white Nectar teares,
They will be mixt: this sweet will then be brine,
Theyle crie, Ile chide and say the sinne is thine. (4.1, p. 59)

Here the involuntary nature of maternal love is signified not only by Grissil's tears, but by her breasts, so that milk and tears become related images which signify simultaneously the plenitude of the mother's body and her grief, amplified by the conventional association of milk and blood that links maternal sacrifice with a mother's desire to nourish her child. The idea was so fully accepted in the period that the transformation could apparently be experienced as physical sensation according to the writer Dorothy Leigh: 'will she not blesse it [her child] every time it sucks on her breast, when she feels the blood come from her heart to nourish it?'[46]

Grissil describes herself in terms which, in keeping with the necessarily voyeuristic nature of the wife-taming play, take much of their effect from the sexual frisson generated by combining the spectacle of her grief with a rhetorical assertion of the material, brimming, maternal body, spoken by the character humiliated on her knees, surrounded by a stage full of men. The abjection of the mother figure induces both pleasure and guilt in the spectator, who is drawn into complicit pleasure at both sensations by the husband's asides: 'My cheeks do glow with shame to hear her speak. / Should I not weep for joy my heart would break' (4.1, p. 55). Grissil's overflowing breasts and eyes, signifiers of maternal abundance, suffering and nourishment are eroticised and transformed into emblems of women's weakness. Grissil is returned to the condition of girlhood, sobbing and sexily submissive in the thrall of the men who dominate the stage, tested to the point where the mother is broken apart so that the girl is rediscovered.

In this play which engages with contemporary debates and jokes about other aspects of women's power (Gwenthian, Grissel's foil in the play, refers contemptuously to the heroine as a 'ninny pobbie foole'), the heroine's potential to be a mother is appropriated by her husband at every level (3.1, p. 202). His empowering 'knowledge' of women's instinctual behaviour facilitates cynical manipulation: 'She'll return,' he assures his companions after he has banished her from sight of her children, 'I know a tender mother cannot part / With such a patient soule, from such sweet soules' (4.1, p. 80). Grissil's battle to control her maternal desire culminates in physical collapse when her children are finally taken away, though she still asserts obedience to her husband who is watching her, in disguise: 'Why should I grieve / To lose my children? no, no; I ought rather / Rejoice, because they are borne to their father' (4.2, p. 64).

Dekker's play was written for a diverse, paying audience, whose political and social sympathies might vary. It was clearly popular. According to Harry Keyishian, 'in 1600 Henslowe paid out a substantial sum to stay its printing, an indication that its three theatrewise authors had turned out a commercially successful work on a sure-fire subject'.[47] The play's preoccupation with the control of the mother's body has analogues in other contemporary publications from the expanding range of obstetric manuals to the conduct books that itemise the duties of the mother within the family. The period between Phillip's play and Dekker's comedy also saw an increase in the legal penalties for female adultery.[48] The development of Puritan ideas certainly accounts for closer attention to maternity and its responsibilities, and indeed may explain a more profound concern for the physical health of mothers and children, but does not really account for the fascination, in so many different cultural products, with the control of the mother's body and its processes.

In E. Ann Kaplan's discussion of motherhood in twentieth-century films, she suggests that that such preoccupations might reveal an underlying anxiety:

> in [the psychoanalytic] view, such representations would manifest increasing unconscious fear of the mother – indeed a pathological fixation on her displaced into an obsessive need to control and/or erase her very being, to take charge of the very functions that define her and have created individuals' unbearable dependence on her.[49]

When Dekker, Chettle and Haughton wrote their play, Elizabeth was an old queen with no direct heir, and England teetered fearfully on the brink of political instability. The woman who had presented herself as mother figure to the nation for half a century was the subject of an enduring veneration which had been carefully cultivated through skilful public relations, but which had now become the focus of deep anxiety as her subjects contemplated a future with no clear successor. Such anxiety found expression, it might be argued, in cultural productions. Gwalter's alternating veneration and torture of Grissil can be understood with reference to Melanie Klein's observation that idealisation is always a counterpoint to persecution, and the play can be read as expressive of tensions generated by the dangerous and always imminent possibility of the queen's demise, as her 'body natural' threatened to fail the nation.[50] It is possible to argue, analogously, that while the natural, instinctive, desiring body of the mother visibly breaks down in the play, it is later recuperated as a safe idealisation in the emblematic finale of the triumphant closing scene when Grissil, tamed and no longer displaying the physical markers of fragile maternity, is venerated as the reassuring embodiment of an enduring ideal.

The wife and the nurse in Romeo and Juliet

The story of Grissil expresses a potential tension between the different identities that constitute the role of mother. In different ways, both plays about her attend to this through comic narrative processes that split the mother into constituent elements (nurse/wife/instructress) and then bring about a controlled reunification that confirms the husband's power. Shakespeare's *Romeo and Juliet* utilises the same idea from a different perspective by creating a situation where those constituent identities never come together and, indeed, are inhabited by different dramatic characters. The absence of a unifying maternal presence that brings together the functions of nurturer and wife is, in part, what turns the play to tragedy.[51]

Romeo and Juliet makes use of conventional comic structures and characterisation; as Susan Snyder points out, the play is structured around a familiar comic impulse towards 'marriage and social regeneration' but 'the game turns into sacrifice'.[52] Snyder quotes Madeline Doran's observation that 'we are in the region where comedy and tragedy are cut from the same cloth', and notes that 'the very features that distinguish this subgenre from the more dominant fall-of-the-mighty strain move it closer to comedy: its sources are typically novelle ... its situations are private rather than public, its main motive force is love'.[53]

Shakespeare's immediate source for the play, Brooke's poem written in 1562, casts the story as a tale of regrettable filial (and Catholic) irresponsibility: 'a couple of unfortunate lovers, thralling themselves to unhonest desire, neglecting the authoritee and advise of parents and friendes, conferring their principall counsels with dronken gossyppes and superstitious friers (the naturally fitte instruments of inchastitie)'.[54] The poem shares, with other literary products of the period, including Phillip's *Grissil*, a concern with children's behaviour. Stories about deviant children were as popular in the 1560s as those celebrating virtuous behaviour. *Nice Wanton* is only one example of a rich vein of material which shares the thrust of Protestant polemic with Brooke's poem. It is a moral play which firmly places the responsibility for unruly children upon inadequate mothering and demonstrates its awful consequences. Written at about the same time as Brooke's poem, the play follows the fortunes of 'two children brought up wantonly in play, / Whom the mother doth excuse, when she should chastise' and mediates a Calvinist assertion of predestination and an emphasis upon the moral implications of good parenting which might enable a child to gain access to God's saving grace:

> The Prudent Prince Soloman doth say,
> He that spareth the rod, the child doth hate,
> He would youth should be kept in awe alway
> By correction in time at reasonable rate:
> To be taught to fear God, and their parents obey,
> To get learning and qualities, thereby to maintain
> An honest quiet life, correspondent alway
> To God's law and the king's, for it is certain,
> If children be nosled in idleness and ill,
> And brought up therein, it is hard to restrain,
> And draw them from natural wont evil:[55]

The greatest danger here is that children are 'nosled'. The word is a corruption of 'nursled', linking it to the abundance of the mother's breast in both its actual and metaphorical significance, and its implication is that there are certain kinds of motherly behaviour which are, albeit unintentionally, dangerous and corrupting. This is not entirely a Protestant idea; the humanist Vives was concerned about its consequences early in the sixteenth century: 'Bodies are as much delights as weaknesses: and so mothers damn their children when they nurse them voluptuously ... The child the mother holds dearest is usually the worst of the lot'.[56]

The *Oxford English Dictionary* shows that 'nursled' in many of its variants 'had great vogue from about 1530 to 1650' meaning 'to train, educate, nurture in some opinion, habit'.[57] However, the examples it gives suggest a more specific meaning associated with the condemnation of (predominantly Catholic) heresy. In 1553 John Bale wrote of 'people nusled up from their youth in calling upon dead men and ymages' and in 1587 Holinshead, in his post-Reformation rewriting of English history, wrote of those 'nuzled in papistrie'.[58] The 1573 interlude *New Custom* has the Protestant figure, Light of the Gospel, accuse his enemy, Perverse Doctrine, of being 'Born to all wickedness, and nusled in all evil'.[59] Always implicit in such use of the word, too, is its association with bestial activity, associated with maternal tenderness but also with sex and death.[60] And, of course, the word has clear and traditional links with the act of nursing, nuzzling at the breast.[61] I have explored these meanings at some length because they indicate the complexities of the idea of nursing in this period. Its implications are at once sensual, emotional, religious and political; they signal both comfort and danger. Without the modifying possibilities offered by that other aspect of motherhood which is demonstrated as a duty to civilise and socialise the child, it becomes an unstable and worryingly un-Protestant concept.

A moral play like *Nice Wanton*, with a Calvinist agenda, demonstrates that bad mothering is caused not necessarily by parental viciousness but by a lack of enlightenment. The errant mother in the play is bewildered by the causes and effects of her children's behaviour:

> My children or I be cursed, I think;
> They be complained on, wherever they go,
> That for their pleasure they might drink.
> Nay, by this the poor souls be come from school weary;
> I will go get them meat to make them merry.[62]

In *Romeo and Juliet*, the Nurse, whose motives, like those of the mother in *Nice Wanton* are clearly well-meaning and loving, plays a determining part in facilitating the tragic outcome of the story. The play depicts a collapse of maternal authority. If this is so, it is because motherhood is compromised in this story where maternal desire is separated from, and more privileged than, the corrective and civilising effects of wifely duty. As an embodiment of dangerous destabilisation in this play, the Nurse's function is paramount. She is a character whose classical antecedents in Greek and Roman comedy are mediated through later Italian novelle to merge with the unruly woman figures in pre-Reformation theatre.[63] Susan Snyder suggests that the figure recalls 'comedy's ancient roots in fertility rites' in her conventional association with female sexuality and bodily excess.[64] Her carnivalesque characteristics link her with the medieval notion of the world-turned-upside-down where women have power over men, and servants control their masters. The grotesque, bestial aspects of the maternal are celebrated in the Nurse as comic because they can be separated off from other, more cerebral and affective, aspects of the maternal paradigm. In contemporary practice, nurses were selected for material qualities: their temperament and breeding; their health and the look of their breasts. Obstetric texts on wet-nursing stress the importance of these when selecting that elusive creature, the ideal nurse. Guillemeau insists that her birth and parentage must be discovered, her person and behaviour observed, her milk and children inspected. Redheads are risky because of a traditional link with lascivious behaviour. The breasts must be closely examined; nipples 'ought to be somewhat eminent and with a ruddie colour like a strawberrie'.[65] The selection is entirely in terms of bodily potential. For example:

> Now in choosing a Nurse there is foure things observable . . . First, concerning her parentage, she must come of good kindred, and honest parentage, that is not stained with any vice, for often times we see that although the Father and Mother be healthy and strong, and ready witted, yet oftentimes the children are weak and sickly, or else fools . . . Touching her person, for her Age, she should be at her full growth, about 22 yeare of Age, and she will continue good until she be forty years.[66]

In *Romeo and Juliet*, the Nurse's own iteration of her function confirms this link with the creatural and the grotesque. She refers to her breast as 'the dug', a term only ever used with reference to lactation, and then most commonly in association with beasts.[67] Attention is drawn repeatedly to her material body, usually with a bawdy association which confirms the grotesque, subversive aspect always implicit in her stage presence: 'Now afore God, I am so vexed that every part about me quivers' (1.4.158). More delicately, the intimacy of the language in which her relationship with Juliet is constructed affirms an instinctive, natural basis for affection – 'What, lamb! What, Ladybird!' (1.3.3) – that is enhanced by her memories of physical bonding with her charge: 'Thou was the prettiest babe that e'er I nursed' (1.3.62). Her detailed account of Juliet's weaning reiterates this closeness while at the same time disclosing its limitations; her coarse amusement at the memory of the thwarted child's frustration at the trick of applying bitter wormwood to the 'dug' is ominous, its significance perhaps underlined by the familiar quality of that herb as an emblem associated with grief and bitterness.

As in Phillip's moral play, motherhood is divided into constituent and conflicting parts in this play, but this time not in an organised way from a moral point of view. It is the structures of the social world of the play which create a gap between the wifely concerns of Lady Capulet, whose social and political duty is to facilitate her husband's dynastic ambitions, and the Nurse's emotional and physical relationship with Juliet which recalls the 'voluptuous' maternal intimacies that worried Vives. This gap is indicated in Lady Capulet's difficulty in remembering her daughter's birthday, something the Nurse knows well and recalls through a train of affectionate and personal memories which establish a history to her relationship with Juliet that is missing from that between Juliet and her mother.[68] As Gail Kern Paster says, Lady Capulet becomes 'a more or less secondary effect of patriarchal rule once her womb is vacated and responsibility for her baby's survival given over to a servant'.[69] Sasha Roberts sees this fragmentation of the family in the play as an engagement with contemporary social anxieties about the collapse of family structures, and Rachel Trubowitz writes of contemporary 'cautionary tales about wet-nurses that link non-breast milk with social instability'.[70] Estrangement caused by sending children to nurse was a staple tenet of the argument for maternal nursing in the period.[71] Elizabeth Clinton argues that no mother will willingly separate from her child: 'This she may feign to do upon a Covetous Composition, but she frets at it in her Mind, if she has any Natural Affection'.[72] *The Happie Deliverie of Women* warns that, 'every mother should nurse her owne child: because her milk . . . will bee alwaies more naturall and familiar unto him, than that of a stranger: and also by nursing him her selfe, *she shall be wholly accounted his mother*'[my italics].[73]

Maternal authority is always compromised in *Romeo and Juliet*; first because motherhood is always figured here through two characters – no one woman can be *wholly* accounted Juliet's mother – and secondly, because maternal authority is always in fact a version of patriarchal authority. Lady Capulet's wifely function is to rearticulate her husband's dynastic concerns to marry his daughter to the right man, in language designed to suit her daughter's emotional needs. Roberts shows how interpretations of the mother/daughter relationship offer a variety of possibilities, from the vilification of the mother as uncaring and absorbed in the patriarchal concerns of her husband, to recovering her as another victim of those concerns. In the latter analysis, she is unable to express her maternal anguish at the circumstances in which she is unwillingly complicit, so she is made, in performance, to demonstrate it through movement and gesture.[74] Either interpretation, though, stresses her ultimate inadequacy; her lack of engagement with the details of Juliet's childhood and the continuous assertion of the powerful emotional bond between the girl and her wet nurse upon the stage suggest a lack of maternal resource in the real mother and these details undermine any attempt to read her silence as a wifely sacrifice of her maternal desires. Grissil, in both plays, articulated her lack of access to her children as a physical and emotional loss; Lady Capulet never speaks of it, so that her inadequacy is enigmatic.

A nurse's function is physiological, her body is her *raison d'être*, a substitute for the mother's body but, crucially, not the mother. As a substitute she, also, is never quite adequate. Partly this is because she is of a different social class from that of the child with whom she is so intimate. Much of her comic value was, by tradition, based upon that difference, so that not only the plot but the very conventions which inform her construction bar the Nurse from any serious maternal function. The limitations of her class are evident in Act 1 Scene 3, where her comic interventions are at odds with the seriousness of the prospect of marriage being discussed. The scene is set up in such a way that Juliet at first appears to be securely supported by both mother figures in the safety of a domestic, private space where women can talk freely about love and sex. Nevertheless, the gaps are evident. The Nurse's poignant reference to her dead daughter, Susan, offers a brief, pathetic glimpse of a social world where poverty and grief are associated with the demands of those who are socially and economically more privileged. The context of the bawdy joke of the child falling on her back involves the Nurse recalling a world away from that of the court in which she is presently situated; a memory of lower-class family life which includes a surrogate daughter for whom there is much affection (they nickname her 'Jule') but in whom the step parents are allowed no investment other than emotional interest, which in the play becomes itself problematic. The Nurse can only joke about Juliet's planned future; her status permits her no power to determine its outcome.

The fact that she does become involved in Juliet's plans promotes disaster: her overstepping of her designated role is integral to the chain of events that shifts the narrative from comedy to tragedy. Her efforts to bring Romeo and her charge together are temporarily effective but also pathetically comic; in Act 2 Scene 4, for example, she is clearly out of place in the sparky public world of Romeo and his gallant friends. The scene where Mercutio teases her is both funny and pitiable as she is outwitted and ridiculed by the young men, unable to speak of Juliet except in terms of inappropriate intimacy – 'Well, sir, my mistress is the sweetest lady. Lord, lord! When t'was a little prating thing' – and only able to demonstrate her frustration at the treatment she gets from the gallants by reference back to her body grotesquely 'quivering' with rage. Julia Kristeva suggests that comedy in this play is always compromised: 'are not all comic scenes dominated by fury rather than joyous laughter?' Her analysis explains why the comic figure here is always somehow out of place and it is at that disjunction between two genres of comedy and tragedy that the pathos of the story becomes especially poignant.[75] The Nurse's limitations are recognised even by Juliet. When she is forced to agree to marry Paris, it is to her real mother that Juliet first appeals: 'O sweet my mother cast me not away' (3.5.198). She only turns to the Nurse when her mother has rejected her plea.[76] At this point in the play the Nurse is all that Juliet has, and her final inadequacy at this desperate moment provokes an outraged response – 'Ancient damnation! O most wicked fiend' (3.5.235) – which draws attention to the subversiveness and grotesquery of the figure, whose powerlessness and limited understanding becomes a kind of unintentional cruelty as the play turns inevitably towards a tragic closure.[77]

As Protestant ideals were absorbed into mainstream culture and practice the mother figure acquires a new social meaning in plays where the family and its configuration and control are a central concern. Traditions associated with the representation of motherhood were adapted to articulate new preoccupations in a change from a theatre concerned with religious and moral edification to a commodified entertainment which generated pleasures through its engagement with contemporary social and political concerns. Dramatists were able to explore the problematics of maternity that were being addressed in other contemporary discourses, to take risks with the fusion of genres as Shakespeare does in *Romeo and*

Juliet, or the sexualising of spectacle, in order to elicit a complex emotional reaction from an audience that appreciates the impossibility of reconciling the many identities that the complete mother must inhabit: the limits, in practice, of achieving that ideal. As some dramatists shifted away from the retelling of old tales towards the representation of their own social world in the domestic tragedies and city comedies that are the subject of the next chapter, their change of emphasis provoked some adjustment in the representation of the relation between ideal maternity and its everyday expression.

Notes

1 William Shakespeare, *The Comedy of Errors* (1.1.46–7) in Stanley Wells and Gary Taylor, *The Oxford Shakespeare: The Complete Works* (Oxford: Clarendon Press, 1988), pp. 259–77.
2 See Elaine Hobby, ed., *The Midwives Book, or the Whole Art of Midwifry Discovered: Jane Sharp*, Women Writers in English 1350–1850 Series (Oxford: Oxford University Press, 1999), pp. xi–xiii, for a discussion of the rarity of the male midwife.
3 The image was also read, as Naomi Yavneh points out, as an allegory of holy communion. See Naomi Yavneh, 'To Bare or Not To Bare: Sofonisba Anguissola's Nursing Madonna and the Womanly Art of Breastfeeding', in Naomi J. Miller and Naomi Yavneh, eds, *Maternal Measures: Figuring Caregiving in the Early Modern Period* (Aldershot: Ashgate, 2000), p. 70.
4 See Bellini's *The Madonna of the Meadow* and other depictions of the Virgin with her baby in *The Image of Christ* (the catalogue of the exhibition *Seeing Salvation*) (London: National Gallery Company Limited, 2000). Quotation from John Donne, 'Deaths Duell', in *Selected Prose*, ed. Neil Rhodes (Harmondsworth: Penguin, 1987), p. 313.
5 This example is from the Ludus Coventriae 'The Death of Herod', in Peter Happé, ed, *English Mystery Plays* (Harmondsworth: Penguin, 1985), p. 336.
6 Aeschylus, *The Oresteia*, trans. Robert Fagles (London: Wildwood House, 1976), ll. 883–5.
7 Marina Warner, *Alone of All Her Sex: The Myth and Cult of the Virgin Mary* (London: Picador, 1995), pp. 201–2.
8 Janet Adelman, *Suffocating Mothers: Fantasies of Maternal Origin in Shakespeare's Plays* (London: Routledge, 1992), p. 5.
9 Gail Kern Paster, *The Body Embarrassed: Drama and the Disciplines of Shame in Early Modern England* (Ithaca, NY: Cornell University Press, 1993), p. 215.
10 W. Gouge, *Of Domesticall Duties* (London, 1622), p. 508.

11 See Audrey Eccles, *Obstetrics and Gynaecology in Tudor and Stuart England* (London: Croom Helm, 1982), ch. 1, for a discussion of obstetrical textbooks in the period.
12 See J. W. Ballantyne, 'The "Byrth of Mankynde" (Its Authors and Editions)', *Journal of Obstetrics and Gynaecology of the British Empire* 10:4 (1906), 297–325. Ballantyne lists editions updated in the years 1540, by Richard Jonas, then 1545 (Raynalde's translation), which reappeared in 1552, 1560, 1565, 1598, 1604, 1613, 1626, 1634 and 1654. Elaine Hobby's new edition of this text, *The Birth of Mankind*, is forthcoming (Ashgate).
13 Quoted in Ballantyne, 'The "Byrth of Mankynde"', p. 191.
14 A side note reads, 'the difficulty of finding a good nurse'. Jacques Guillemeau, *Childbirth, or The Happie Delivery of Women, to which is added, a treatise of the diseases of infants and young children. Written in French and translated into English* (London, 1612), book 3, ch. 1, p. 10.
15 See Erasmus, 'The New Mother', in *The Colloquies of Erasmus* (Basel, 1526), trans. Craig R. Thompson (Chicago: University of Chicago Press, 1965), from p. 267.
16 Elisabeth Badinter, *The Myth of Motherhood: An Historical View of the Maternal Instinct*, trans. Roger DeGaris (London: Souvenir Press, 1981), p. 42.
17 Dorothy McLaren, 'Fertility, Infant Mortality and Breastfeeding in the Seventeenth Century', *Medical History* 22 (1978), 378–96.
18 Elizabeth Clinton, *The Countess of Lincoln's Nursery* (Oxford, 1662) Harleian Misc. vol. 4, p. 25. The quotation is from the introduction, which is dedicated to Bridget, Countess of Lincoln, by Elizabeth Clinton, who was Bridget's mother-in-law.
19 Clinton, *The Countess of Lincoln's Nursery*, p. 25.
20 In Valerie Fildes, *Wet Nursing: A History from Antiquity to the Present* (Oxford: Basil Blackwell, 1988), p. 82. See also Patricia Crawford, 'The Sucking Child', in *Continuity and Change*, 1 (1986), pp. 83–4. Also Michael Anderson, *Approaches to the History of the Western Family 1500–1914* (London and Basingstoke: Macmillan, 1984), pp. 59–61 for earlier debates on early modern breastfeeding practice.
21 Gouge, *Of Domesticall Duties*, p. 239.
22 Keith Thomas, *Man and the Natural World* (London: Penguin, 1987), Ch. 3, p. 92.
23 Gouge, *Of Domesticall Duties*, p. 289.
24 I refer to the translation by Richard Aldington, vol. 2 (London: Folio Society, 1957), p. 657.
25 Aldington, *The Decameron*, p. 657.
26 Geoffrey Chaucer, *Canterbury Tales*, ed. A. C. Cawley (London: J. M. Dent and Sons Ltd., 1978), p. 254.
27 See Cristelle L. Baskins, 'Griselda, or the Renaissance Bride Stripped Bare by her Bachelor in Tuscan Cassone Painting', *Stanford Italian Review*, 10:2 (1991), 159.

28 John Phillip, *The Commodye of pacient and meeke Grissil*, eds R. B. Mckerrow and W. W. Greg (London: Malone Society, 1909). All subsequent quotations are from this edition. Thomas Dekker, Henry Chettle and William Haughton, *Patient Grissil: A Comedy*, repr. from the black letter edition of 1603 (London: Shakespeare Society, 1841). All subsequent quotations are from this edition.
29 Baskins, 'Griselda', p. 171: 'Petrarch as well as other readers, reserved some doubt about the legibility of Griselda's nudity as an *exemplum virtutis*. It seems that the literary critics and the social historians, in their eagerness to claim either ennobling meaning or to find illustrations of social practice, reduce the powerfully conflicting investments of the textual and pictorial representations of Boccaccio's tale of Griselda'.
30 For a discussion of the representation of the maternal body by boy actors, see Peter Stallybrass, 'Transvestism and the "Body Beneath": Speculating on the Boy Actor', in *Erotic Politics*, ed. Susan Zimmerman (London: Routledge, 1992), pp. 64–83.
31 Linda Woodbridge, *Women and the English Renaissance* (Brighton: Harvester Press, 1984), p. 212.
32 See J. Wimsatt, 'The Blessed Virgin and the Two Coronations of Griselda', *Mediaevalia* 6 (1980), pp. 187–207, for a discussion of the Griselda story as Christian allegory. Also, Francis Lee Utley, 'Five Genres in the Clerk's Tale', *Chaucer Review* 6 (1972), 198–228.
33 David Bevington discusses this play as a 'children's court play', dating it between 1558 and 1569. Bevington, *From Mankind to Marlowe*, p. 62.
34 See Bevington, *From Mankind to Marlowe*, pp. 9–10, for plays which mix abstractions and concrete figures as 'hybrid moralities'. Also Sylvia D. Feldman, in *The Morality-Patterned Comedy of the Renaissance* (The Hague: Mouton, 1970).
35 Megan Matchinske, *Writing, Gender and state in Early Modern England* (Cambridge: Cambridge University Press, 1988), pp. 55–67 and p. 86.
36 See C. D. N. Costa, ed, *Seneca* (London: Routledge and Kegan Paul, 1974), p. 98, for the Nurse as a stock character and pp. 103–9 for her function in *Medea*.
37 Bruno Bettleheim, *The Uses of Enchantment: The Meaning and Importance of Fairy Tales* (London: Penguin, 1976, repr. 1991), p. 69.
38 Megan Matchinske quotes a letter from Margaret Clitherow to her daughter that links the sufferings of childbirth to the pains of separation and death, thus leading to salvation: 'I wyll not feare the colde swet but wyll taketh them as throwes yn chyldbedde by whych our sowle ys brought out of a korrup bodye ynto felycyte'. Matchinske, *Writing, Gender and State*, p. 84.
39 In *The Comedy of Errors*, the Abbess herself likens the restoration of her husband and children to her as a kind of replayed birth as she invites her audience to a 'gossips feast' to celebrate 'after so long grief, such nativity' (5.1.403–4).

40 The fantasy of total control of wives by their husbands appears in popular literature as Protestant ideals spread. Valerie Wayne quotes Edmund Tilney: 'The wise man may not be contented onely with his spouses virginitie, but by little and little must gently procure that he maye also steale away hir private will, and appetite, so that of two bodies there may be made one onelye hart, which she will soone doe, if love raigne in hir'. Valerie Wayne, quoting *The Flower of Friendship* (1568), 'Advice for Women from Mothers and Patriarchs', in *Women and Literature in Britain 1500–1700*, ed. Helen Wilcox (Cambridge: Cambridge University Press, 1996), p. 67.

41 Thomas Dekker, Henry Chettle and William Haughton, *Patient Grissil: A Comedy*, repr. from the black letter edn of 1603 (London: Shakespeare Society, 1841).

42 See Bevington, *From Mankind to Marlowe*, p. 62, for a discussion of the dispersal of female roles in boys' plays.

43 Viviana Comensoli finds a psychological struggle in the husband's behaviour. She acknowledges that this analysis cannot account for his excessive violence, however, which she sees as engaging with contemporary discourses: 'While the portrayal of Gwalter's excessive behaviour introduces a psychological dimension rooted in the tensions generated by the ideologies of gender and class, the psychological interest is eclipsed by the commonplace denunciation of violent husbands found in the conduct books and other discourses'. Viviana Comensoli, *'Household Business': Domestic Plays of Early Modern England* (Toronto: University of Toronto Press, 1996), p. 58.

44 Comensoli reads Gwalter as 'under profound emotional stress' here, which explains why he 'turns Grissil into an object for the court's pleasure'. Comensoli, *'Household Business'*, p. 57.

45 Kathleen McLuskie, *Renaissance Dramatists* (Hemel Hempstead: Harvester Wheatsheaf, 1989), p. 140. Comensoli notes that 'Grissel's rebellion clashes with the homiletic overtones of the testing' and sees this as exposing 'a principal cause of domestic strife, namely, the hierarchical structure of marriage and society which threatens the powerless'. The problem is that her powerlessness is made so attractive in this play by dint of the pleasures offered by the spectacle of her submission. Comensoli, *'Household Business'*, p. 60.

46 Dorothy Leigh, *The Mother's Blessing*, 14th edn (1629), ch. 3, p. 10 in Betty Travitsky, ed., *Mother's Advice Books* in *The Early Modern Englishwoman* series 1, part 2, vol. 8 (Aldershot: Ashgate, 2001).

47 Harry Keyishian, 'Griselda on the Elizabethan Stage', *Studies in English Literature 1500–1900* 16:2 (spring 1976), 253–61.

48 For a discussion of the punishment of adultery in the period, see Keith Thomas, 'The Puritans and Adultery: The Act of 1650 Reconsidered', in Keith Thomas and Donald Pennington, eds, *Puritans and Revolutionaries* (Oxford: Clarendon Press, 1978), pp. 257–82.

49 E. Ann Kaplan, *Motherhood and Representation* (London: Routledge, 1992), p. 68.
50 Melanie Klein, 'A Study of Envy and Gratitude', in *The Selected Melanie Klein*, ed. Juliet Mitchell (London: Penguin, 1986).
51 All quotations from the play will be taken from William Shakespeare, *Romeo and Juliet*, New Penguin edn, ed. T. J. B. Spencer (London: Penguin, 1967).
52 Susan Snyder, *The Comic Matrix of Shakespeare's Tragedies* (Princeton: Princeton University Press, 1979), p. 58.
53 Snyder, *The Comic Matrix*, p. 56. Snyder quotes Madeline Doran, *Endeavours of Art* (London: Wisconsin University Press, 1954), p. 137.
54 G. Bullough, *Narrative and Dramatic Sources of Shakespeare*, vol. 1 (London: Routledge and Kegan Paul, New York: Columbia University Press, 1957), p. 284.
55 *Nice Wanton*, eds R. Dodsley and W. C. Hazlitt, *A Select Collection of Old English Plays*, 4th edn (London: Reeves and Turner, 1876), Prologue.
56 In Elisabeth Badinter, *The Myth of Motherhood: An Historical View of the Maternal Instinct*, trans. Roger DeGaris (London: Souvenir Press, 1981), p. 33.
57 *Oxford English Dictionary* online.
58 *Oxford English Dictionary* online. There are many examples of this use in Reformation and post-Reformation propaganda. For example, in 1545, 'Thus for greasy lukers sake the greasy canonistes nosel the people in idolatry'.
59 Anonymous, 'New Custom', in Dodsley and Hazlitt, eds, *A Select Collection of Old English Plays*, p. 44.
60 *Oxford English Dictionary* online. Nashe writes of 'The Dogge nussling his nose under the necke of the Deare' in 1594, and Shakespeare deploys the word in a glorious and complex image in *Venus and Adonis*: 'And nousling in his flanke the loving swine / Sheathed unaware the tusk in his soft groine' (l. 1115).
61 A nice use of the word in this sense comes in the prologue to Marston's *Antonio's Revenge* (1602), where a character is 'nuzzled twixt the breastes of happiness'.
62 Dodsley and Hazlitt, eds, *A Select Collection of Old English Plays*, p. 168.
63 Snyder, *The Comic Matrix*, p. 64.
64 Snyder, *The Comic Matrix*, p. 64.
65 Guillemeau, *Childbirth, or The Happie Delivery of Women*, p. 10. Also Patricia Crawford, 'The Sucking Child', in *Continuity and Change* 1 (1986), 23–54 and 83–84.
66 Guillemeau, *Childbirth*, p. 10.
67 See J. Barry Webb, *Shakespeare's Erotic Word Usage* (Hastings: Cornwallis Press, 1989), p. 36, where he describes 'dug' as primarily referring to animals. Quoted in Snyder, *The Comic Matrix*, p. 65.

68 Gail Kern Paster describes how the nursing relationship 'calls a quintet of actors into being: the two "blood" parents, the two surrogate "milk" parents of nurse and husband, and the infant girl in their care'. Paster shows how in this scene the Nurse's story about Juliet's fall excludes Lady Capulet to the extent that her role is 'distinctly diminished and occluded'. Paster, *The Body Embarrassed*, p. 221.
69 Paster, *The Body Embarrassed*, p. 225.
70 Rachel Trubowitz, 'Nursing Mothers and Others', in Naomi J. Miller and Naomi Yavneh, eds, *Maternal Measures: Figuring Caregiving in the Early Modern Period* (Aldershot: Ashgate, 2000), p. 83.
71 Sasha Roberts, *William Shakespeare: Romeo and Juliet* (Plymouth: Northcote House, in association with the British Council, 1998), p. 25.
72 Clinton, *The Countess of Lincoln's Nursery*, p. 31. Also Badinter, *The Myth of Motherhood*, p. 42.
73 Guillemeau, *Childbirth*, p. 10.
74 Roberts, *William Shakespeare: Romeo and Juliet*, p. 29.
75 Julia Kristeva, 'Romeo and Juliet: Love-hatred in the Couple', in *Shakespearean Tragedy*, ed. J. Drakakis (London: Longman, 1992), p. 301.
76 Rachel Trubowitz argues that Juliet's estrangement from her family is compounded by what her father sees as 'the likeness she bears to the bawdy Nurse . . . who suckled her'. Rachel Trubowitz, 'Nursing Mothers and Others', in Miller and Yavneh, *Maternal Measures*, p. 84.
77 This might be read as a replay, for Juliet, of what Adelman calls 'two psychic sites of intense maternal deprivation', in that she is rejected for the second time by both the mother who bore her but gave her away to be nursed and the nurse who weaned her with wormwood. See Adelman, *Suffocating Mothers*, p. 5.

5

Motherhood and the household: domestic tragedy and city comedy

> truth in plaine attire is the easier knowne[1]
> Robert Armin on the crime and execution
> of Elizabeth Caldwell

The household in context

Domestic tragedies and city comedies do not adapt existing literary narratives, but emerge out of an engagement with contemporary circumstances and, in the case of domestic tragedies, often represent real events. They are not situated in some imagined other place, but in locations and spaces familiar to members of a contemporary audience with whose social world they are likely to engage. These plays emerge in the period between 1590 and the second decade of the seventeenth century at a time when the commercial theatre had, says Catherine Richardson, 'grown immeasurably in confidence' and embedded itself into its local environs so that 'the portrayal of the domestic environment and the pull of local and contemporary narratives seem particularly intended to invite comparison with experience outside the theatre'.[2] These are plays that represent a recognisable world to a knowing audience – a consequence, in part, of what Richardson identifies as an 'emerging focus' on the 'credibility of representations' which she sees as developing from Renaissance reconsiderations of classical theories of mimesis.

Both dramatic forms begin to appear during a period of social and economic stress, when a variety of adversities including poor harvests and related social and political unrest provoked a series of legislative measures that mark the period as particularly troubled.[3] Historians agree that evidence indicates that disorder was greatly feared.[4] The increasing numbers of dispossessed poor, combined with the bad harvests of the 1590s, provoked a sharp rise in the population of the cities, especially London, as people looked for work, leading to increased anxiety about the maintenance of order.[5] The Poor Laws of 1576 represent early government efforts to keep control, mainly by addressing a perceived need to regulate personal behaviour.[6] This was influenced, as Joan R. Kent has shown, by the desire for a 'moral reformation' expressed by the more Puritan members of parliament, but also by 'social, economic and political considerations' that were equally important as, and perhaps more important than, religious and moral considerations among those who supported the bills. Kent finds that 'Members often seem to have been less concerned about personal morality than about the implications for society of the conduct of the individual'.[7]

Protestant emphasis upon individual responsibility to uphold 'God's Law and the king's', and the tendency of this idea to be associated with the regulation of family, inevitably placed an emphasis upon the consequences of personal conduct.[8] This included the need for the heads of families to set a clear moral example for, and to take responsibility for, the wives, servants and children in their care.[9] Such dominant ideas engaged with what Keith Thomas calls 'a growing idealisation of married love and domestic life', placing responsibility for social stability with the family, and encoding its regulation in legal proclamations. Thomas acknowledges the influence of Protestant ideas, but stresses that 'Protestants and Catholics alike laid increasing emphasis on the blessings of mutual society and companionship' in marriage, suggesting caution against reading this new emphasis as an exclusively Protestant phenomenon.[10] Regulation of what we would now call 'private' behaviour was also understood to be a right of all the local community. Philip Julius noted in 1602 that, 'In England, every citizen is bound by oath to keep a sharp eye at his neighbor's house'.[11] This interest was manifest in rituals like the 'skimmington', which involved the public humiliation and punishment of husbands and wives suspected of disruptive behaviour. As Karen Newman points out, such events offer evidence that neighbours and local people assumed that they had a right to interfere in personal matters, and also assumed that their intervention was necessary.[12] Martin Ingram has shown that 'Domestic relations were . . . on the borders of public and private morality in the period' and in Ariès' more generalised analysis, the negotiation of these borders is shown to generate both potential tensions and opportunities: 'One of the individual's primary missions was still to acquire, defend or increase his or her social role within the limits of the community's toleration... [A]s the inequalities between people in different walks of life grew more pronounced, there was greater room to manoeuvre within those communal boundaries'.[13] The idea of 'abroad', the world outside the house, thus operated as both threat and control; the potentially disruptive dangers of the outside existed alongside the comforts and opportunities offered by a supportive social network.

Domestic tragedies and city comedies present mothers whose meaning is adjusted to represent a dramatised world in which social and economic considerations predominate. The significance of the mother, the ideas and principles that she embodied, shifts in these plays to accommodate an understanding of maternity as a fundamentally social function that is important in ensuring stability in the wider world. The complex social structures in such a world are always clearly adumbrated in this drama, with the family as the smallest unit of an integrated social world placed in a realised geographic locality and based upon economic interdependence. Locale is created through reference to recognisable neighbourhoods: to the length and time it takes to move around them, to the kind of people who might be typically found working or moving within them. Neighbourhoods, in turn, are the location of the households where the main events of each play are set. A household signifies both the materials that comprise it (buildings, rooms, furniture, belongings) and the people who inhabit it: the family, servants and visitors who link it with the world within which it exists and which impinges upon it.[14] As Martin Ingram points out, 'Domestic relations were... on the borders of public and private morality in the period', implying a link between the internal functions of the household and their wider social context.[15] The geographic setting in which the drama is played out thus offers a connective structure that brings together the social world of each play and details of the household and the family that is its subject. Furthermore, such a structure links the theatre with the world outside its walls. Alison Findlay has pointed out the importance of 'the interaction between setting and venue' in creating 'the distinctive life' of a dramatic work.[16] The dramatic representation of real and familiar settings in these plays constructs a kind of intimacy between audience and dramatic action that invites contemplation of the events of the play in relation to the ideas and discourses that contextualised the experience of everyday life.

Contemporary conduct books associated good motherhood with wifely duty. Potential tensions between the roles of wife and mother were addressed in such texts by confirming that a woman's first duty was to her husband, but they also emphasised the importance of mutual love and respect in marriage. Such texts also see the role of the wife and mother in part as acting as a kind of physical signifier of her husband's wealth, status and piety. This is, they say, manifest in her behaviour, her speech, her dress; the way she manages her household and the way she brings up her children. For example, in 1591 Phillip Stubbes celebrated his wife's governance of her household: 'Shee would suffer no disorder or abuse in her house, to be either unreproved or unreformed'.[17] The wife and mother is seen as an ambassador for her husband's household: a signifier of the social and economic stability which is associated with the ideal home, the ideal Protestant family.[18] The idea that the roles of wife and mother are complementary, indeed integral to one another, is fundamental to the depiction of social relations in domestic tragedies and city comedies. The tension between maternity and wifehood that offered a fruitful organising dynamic for the romantic and comic narratives discussed in the previous chapter is replaced in the plays discussed here by an emphasis on a woman's social meaning as a signifier of her husband's social and economic status and success, of his household and his family. Being a good wife *is* being a good mother in these plays: the maternal body presents not a threat but a comfort. It is, however, in peril. These plays stress the vulnerability of the mother – the dangers that threaten her outside her home and that therefore jeopardise the fragile stability of the social structures which depend upon her.[19]

Motherhood and domestic space

Domestic tragedies typically advertised themselves as a satisfying combination of reportage, titillation and moralising.[20] These plays, which usually purport to represent actual, more or less recent events, depend for this exotic mix of effects upon the evocation of a world that is recognisable and familiar to an audience in terms of dominant ideas and perceptions, if not actually known through material experience. They tend to construct an audience that knows better than the individuals impersonated on the stage, by deploying a clear moral dynamic, abetted through the use of convention and typology. Richardson identifies this as a link 'between representation and ethical function [that is] didactic in motivation and ecclesiastical in form' and sees this as deriving in part from the pamphlet writers whose work informed many domestic tragedies: 'pamphlet writers borrow the rhetorical structures of the sermon to legitimise their representation of sensational material'.[21] In such a context the consequences of social and economic upheaval are recast in terms of sensational stories in which the titillation is rendered acceptable by the moral context. The traditional notion of motherhood as a vulnerable condition for a woman, and the conventional dramatic operation of the mother figure as the locus of emotional tension, offered dramatists a set of conventions around which to organise the emotional and moral concerns of the play.

A Warning for Fair Women represents for the stage the notorious events of 1573, recorded by Holinshed, which culminated in the hanging of a minor merchant's wife, the mother of his three small children. Anne Sanders was allegedly involved in the planning of her husband's murder and accused of an affair with the murderer, Browne, but there appears to have been a financial motive behind the murder; in fact its planning and execution allegedly involved several transactions between the parties involved. Ann denied knowledge of the murder right up to the last moment before her execution, when she confessed.[22] In this play there is no conflict between a mother's duties to her children and those she has to her husband. Indeed, motherhood is shown to be part of what it means to be a good wife, both within her husband's household and in the wider social context of the play.

When Anne first meets the man who will be her lover, she is sitting outside the door of the house she shares with her husband, the doorway becoming a metonym for the household which she manages and to which she is bound, for as Nicole Castan has pointed out, 'the woman was . . . both the servant and mistress of the household'.[23] She is sitting on the threshold with her child: 'Enter Anne Sanders with her little sonne' (l. 321). The scene thus begins with an emblematic tableau which links the mother with the household and with social stability, implied in the presence of the small boy who will inherit all that the household represents. The importance and the vulnerability of Anne's situation is implied by the liminality of her placement both literally, at the doorway which divides the household from the street, and figuratively, as the mother entrusted with realising the stable transfer of social and material status from one generation to the next. The domestic space that Anne should occupy is rhetorically drawn as she discusses the timing of supper with her son when his father returns from 'th'Exchange' and asks him to 'go bid your sister see / My Closet lockt when she takes out the fruite', the dialogue evoking a homely sense of a comfortable and well ordered house where everything is in its place (ll. 323–41).[24] But the privacy of the house, signified yet again by the doorway, is placed in the context of the public street where the mother and her child are vulnerable to the threats and infringements of the outside world.[25] Alison Findlay discusses a version of the city as 'a unified and autonomous masculine subject', suggesting that 'London does not appear to offer a home to early modern women'. Something of that hostility to the woman's safety is present in the threatening person of Anne's future lover, Browne.[26] The dialogue between them when they meet reinforces this sense of threat; there are references to Browne coming to 'drive her from her door', and Anne herself refers to the dangers of women sitting alone 'at any doore'.[27] There is a tension between the public aspect of the positioning of mother and son, and the private intimacy of the affectionate banter between them, which opens the scene. The boy is only on stage for ten lines, which is enough to offer up a pleasurable glimpse of motherhood at its most ideal before Browne appears to disrupt the scene and the plot begins the push to its gloomy conclusion. By showing Anne as a wife vulnerably positioned both in terms of her function as mother and housekeeper before her fall, the dramatist creates a moral and an emotional landscape which will inform an audience's reading of her subsequent behaviour. The moment is recalled in a later scene where the murderer is stirred to guilt by the sight of the child (ll. 1614–15). City, child and house will become related signifiers of the downfall of the adulterous mother and the family and household broken apart by her crime.

The play thus invites a moral reading that chimes with the concerns expressed in many of the conduct books and moral literature of the time. Dod and Cleaver, the writers of *A Godlie Forme of Householde Government* (1561), underline the significance of the link between wife and house: 'we call the wife the Hus-wife, that is, house-wife not a street-wife, one that gaddeth up and downe'.[28] H. H. Adams describes the typical structure of domestic tragedy as a sequence of 'sin, discovery, repentance, punishment, and expectation of divine mercy', in which the moral framework is predominant, though he finds reference to social experience in characterisation, suggesting that Anne's son is 'drawn from life'.[29]

However, the social setting and the 'truth' of the subject matter make these plays primarily social dramas in which even motivation to murder is given a clear social context: Anne's accomplice is helping the murderer because she needs to make money for a dowry for her daughter. (l. 464). A sense of financial desperation socialises the crime, which might be the result of sin but is also a consequence of social need. But the conventions of the morality play also have a role in structuring the narrative: Anne is shown to be already fallen by reference to conventional signifiers of feminine malignity in an early scene in which her vanity, as well as her greed, is demonstrated by a desire for expensive clothes (l. 590).

That the narrative shifts between the structures of morality form and a story taken from life is evident in a structure where the narrative is punctuated by a series of dumb shows which are a startling contrast to the more homely visual image of the mother and son discussed above. Kate McLuskie says that this indicates how 'the tension between true reportage and the need to set a moral example was difficult to achieve in the theatre'.[30] She shows how, in this play, such tension is resolved by 'separating the two into parallel actions which contrast the true story of Anne Sanders' adultery with a series of allegorical dumb shows depicting the conflict between Lust and Chastity', and concludes that 'the author of *A Warning for Fair Women* was only partly successful in resolving the conflict between morality and style'.[31] McLuskie sees this conflict as generated by the different expectations of a heterogeneous audience. Nevertheless, it is possible to argue that the allegorical scenes which punctuate the narrative work by heightening the sense that the story itself is true, and not only more shocking but more theatrically satisfying because of it. The allegory serves to set the action against a detailed moral framework, and, as McLuskie shows, to fill in some difficult gaps in the narrative not accounted for by the sources, but the conventions it utilises also engage with the social concerns of the play.

The first dumb show, orchestrated by the figure of Tragedy, who enters the stage 'with a bowle of bloud in her hand', depicts Ann thrusting away Chastity at a feast where she succumbs to Lust and then falls asleep with her lover Browne. The depiction of adultery in relation to gluttony as well as lust, in the context of an ordinary domestic setting, evokes the social implications of their actions alongside the moral operation of conventional allegory (l. 845).[32] The work of a good wife and mother (the preparation of food; the entertainment of guests; the sexual comfort of a husband) is turned upon itself in the dumb show in a home that is transformed, as Tragedy makes clear, into a 'fatal house' through the corruption of the wife and mother at its heart.[33] The play barely mentions that the real Anne Sanders was heavily pregnant at the time her husband was killed, a fact that does not emerge in the play until Anne's trial, where in the narrative it serves as an affirmation of her guilt.[34] The drama prepares for the revelation of her pregnancy through the dumb show, so that it is possible to make a visual link between Anne's symbolic sleeping with her lover, her real lying-in and her alleged crime, something which is confirmed rhetorically by the lords who examine her at her trial. When she denies that she received a token confirming the murder because 'I kept my childbed chamber at that time' she is warned to 'clog not your soule / With new additions of more heinous sinne' and told that she is suspected of adultery (ll. 2347–8). Thus the home is infiltrated by the adulterer, and the family it embraces is polluted by adultery. The body of the mother and the household thus become entwined in meaning, the one signifying the other, the one destroyed with the other.

Viviana Comensoli has explored this analogy in some detail with reference to Heywood's *A Woman Killed with Kindness*, where the adultery of Anne Frankford is condemned by her husband in terms which suggest that 'the contamination of Anne's body is one and the same with her "infect[ion]" of Frankford's property' and shows how 'Heywood carefully maps the refuges of civility and privacy that have been corrupted, Frankford's entrance of his house paralleling Wendoll's [the lover's] penetration of Anne's body'.[35] *A Warning for Fair Women* does not sexualise its subject matter to the same extent. The analogy is there in the sense of 'a violation which is transferred from human interaction to the space in which it takes place', but the sexual sin is separated out, enacted in the dumb shows while the main narrative deals with its consequences – the murder, grief, illegitimacy and household and family breakdown that follow.[36] The moral content shifts between an exhibition of family disintegration (and its social implications) and a bleak morality, heightened by the dumb shows, which demonstrates the consequences of sin for the individual sinner. The scene of Anne's final repentance when her three children are brought to say goodbye to her before her execution combines both. Anne pays for her crime not only with her life but by losing her right to motherhood, acknowledging this in her response to her children's distressed cries of 'Oh mother, mother': 'Oh my deare children! I am unworthy of the name of mother' (ll. 2659–61). She advises them to learn by 'your mother's fall', 'to follow vertue and beware of sinne' (ll. 2666–7).[37]

Throughout this play, Anne moves further and further out into public space as her adultery and its consequences propel her away from the intimate spaces of the home and into the city that provides the forum and the audience for her execution. The farewell scene is public, both because it is set in prison and the farewells take place before onlookers, and because Anne addresses the theatre audience in imitation of an actual scaffold speech (taken from accounts of the real Anne's last words). There is a terrible tension between the intimacy of her farewell to her children and the public space in which it happens. The children become, however unwillingly, an aspect of the moral here; their distress is another indication of the perversity of a crime which has broken a household.[38] The theatrical nature of Elizabethan judiciary executions is here appropriated by the theatre in a kind of dramatic ritualising of ritual itself. J. A. Sharpe identifies a change in the significance of executions in the sixteenth century, noting that 'the person being executed became the central actor in a theatre of punishment', and that the 'public execution . . . was in fact a highly structured ritual in which the authority of the state was demonstrated in a dramatic fashion, to the public at large'.[39] These grim rituals dramatised a personal story of corruption through the condemned person's forced iteration of their own sinful past, situating themselves and their transgression within the context of the social world that they had wronged and demonstrating the concern of the state to regulate its microcosmic analogue, the household. Translated into dramatic spectacle the public rite creates a frightening clash between the private family – the mother and her children – and the society that has condemned her, revealing their terrible isolation in the midst of a collective wider and wiser world.[40] The presence of Anne's children adds further resonance, not only creating emotional tension, but emblematising the social consequences of the adultery which led to murder: the shattered family disintegrates publicly as the doubly bereaved children receive their mother's final embrace:

So God send down his blessing on you al:
Farewel, farewel, farewel, farewel, farewel.
(She kisses them one after the other)

Nay stay not to disturbe me with your teares,
The time is come sweete hearts, and we must part,
That way you go, this way my heavie heart. (ll. 2710–15)

Ann presents her children each with a book of 'holy meditations', and exhorts them to 'Sleepe not without them when you go to bed, / And rise a mornings with them in your hands' (ll. 2708–9). In this, she imagines the children in their beds protected by the meditations that will keep them 'safer than in faire buildings'. She re-places them, in her imagination, at the secure heart of some new home.

In *A Warning for Fair Women* the mother, by sitting at her open door, talking in the street, becomes the means by which corruption enters and pollutes the home. In the anonymous *A Yorkshire Tragedy*, a mother again is destroyed and familial and social relations disintegrate. But here the mother is not corrupted by crime, but attacked where she should be most safe, by one who should protect her. The play is based upon the true story of the Calverley murders, where in 1605 a Yorkshire gentleman killed his wife and two of his children, and set off to kill the third, a baby at nurse, but was apprehended before he reached the child. The story is also the subject of a comedy, *The Miseries of Enforced Marriage*, written by George Watkins in 1607, where the course of events is altered to provide a happy ending.[41] In both plays there is an emphasis upon social and family relations which is crucial to the plot in that Calverley broke off an engagement before his eventual prudent marriage to a relation of his guardian; his unhappiness has made him profligate and criminal and is, as Comensoli puts it, 'a source of profound distress'.[42]

The play presents the story of the crime as a dismal celebration of the household and of the cohesive forces created by its place in a wider social context. Comensoli points out that 'the principal characters are named according to their domestic or social roles (Husband, Wife, Maid, Gentleman, and so on)' and that the word 'home' or 'house' is repeated throughout the play, reinforcing its focus on the household.[43] Friends and family continually admonish Calverley for not treating his wife as she deserves, and a sense is created of a society working hard to contain and support a relationship that is under strain because of the aberrant behaviour of the husband. Though he accuses his wife of being a whore who has bred him bastards, and refuses to recognise her, the household and the social network into which it is embedded work to support her.[44] When Calverley physically threatens his wife with a dagger, it is a servant who enters the room hastily to intervene: the household acts to protect the wife and mother who is literally and metaphorically at its centre (v, 33).

Calverley's wife demonstrates an understanding of her proper place as a wife and a mother in the power structures of the family. While she hints at the emotional turmoil that her husband's behaviour has caused her as a mother, she subjugates it to the demands of duty:

> If thou suspect it but a plot in me
> To keep my dowry, or for mine own good,
> Or my poor children's (though it suits a mother
> To show a natural care in their reliefs)
> Yet I'll forget myself to calm your blood. (iii, 63–7)

However, she qualifies this, bringing together the desires of the mother and the duties of a wife, by associating her wish to protect her children with a commendable sense of family duty and household obligations. Her concern for her children is linked with their social standing and the importance of continuity and household:

> What shall become of me and my poor children,
> Two here and one at nurse, my pretty beggars?
> I see how ruin with a palsy hand
> Begins to shake the ancient seat to dust. (iii, 88–91)

The mother's love for her children is thus integral to her wider concerns and duties as a wife, an integrity of family and household that is broken apart in the climactic fifth scene, in which the murders are depicted. A mix of realistic and emblematic moments signifies the social, moral and emotional implications of the murder.

The scene opens with a tableau that signifies domestic harmony, a household quietly operating as it should: 'Enter a maid with a child in her arms, the mother by her asleep'. The women inhabit a private space, protected by the house, safe to sleep and to nurse. This static, emblematic moment is broken by frenzied action (the dramatist utilising the same convention as that deployed by Dekker in his Grissil play) when Calverley enters with a weapon. The mother wakes at the crying of her children and leaps from bed to 'catch up' the younger, which is stabbed in her arms. As this happens she is injured and sinks down – creating for a moment the ghost of a *pietà* – before her husband wrenches her child from her. The traditional associations of the maternal body with sacrifice and division are recalled here in a new context in which the mother simultaneously stands for a social ideal and demonstrates the fragility of that ideal in her suffering. Richardson shows how the setting of this scene also contributes to this, notably 'the familiar image of the bed alters the tone of this scene . . . it brings into play the two key iconographical manifestations of such an object, the deathbed and the childbed, recalling the rites of passage around which family and household figure and refigure themselves'. At the same time, the household exhibits a kind of resilience to the terror at its heart: 'For the only time in the play, a household as a dynamic of individuals collaborate to defend the Wife and children as the hope on which their future as a group depends'.[45] The Wife demonstrates a complementary practical resilience which compromises – or perhaps extends – the image of her fragility, for, as Comensoli has argued, her effort to retain something of what has been lost is demonstrated in the play by her continued loyalty to her husband, for whose life she pleads, and from whom she says parting is the worst suffering of all: 'More wretched am I now in this distress / Than former sorrows made me' (v, 61–2). The Wife upholds social, family and political structures, subordinating first her concern for her children to the demands of her mad husband and then her desire for her husband's continued life to the demands of the law. But she is no passive victim. She has taken steps to ensure that a transfer of family land prevents her destitution, and in doing so effectively retains her status as the centre of a home. And for Comensoli, the Wife's declaration of love and forgiveness has a strategic function in that it 'preserves not only her reputation but her lands'.[46]

Motherhood in this play is social in its orientation: the conservation of land is as integral to the wife's role as the care of her children. In this play the mother is threatened by a different kind of corruption from that of *A Warning for Fair Women* and her loss is that of a victim, albeit a canny one, rather than a felon. Both mothers figure the vulnerability at the heart of a household, and the significance that such vulnerability has for the good order of the society in which it is situated. But if Comensoli is right, *A Yorkshire Tragedy* adds a hard edge to that vulnerability in the mother's calculated determination to protect herself and her surviving child. It also demonstrates the value of a practical concern

Motherhood and the household

for economic survival. This can be set alongside the preoccupations of conduct books that advocate the careful regulation of household and family for spiritual reasons, but also as a means by which wider anxieties about social order and the good management of society should be addressed. Margot Heinemann sees the drama of this period as presenting 'a society changing from one regulated by inherited status to one ruled increasingly by the power of money and capital, with much greater social mobility and, hence, with an increasing sense of opportunity and insecurity'.[47] The Wife in this play acts pragmatically in response to potential insecurity in the face of change. In doing so her representation shifts away from the paradigm of ideal, tragic motherhood which is emblematically asserted at the moment of her husband's attack, towards that of a practical and organised housewife.

Motherhood and domestic economy

City comedies offered their audience a satirical representation of a familiar, rather than an ideal, world, in which the economic preoccupations of a mercantile and ambitious group are embedded in their social and family relations and ambitions.[48] Middleton's *A Chaste Maid in Cheapside*, written in 1613, has at its heart a plot that, like *Romeo and Juliet*, pits the aspirations of romantic love against the material and social demands of parents.[49] The story is of an avidly upwardly mobile goldsmith, Yellowhammer, and his equally ambitious wife, Maudline, who enrich themselves through the advantageous marriages of their children. Their daughter Moll is intended for Sir Walter Whorehound, a philandering knight. Sir Walter already has a mistress, Mrs Allwit, whom he keeps, along with her husband, who boasts that he need not even impregnate his wife, so generous is Sir Walter on his behalf. Sir Walter's continued good fortune depends upon the sterility of his relative Sir Walter Kix. Moll Yellowhammer, meanwhile, is in love with a young man whose older brother, Touchwood Senior, is happily married but produces too many children and so is forced to live apart from his wife, satisfying his desires instead by impregnating country girls in impressive numbers.

As is clear from this synopsis, this is a play which focuses upon kinship and sexuality, placing both within the context of the economic strategies of the urban middle classes. In this play, marriage is a market and children are commodities or liabilities in a world where, for the most part, affective relations are subordinated to the desire for material gain. Middleton uses the bare bones of the comic romance to produce a witty travesty of the family ideal promoted in the conduct literature and elsewhere.[50] The wife is, indeed, the 'helpmeet' so popular in the conduct books, but this role is debased in the play, where the promotion of household economy and social advancement involves the selling of her children.[51] The mother is a kind of bawd, hounding her daughter into marriage by way of sexual jokes and parental pressure:

> We are honour'd then, if this baggage would be humble,
> And kiss him with devotion when he enters.
> I cannot get her for my life
> To instruct her hand thus, before and after,
> Which a knight will look for, before and after.
> I have told her still, 'tis the wavings of a woman
> Does often move a man and prevails strongly. (1.1.36–42)

It was earlier argued that in *Romeo and Juliet* the maternal is estranged and inadequate, polarised into the roles of the wife and the nurse. In this play Mrs Yellowhammer approximates the antitype of both, coming close to the Bawd in Shakespeare's *Pericles* ('Come, you're a young foolish sapling and must be bowed as I would have you').[52] She has the none of the capacity for nurture and affection that created the sense of an emotional relationship between Juliet and her nurse, and her wifely dynastic ambitions have degenerated into a grasping materialism which values her daughter as 'baggage' in an economic transaction: 'you are dull. Nothing comes nimbly from you; you dance like a plumber's daughter; and deserve two thousand pounds in lead to your marriage, and not in goldsmith's ware' (1.1.13–16).

Her conspicuous lack of the traditional qualities of motherhood is, of course, what makes Mrs Yellowhammer such a comic success. When she retrieves her daughter from an attempted elopement and enters the stage dragging Moll by the hair, the effect is funny rather than distressing, provoking a pleasurable frisson of shock at her outrageous unmaternal behaviour. Even when pursued by a remonstrating waterman who tells her that she is a cruel mother, and with her husband enjoining her to 'Hold, hold', she relentlessly follows her aim of promoting her family out of the citizenry and into the nobility and presents her bedraggled, weeping daughter to her suitor: 'I have brought your jewel by the hair' (4.3.25). Her husband's ineffectuality is, part of the joke, but the joke has its black side because its roots lie in the same typological tradition that informed depictions of Noah's relationship with his wife before the flood.[53] The Waterman's appeal to Mrs Yellowhammer's maternity is ironic in the rapacious world of the play, where parents sell their daughters for economic and social gain, and the joke runs on through the play. Even Maudline's grief at her daughter's supposed 'death' is comically coloured by her preoccupation with its financial significance: 'We'll not lose all at once, somewhat we'll catch' (5.3.115). Gail Kern Paster says that this play represents a society where 'social authority – here represented by the older generation – uses the discourses of nature oppressively to serve its own selfish ends'.[54] Certainly, the mother here is a grotesque incarnation of the topsy-turvy values displayed in the play, not so much an emblem as a counter-emblem, not radiating meaning but inviting judgement: the site where ideal maternity collapses into travesty.

Travesty had a traditional function in religious ritual and drama, making use of a Manichean version of psychomachia which reminded an audience of the presence of evil even when the world might seem at its brightest, for example at the moment of Christ's birth. Though written well after the Reformation, *A Chaste Maid in Cheapside* appears to incorporate this tradition into its structure, sometimes offering startling similarities to earlier texts, not necessarily because these plays were known by Middleton, but perhaps because the thrust of such narratives had become part of a widely available dramatic vocabulary associated with a form of satire which emphasised the gaps between religious and moral ideals and the actual shortcomings of human conduct.[55] The childless Lady Kix laments, like the biblical Rachel or the mothers of the innocents, for the children she does not have, but the symbolism of her lack of 'blessings' is undercut by a bawdy joke which privileges the sexual and economic implications of her condition: 'Can any woman have a greater cut?' (1.2.139). When Touchstone Senior bewails, in an aside, the consequences of his alarming fertility, he does so in lines which are almost exactly those expressed by the Sheep stealer, Mak, in the *Second Shepherd's Play*: 'Every year a child, and some years two, / Besides drinkings abroad, that's never reckon'd; / This gear will not hold out' (1.2.15–17). Compare Mak's complaint:'And ilk year that comes to man / She brings forth a lakan – / And, some years, two. / But were I now more gracious, and richer by far, / I were eaten out of house and of harbour. / Yet she is a foul dowse'.[56]

There are tropes in *A Chaste Maid in Cheapside* that are very like those in the earlier play. For example, an unmarried country girl tricks two promoters who are invigilating observance of the rules of Lent into taking her unwanted baby by concealing it in a basket under a loin of mutton.[57] The *Second Shepherd's Play* has at its dramatic climax a sequence where the sheep-stealer and his wife conceal a stolen lamb, swaddled in a cradle, pretending it is their own new-born child, in a subversive imitation of the nativity scene which will end the play. The play on such conventional symbolism in *A Chaste Maid* brings together grotesquely the helplessness and promise of a new-born child and its unwantedness in a world which is so governed by material preoccupations that motherhood no longer carries any emotional or spiritual significance. The girl who plays the basket trick is proud of her 'wit' in devising the game, celebrating it in an aside to the audience, but its resonance goes further than a practical joke, both reducing the baby to the level of the meat she pretends to be selling and elevating it to the status of a sacrificial victim.[58] In an earlier scene, Touchwood Senior is confronted by a girl carrying his latest illegitimate baby, who pushes him into negotiation over its upkeep.

There is a connection between illegitimacy and whoredom in the play which consistently places the mothers of bastards as tricksters, something unlikely to reflect social reality but which nevertheless appears to be engaging with a contemporary problem and perceptions arising from it. Hoffer and Hull offer an extensive analysis of the incidence of infanticide in the period, and of contemporary social and legal responses to it, drawing attention to a gradual broadening of the definition of infanticide which made it more difficult for women to defend themselves. This law, they argue, reveals an assumption that mothers (overwhelmingly likely to be poor and unmarried) would attempt to disguise their crimes and to trick their way out of prosecution.[59] The historian Keith Wrightson discusses the peculiar statistical blip at the turn of the sixteenth and seventeenth centuries where there is a sharp temporary rise in bastardy.[60] This he links with economic decline, which he argues led to instabilities in the courtship of the poor.[61] In *A Chaste Maid* it is poor country girls who produce properly illegitimate offspring, but the association of their plight with whoredom repeats the premises which are evident in the moral literature of the period. Wrightson reminds us that, 'to the religious moralists of the period, illegitimacy was merely a sub-category

of the general and perennial problem of 'whoredom', and that
unmarried women who had babies were severely punished:

> Some girls, however, became . . . the mothers of bastards. There
> tolerance ended. They were likely to be brought before the church
> courts, questioned and ordered to do penance in public. If there was
> a danger that their children would fall upon the parish poor rates,
> they might be brought before the Justices of the Peace, and perhaps
> committed to a house of correction . . . [I]t is scarcely surprising that
> some girls faced with these terrors concealed their pregnancies, bore
> their children alone and then exposed, abandoned or deliberately
> killed them.[62]

An ideological narrative which linked bastardy with promiscuity
and the selling of sex is reinforced in other literature of the period,
for example in ballads such as *No Natural Mother but a Monster*,
which tells the story of a servant girl's impregnation by her master,
the abandonment and subsequent death of her baby, and her
consequent execution for infanticide, as one of her 'unbridled will'
and 'wild carriage'. Told in the first person, the ballad resembles
the first song of Phillip's Grissil, though here the girl falls despite
good parenting, rather than learns virtue from it:

> My parents me vp brought,
> carefully, carefully,
> Little (God wot) they thought,
> that I should euer
> Haue run so bad a race,
> To dye in such a place,
> God grant all Maidens grace,
> To take example.[63]

Protestant ideas about the function of family are here mediated
through Calvinist notions of election and grace to explain the girl's
transgression. Her inability to marshal what should be 'natural'
to a woman, either in terms of stifling sexual impulses or of
summoning proper maternal feeling, becomes malignant; the threat
always implicit in a woman's potential for maternity is carried
through and ends in murder.

In his play, as in the ballad, Middleton represents a similar
ideological thrust to that of Puritan narratives on the regulation of
maternity, engaging with contemporary concerns by reference to

the traditions and conventions of earlier moral and religious dramatic narratives. It thus displays a powerful moral base (but not a prescriptive one) against which an audience is encouraged to appreciate the satirical comedy.[64] Situating *A Chaste Maid in Cheapside* within the frame of the religious festival of Lent contextualises the narrative within it, which operates not to offer a series of universal and dogmatic truths but to invite an audience to test what is enacted before them against a moral dynamic informed by Protestant ideals. If, as Ariès says, 'living became a way of externalising one's inner life and virtues . . . Hence a great deal of attention was paid to what went on in routine home life and daily intercourse', then this play humorously exposes the aspirations and values of the world it satirises.[65] This is evident in the famous scene where the christening of Mrs Allwit's latest baby by Sir Walter is attended by gossips and Puritan well-wishers, described by Alan Brissenden as a 'mockery of true spiritual values . . . where a whoremaster stands godfather to his own bastard, Puritans get drunk and a cuckold beamingly takes the credit for a child not his own'.[66] Here, maternity as any kind of idealised condition is conspicuously missing. The opening stage directions ask for 'a bed thrust out upon the stage, Allwit's Wife in it. Enter all the Gossips'.[67] It is the spectacle which is crucial here. The mother is accompanied by her gossips, so that the representation is of a social event. This is emphasised in a curious prelude to the scene where the baby, carried by a midwife across the stage and off again, is followed by the gossips, who are jostling one another, arguing exaggeratedly about social precedence. The significance of the bed is paradoxical too, in that while it functions as an image of household order and process, in Richardson's formulation, it is also likely to carry more bawdy connotations. Sasha Roberts has discovered contemporary beds that are decorated with figures linked to 'rioting and revelling, to sex and excess'.[68]

This nice juxtaposition of meanings works in the same way as the sleeping scenes in the domestic tragedies discussed earlier: emblematising an ideal and immediately undercutting it with a noisy reality. The same characters, the mother, the nurse, the child, apply. The scene occupies the same domestic space. But the emblematic prelude serves to show that the ritual here is spiritually and morally redundant: important to the participants only in economic and social terms. Mother and baby are not shown together; instead there is an ostentatious over-preponderance of nurses: a wet nurse and a dry nurse whose jobs presumably combine to make the mother redundant. It is tempting to read them as dramatised incarnations of what Janet Adelman has described as 'psychic sites of separation' from the maternal, emphasising the emotional and literal distance between the mother and her offspring.[69] Mistress Allwit's 'lying in' becomes merely an opportunity for pretentious display. The talk is of the expense of the gifts, the quality of the food (and the guests' greedy consumption if it), the price of marriage.[70] A travesty of the spiritual values implicit in the christening ritual is thus organised around the figure of the redundant mother whose bedroom has become the site of conspicuous consumption.

Like domestic tragedies, this play makes a link between the destruction or the debasement of motherhood and the abuse of spaces, from the degenerate christening party in Mrs Allwit's bedroom where the material excess is the point and where Puritans literally get pissed, through to the impregnation of Lady Kix in the seclusion of her coach, thus ensuring that her husband's inheritance will be retained. In contrast to these homely (albeit abused) spaces, the unmarried girls scrambling for money to keep their children occupy the same streets and public places where crime and corruption are exposed and dealt with by the state.[71] Alison Findlay describes, alongside the 'masculine' city that brings unruly women like Anne Sanders to judgement, its chaotic opposite: 'a feminine urban model related to movement and disorder'.[72] This opposition is borne out in Middleton's comedy, depicted through the unruliness and appropriation of its spaces by its female inhabitants.

Households, along with the rituals and the routines that organise them, are shown to be threatened by the corruption that inhabits the public places in which they are situated. In all the plays discussed in this chapter, the disjunction between a social ideal and a grimmer reality, based in a realised geographical area, is mirrored by a structural tension between recurring significant images – of rooms, of sleep, of food, of children – and a story which shows how the ideal is undermined by the demands of living in a society where the pressures are changing and increasing, and where the mother's place within the family, as keeper of the household, as an upholder of morality, is the focus of increased attention. Such attention offered dramatists new ways of extending the dramatic function of the mother figure across a range of genres. In Chapter 6 the discussion to her potential in high tragedy.

Notes

1. Robert Armin to Lady Chandois, appended to Gilbert Dugdale, *A true discourse of the practises of Elizabeth Caldwell, Ma: Ieffrey Bownd, Isabell Hill widow, and George Ferneley, on the parson of Ma: Thomas Caldwell, in the County of Chester, to have murdered and poisoned him, with diuerse others.* (London: James Roberts, 1604).
2. Catherine Richardson, *Domestic Life and Domestic Tragedy* (Manchester: Manchester University Press, 2006), p. 10.
3. See J. A. Sharpe, *Early Modern England: A Social History 1550–1760* (London: Edward Arnold, 1987). Sharpe discusses many of the contributory factors to the problems of the period, including plague, crop failures in the 1590s, and political and social symptoms of unrest such as the Essex Rebellion of 1601. He charts attempts to control what was perceived as increasing social instability in the Poor Laws of 1598 and 1601 and more particular legislation such as the Bigamy Act of 1604.
4. Sharpe, *Early Modern England*, pp. 149–51, and Keith Wrightson, *English Society 1580–1680* (London: Hutchinson & Co., 1982), pp. 121–48.
5. Sharpe, *Early Modern England*, pp. 149–51.
6. This is discussed as a contributing cause for bastardy in Peter C. Hoffer and N. E. H. Hull, *Murdering Mothers: Infanticide in England and New England 1558–1803* (New York: New York University Press, 1984), Ch. 1.
7. Joan R. Kent, 'Attitudes of Members of the House of Commons to the Regulation of "Personal Conduct" in Late Elizabethan and Early Stuart England', *Bulletin of the Institute of Historical Research* 46, (1973), 42.
8. *Nice Wanton*, eds R. Dodsley and W.C. Hazlitt, A selection of Old English Plays, 4th edn (London, 1876), prologue.
9. Kent, 'Attitudes of Members of the House of Commons', pp. 55–6. Kent discusses proposed bills to make masters answerable for the offences of their children and servants (1610) and to make husbands responsible for the conduct of their wives (1601).
10. Keith Thomas, 'The Puritans and Adultery: The Act of 1650 Reconsidered', in *Puritans and Revolutionaries: Essays in honour of Christopher Hill*, eds Donald Pennington and Keith Thomas (Oxford: Clarendon Press, 1978), p. 259.
11. Richardson, *Domestic Life and Domestic Tragedy*, p. 33.
12. Karen Newman, *Fashioning Femininity and English Renaissance Drama* (Chicago: Chicago University Press, 1981), pp. 28–9.
13. Martin Ingram, *Church Courts, Sex and Marriage in England, 1570–1640* (Cambridge: Cambridge University Press, 1987), p. 142. Also Phillipe Ariès, introduction to *A History of Private Life, Volume III: Passions of the Renaissance*, ed. Roger Chartier, trans. Arthur Goldhammer (London: Belknap, 1989), p. 3.
14. For a discussion of the composition of family households see Ingram, *Church Courts, Sex and Marriage in England, 1570–1640*, pp. 126–7. Much

of my appreciation of the early modern household results from discussions with Catherine Richardson as she worked on the thesis which became *Domestic Life and Domestic Tragedy*.
15 Ingram, *Church Courts, Sex and Marriage in England, 1570–1640*, p. 142.
16 Alison Findlay, *Playing Spaces in Early Women's Drama* (Cambridge: Cambridge University Press, 2006), pp. 10–11.
17 Quoted in Suzanne Trill, Kate Chedgzoy and Melanie Osborne, *Lay by your needles Ladies, Take the Pen: Writing Women in England 1200–1700* (London and New York: Arnold, 1997), p. 58.
18 'Household' is used here to indicate the social and economic unit which comprises a family, their servants and their guests. 'Family' refers to the network of relationships between the people who inhabit the household.
19 Catherine Belsey sees anxiety about the household and the mother's place within it as symptomatic of 'a direct connection between the emergence of family values and the increasing perception of the loving family as a place of danger'. Catherine Belsey, *Shakespeare and the Loss of Eden* (Basingstoke: Macmillan, 1999), p. 23.
20 For example, the title page to the 1592 edition of *Arden of Faversham* reproduced in *Three Elizabethan Domestic Tragedies*, ed. Keith Sturgess (Harmondsworth: Penguin, 1985).
21 Richardson, *Domestic Life and Domestic Tragedy*, p. 11.
22 *A Warning for Fair Women*, ed. Charles Dale Cannon (The Hague: Mouton, 1975). All subsequent references are to this edition.
23 See Nicole Castan, 'The Public and the Private', in Ariès, *A History of Private Life*, pp. 408–9.
24 Ceremonies and practices associated with food and feasting draw attention to the efficient operation of the household in many domestic tragedies, notably Heywood's *A Woman Killed with Kindness*, as Richardson has shown in some detail in *Domestic Life and Domestic Tragedy*. Also see Viviana Comensoli, 'Household Business': *Domestic Plays of Early Modern England* (Toronto: University of Toronto Press, 1996), pp. 70–2. In *A Warning for Fair Women*, the innocuous mention of 'supper' links with the later spectacle of the 'bloody banquet' in the first dumb show, creating the disturbing effect that Comensoli describes as 'the dramatisation of the household not as the seat of civility, as it appears to be in the play's opening scenes, but of distortion and incongruity'. Comensoli, *Household Business*, p. 95.
25 Richardson describes 'the stage-like qualities of the street' in *Domestic Life and Domestic Tragedy*, p. 42.
26 Findlay, *Playing Spaces in Early Women's Drama*, p. 181.
27 See ll. 375 and 396. The fragility of the doorway and its association with the intervention of the public into the private is well illustrated in Karen Newman's account of a skimmington in Wiltshire in 1628, where a crowd first 'pressinge hard' against the targeted house eventually 'brake open [the owner's] chamber door upon his wife'

before dragging her out into the street to assault her. See Newman, *Fashioning Femininity and English Renaissance Drama*, p. 28. It is telling in this play that in the first dumb show the malefactors are invited through the 'fatall doore' to act out their crime: Tragedie and Lust bring them into the house. *A Warning*, l. 797.
28 John Dod and Robert Cleaver, *A Godlie Forme of Houeholde Government: For the ordering of private families according to the direction of God's word* (1561), p. 218.
29 H. H. Adams, *English Domestic or, Homiletic Tragedy 1575–1642* (New York: B. Blom, 1965), pp. 7 and 124.
30 Kate McLuskie, *Dekker and Heywood*, English Dramatists series (London: Macmillan, 1994), p. 85.
31 McLuskie, *Dekker and Heywood*, p. 85.
32 This effect is confirmed in the ensuing scene, where Sanders and companions, returning home from work, talk of households and hospitality and their wives.
33 *A Warning*, induction, p. 2.
34 *A Warning*, Appendix D, p. 219. Anne uses childbirth in her defence in *A Warning*, l. 2344.
35 Comensoli, *Household Business*, pp. 73–4.
36 From Richardson, Domestic Life and Domestic Tragedy, writing of Heywood's *A Woman Killed with Kindness*, p. 166.
37 All this happens in the sources, too. The clerics who brought Anne and Mrs Drurie to repentance were horrified at the lack of religious understanding of both women and had to work very hard to extract and to create suitable confessional material. Golding's 'A Brief Discourse', one of the sources for the play, says that the dean of St Paul's, together with three assistants, 'laboured very painfully to instruct them aright: for (God wote) they founde all the three prisoners very rawe and ignorant in all things perteyning to God and to their soule health, yea and even in the very principles of the Christen religion'. *A Warning*, Appendix D, p. 223.
38 Heywood's *A Woman Killed with Kindness* makes similar use of children.
39 Sharpe, *Early Modern England*, pp. 111–12.
40 According to the sources, the streets and houses around the gallows were crowded with spectators.
41 George Watkins, *The Miseries of Enforced Marriage*, 1607, pub. by the Malone Society (Oxford: Oxford University Press, 1963).
42 Comensoli, *Household Business*, p. 98.
43 Comensoli, *Household Business*, p. 99.
44 Anon., *A Yorkshire Tragedy*, ed. A. C. Cawley and Barry Gaines (Manchester: Manchester University Press, 1986); all subsequent references are to this edition. See also *Three Elizabethan Domestic Tragedies*, ed. Keith Sturgess (Harmondsworth: Penguin, 1983), p. 158.
45 Richardson, *Domestic Life and Domestic Tragedy*, p. 188.

46 Comensoli, *Household Business*, p. 102.
47 See Margot Heinemann, *Puritanism and Theatre: Thomas Middleton and Oppositional Drama under the Stuarts* (Cambridge: Cambridge University Press, 1980), p. 66.
48 Wendy Griswold has argued that the specificity of the geographical location is crucial in setting up the social concerns of city comedies. Wendy Griswold, *Renaissance Revivals: City Comedy and Revenge Tragedy in the London Theatre 1576–1980* (Chicago and London: University of Chicago Press, 1986), p. 17.
49 Thomas Middleton, *A Chaste Maid in Cheapside*, in *Thomas Middleton: Five Plays*, eds Bryan Loughrey and Neil Taylor (London: Penguin, 1988), pp. 163–238. All subsequent quotations are taken from this edition.
50 Griswold discusses the problem of attempting to discover a moral argument in this play. Griswold, *Renaissance Revivals*, p. 25. See also Heinemann, *Puritanism and Theatre*, p. 15.
51 The notion of the wife as 'helpmeet' is turned to a joke by Swetnam, who says that the extent of their help is to 'spend and consume that which man painfully getteth'. See extract from Swetnam, 'The Arraignment of Lewd, Idle, Froward and Unconstant Women', 1615, in Trill, Chedgzoy, and Osborne, *Lay by your needles Ladies, Take the Pen*, p. 82. The joke here is, as Diane Purkiss points out, not about women so much as about the 'morally earnest discourse which glosses helpmeet more diversely'. See Diane Purkiss, 'Material Girls: The Seventeenth Century Women Debate', in Clare Brant and Diane Purkiss, eds, *Women, Texts and Histories 1575–1760* (London: Routledge, 1992), p. 73.
52 William Shakespeare, *Pericles*, ed. Suzanne Gossett (London: Arden Shakespeare, 2004), 4.2.79. This image is in itself a reversal of the usual exhortation to 'bend children' to virtue rather than 'natural wont evil'. See *Nice Wanton* in Dodsley and Hazlitt, eds, *A selection of Old English Plays*, 4th edn (London: Reeves and Turner, 1876), reissued 1964), p. 183, 'A young plant ye may plant and bow as ye will.'
53 The long-suffering husband is a stock character in city comedies, for example, Touchstone in George Chapman, Ben Jonson and John Marston's comedy, *Eastward Ho!*
54 Paster, *The Body Embarrassed*, p. 61.
55 Griswold sees city comedies constructed out of 'both the medieval and modern world pictures, both images of organic community and of acquisitive individualism'. Griswold, *Renaissance Revivals*, p. 54.
56 A. C. Cawley, ed., *Everyman and Medieval Miracle Plays* (London: Dent, 1990), 'The Second Shepherds Pageant', ll. 241–6, p. 90.
57 This similarity has been noted by Alan Brissenden in his New Mermaid edition of the play, *A Chaste Maid in Cheapside* (London: Benn, 1968), introduction, p. xxi.

58 Again, this is similar to the Towneley play where Mak's wife boasts to the audience of her cleverness in devising a ruse to conceal the stolen sheep.
59 Peter C. Hoffer and N. E. H. Hull, *Murdering Mothers: Infanticide in England and New England 1558–1803* (New York: New York University Press, 1984), chs 1 and 4.
60 Keith Wrightson, *English Society 1580–1680* (London: Hutchinson & Co., 1982), pp. 84 and 145.
61 The *Second Shepherds' Play* to which I refer above is similarly situated in a time of dearth, 'for the tilth of our land lies fallow as the floor', where the oppressions of the poor by the state are keenly felt: 'we are so hamyd, for-taxed and ramyd, we are made hand-tamed by these gentlery-men'. Cawley, ed., *Everyman and Medieval Miracle Plays*, 'The Second Shepherds Pageant', ll. 23–26.
62 Wrightson, *English Society*, p. 86.
63 Repr. in *The Roxburghe Ballads*, ed. W. Chappell (London: The Ballad Society, 1899), vol. 9, pp. 425–30.
64 Middleton was married to Ann Marbeck, granddaughter of the Calvinist musician John Marbeck, and there is speculation as to his religious sympathies. (Loughrey and Taylor, *Thomas Middleton: Five Plays*, p. x.)
65 Ariès, introduction to *A History of Private Life*, p. 6.
66 Brissenden, *A Chaste Maid in Cheapside*, p. xxi.
67 Act 3 Scene 2. Ariès stresses the increasingly special place of the marriage bed in the early modern household. Ariès, introduction to *A History of Private Life*, p. 6.
68 Sasha Roberts, 'Lying among the Classics: Ritual and Motif in Elite Elizabethan and Jacobean Beds', in Lucy Gent, ed., *Albion's Classicism: The Visual Arts in Britain 1550–1660* (New Haven and London: Yale University Press, 1995), p. 336.
69 Adelman, *Suffocating Mothers*, p. 5.
70 A reference to Mistress Allwit's lying in 'like a countess' may refer to the famous lying in of the Countess of Salisbury in 1613: 'the Countess of Salisbury lies in very richly, for the hanging of her chamber, being white satin, embroidered with gold (or silver) and pearl is valued at fourteen thousand pounds'. John Chamberlain, *Letters*, ed. N. E. McLure (Philadelphia, PA: American Philosophical Society, 1939), vol. 1, pp. 415–16. See Brissenden, ed., *A Chaste Maid in Cheapside*, p. 50.
71 In contrast, Moll, the play's romantic heroine who is pulled unwillingly and violently into her parents' house at the beginning of the play, gets there on her own terms at the end.
72 Findlay, *Playing Spaces in Early Women's Drama*, p. 181.

6

Typology and subjectivity in *Hamlet* and *Coriolanus*

O mother
What shall I cry?
T. S. Eliot, 'Coriolan II'[1]

The relationship between the representation of motherhood and the construction of dramatic narrative that has been explored in this book, gained resonance from the placing of the mother in contexts that attested to her relationship to domestic and civic spaces, to the economies of society and household. Alongside this developed a dramatic interest in the complexities of the mother's role as experienced by her children. Each of the plays discussed in the previous chapter invites its audience to consider, albeit briefly, the consequences for the child of its mother's negotiation of her domestic, social and moral role. A consistent moral narrative and attention to tradition balance the innovative subject matter to position the audience's reading of each play. In both *Hamlet* and *Coriolanus*, Shakespeare brings this interest in the mother's significance for her children to bear upon two very different extant tragic narratives where there is already a focus upon the mother's influence upon her son. These narratives are developed by Shakespeare in part to tell of the subjective experience of a mother by her son, but both also tend to interrogate that experience by juxtaposing the son's understanding of his mother with competing readings that confuse any clear moral dynamic.

The relations between mothers and sons in these plays is constructed in each play across a narrative which allows them to change through time, and which thus repudiates, even as it acknowledges and appropriates, the fixed meaning offered by typology. Jonathan Dollimore has argued that tragedy shifted from what he calls 'idealist mimesis' to a mimetic drama that was essentially 'realist':

On the one hand didacticism, inherited as dramatic conventions from the morality tradition, demanded that the universe be seen to be divinely controlled; that justice and order be eventually affirmed, conflict resolved, and the individual re-established within, or expelled from, the providential design (idealist mimesis). On the other hand, drama was rapidly progressing as a form with empirical, historical and contemporary emphases – all of which were in potential conflict with this didacticism (realist mimesis).[2]

The theatrical function of motherhood manifests this adjustment by adapting the relations between ideology and typology. Such a shift facilitates what Janet Adelman calls 'a fully developed subjectivity', which she describes as the 'illusion that a stage person has interior being, including motives that he himself does not fully understand'.[3] It makes possible a change of perspective in the dramatic representation of maternity. When Hamlet discusses the 'vicious mole of nature' that spoils the men of Denmark, he describes this ruinous influence by reference to familiar allegory: 'the stamp of one defect / Being Nature's livery or Fortune's star'.[4] This 'defect' is linked to birth and thus to maternity even as Hamlet appears to struggle linguistically to detach the man from the mother: 'As, in their birth – wherein they are not guilty, / Since nature cannot choose his origin'. Whereas in the drama addressed so far in this book, children have functioned to amplify and extend the meaning of the mother, the plays in this chapter demonstrate the meanings that mothers have for their protagonist sons.

Deborah Willis argues that Protestant literature demonstrates a change in constructions of the 'ideal' mother in the second half of the sixteenth century, with a 'new emphasis on the wife's role as a nurturer and caretaker of small children'. Willis says that 'the health and wellbeing of the child came to be viewed as more dependent on the quality of her care'. The corollary of this is that 'New constructions of motherhood as a valued "special vocation", it seems clear, went hand in hand with a new anxiety about women's capacity for malevolent nurture. Maternal power, however generative, could also be used to maim, deform or destroy children under women's care'.[5] As Janet Adelman puts it, '*Hamlet* stands as a kind of watershed, subjecting to the maternal presence the relationships previously exempted from that presence', and certainly the play's complex dealings with the son's response to his mother have long been recognised as a critical issue.[6] In the early twentieth century, A. C. Bradley took a moral view of Hamlet's predicament in which he raises the problem of the relationship between Hamlet and his mother as central to a proper understanding of the narrative structure of the play:

> It was the moral shock of the sudden ghastly disclosure of his mother's true nature, falling on him when his heart was aching with love, and his body doubtless was weakened by sorrow. And it is essential, however disagreeable, to realise the nature of this shock. It matters little here whether Hamlet's age was twenty or thirty: in either case his mother was a matron of mature years. All his life he had believed in her, we may be sure, as such a son would . . . [S]he married again, and married . . . a man utterly contemptible and loathsome in his eyes; married him not for any reason of state, nor even out of old family affection, but in such a way that her son was forced to see in her action not only an astounding shallowness of feeling but an eruption of coarse sensuality, 'rank and gross', speeding post haste to its horrible delight.[7]

Bradley does not acknowledge that Claudius states that his marriage to Gertrude was, whatever else it might also have been, part of a political strategy and it is no longer possible to assume either his romantic identification of the hero as poet, nor his sense of moral outrage.[8] Writing before the popularising of psychoanalysis, Bradley sees Hamlet's crisis in terms of 'moral shock', a clash of ethical and emotional concerns that brings about an inevitable breakdown: 'is its result anything but perfectly natural?'[9] This emphasis upon a link between morality and emotion looks like an attempt to reformulate the play in terms of straightforward moral typology but in fact Bradley has touched on the heart of the problem – that Gertrude frustrates conventional readings of maternity, good or bad. T. S. Eliot acknowledged this when he famously redirected attention away from character to consider the play as artifice and described *Hamlet* as 'most certainly an artistic failure', concluding that while 'the essential emotion of the play is the feeling of a son towards a guilty mother', the play lacks the 'objective correlative' to account for it:

> Hamlet is up against the difficulty that his disgust is occasioned by his mother, but that his mother is not an adequate equivalent for it; his disgust envelops and exceeds her. It is thus a feeling which he cannot understand; he cannot objectify it, and it therefore remains

to poison life and obstruct action ... To have heightened the criminality of Gertrude would have been to provide the formula for a totally different emotion in Hamlet; it is just *because* her character is so negative and insignificant that she arouses in Hamlet the feeling which she is incapable of representing.[10]

For Eliot the play is structurally flawed, incomplete in achieving its aims. This, he speculates, might be due to Shakespeare's reworking of an older revenge play which proved difficult to adapt to the dramatist's chosen focus upon the guilt of the mother, visited upon her son. Eliot contends that 'Shakespeare was unable to impose this motive [guilt] upon the "intractable" material of the old play'.[11]

The structural gap suggested by Eliot is not, however, so much between what Gertrude says and what she means as between what the queen is heard to say and seen to do, and what she means *to her son*. The resulting disruption to narrative consistency provokes both the pleasures and the frustrations created by the play. As Adelman puts it, 'the Gertrude we see is not quite the Gertrude they see'; she suggests that what we see is 'a woman more muddled than actively wicked'.[12] Jacqueline Rose implies this when she takes up Eliot's analysis, showing how he 'suggests that the question of the woman and the question of meaning go together'.[13] Suggesting that for Eliot, 'emotion must be controlled by meaning', she finds instead that a 'dangerous excess' of female sexuality, no longer contained when a woman is widowed, contributes to a breakdown in dramatic structure: 'Femininity ... becomes the focus for a partly theorised recognition of the psychic and literary disintegration which can erupt in any moment into literary form'.[14]

Rose's contention that the sexuality of the mother is made to 'bear the weight' of her son's guilt in the play places an emphasis upon widowhood and its potential to disrupt and complicate issues concerning inheritance and family.[15] Dorothea Kehler associates this with structural differences between the First Quarto and the Folio versions of the play. She argues that the First Quarto could have been written for touring venues in the north of England where audiences were likely to have recusant sympathies and therefore be receptive to a representation of the mother that operates in the traditional, iconic, romantic mode, figuring through maternity the tension between duty and desire.[16] In Q1, argues Kehler, Gertred is 'all mother', committing herself 'unequivocally to Hamlet's cause and promising to keep up connubial appearances only to deceive Claudius' once she discovers that he is a murderer.[17] Her analysis confirms the importance of the construction of the mother for the meaning of the play. For Kehler, the Gertrude of Q1 is designed with a particular audience in mind, figuring anxieties about remarriage in the context of recusant sympathies and associated cultural ideals:

> Even after the Reformation stripped marriage of its status as a sacrament, many sixteenth-century English writers were loath to abandon earlier attitudes. John Webster, the probable author of the thirty-two New Characters appearing in the sixth edition of Overbury's *Characters* (1615) set 'A vertuous Widdow' in opposition to 'An ordinarie Widdow'. Shunning remarriage, the 'vertuous Widdow' whose celibacy is a second virginity, garners up her heart in her children and her Maker. Of particular importance to Hamlet, neither her children's persons nor their inheritance is at the mercy of a new husband or step-siblings.[18]

Kehler's analysis offers a helpful context for the representation of Gertrude but owns that her analysis can do little to address the gap between the mother as represented by the play and as represented by her son:

> While the play's audience, familiar with the trope of the 'lusty widow' and positioned to identify with the protagonist, may accede to the assessment of Gertred they hear from Hamlet and the Ghost, the queen they actually witness is apt to strike them as a basically decent, rather ordinary woman, able to accept guidance from her son and willing to mend her ways.[19]

Readings of all versions of the play have tended to account for Hamlet's description of his mother by seeing the hero as projecting male anxieties (about widows, about sexuality, about the power of women generally) upon his mother with reference to contemporary discourses that typify the mature woman in terms of corruption and lust.[20] This analysis is often linked with the ascription to such figures of a dramatic function that tends to associate feminine freedom with disaster. Lisa Jardine describes as a critical given that 'it is the male characters who perceive free choice on the part of the female character as an inevitable sign of irrational lust, and as the inevitable prelude to disorder and disaster'.[21]

It would thus appear that any critical assessment of the representation of Gertrude must address two related issues. First, the gap that Bradley noted between what the mother appears to be and what her son says she is: a problem for critics, directors and actors who have to justify readings of the play which depend to an extent upon speculative recourse to either historical or psychoanalytic contexts. Secondly, a perceived disjunction in narrative structure; the mother is crucial to the successful operation of narrative while at the same time, if we accept Eliot's position, unequal to it as she is written. These issues taken together suggest that *Hamlet* creates a complex narrative strategy to establish conflict by setting the ideal against what is realised through dramatic action so that the disjunction that was perceived by Eliot as a failure is in fact the very subject of the drama. This is similar to the dynamic that Dollimore identifies in Jacobean tragedy, where 'the play's structure incorporates and intensifies the sense of social and political dislocation which is its subject'.[22] Tragedy, for Dollimore, occurs at this point of dislocation. For earlier dramatists, the Senecan and Aristotelian dramatic models that focus upon a heroic crisis and catharsis predominate. In later plays, however, tragedy is produced out of theatre itself; it is the effect of a disjunction between what we know as spectators and what we are told, and the impossibility of reconciliation between conflicting experiences. Christine Buci-Glucksmann, citing Walter Benjamin's assertion that in *Hamlet*, 'the generality of its time is not mythical but spectral [and] is intimately bound up with the mirror nature of the play', characterises this as the breakdown of an allegorical schema: 'the endless fragmentation of allegory as frozen portrait of horror'.[23] For Buci-Glucksmann, the effect of fragmentation occurs as the consequence of a conjunction of the aesthetic with the metaphysical: 'Allegory . . . consigns reality to a permanent antinomy, a game of the illusion of reality as illusion, where the world is at once valued and devalued . . . [T]he gulf between reality and illusion cannot be bridged: theatre now *knows* itself to be theatre'.[24]

It is a tenet of this book that the allegory embedded in the dramatised mother figure is crucial to determining her meaning. In *Hamlet*, as Adelman points out, the traditional duality is fundamental to the hero's construction of his mother: 'The alternatives that govern the imagination of his mother's body are the familiar ones of virgin and whore, closed or open, wholly pure or wholly corrupt'.[25] In the case of Gertrude (in all extant versions of the play) her meanings are, in fact, irreconcilable in terms of a three-way tension between what a traditional, idealist reading might wish to make of the dramatised mother, the maternal utterances of the stage figure, and her son's construction of her for most of the first three acts, in the context of a play which draws attention to itself as artifice.

Claudius's opening speech in Act 1 Scene 2 of the play confirms what has already been made visible to an audience through the spectacle of a heralded procession of the entire court on to the stage. His immediate affirmation of Gertrude as queen, 'Th' imperial jointress to this warlike state', is separated, by four lines expressing the ambivalent circumstances in which the union has taken place, from his description of her as 'wife' and the important addition that the court has approved the marriage. It is Hamlet's aside, 'A little more than kin, and less than kind' (1.2.65), and his ambiguous response to his mother's remonstrance that death is inevitable, 'Ay, madam, it is common' (74), that begin to undermine the stability which has been established both visually and rhetorically in the opening moments of the scene. Hamlet's brief verbal interjections are either addressed directly to his mother, or are pointed references to his own status as a royal son. Embedded in this first scene, then, is a tension that will inform the entire play: that between Gertrude's role as Claudius's queen and her role as Hamlet's mother. Most simply this can be read as a version of the trope which pits wifehood against maternity, offering the edifying moral spectacle of a woman struggling between her desires and duties like Grissil. But unlike Grissil, Gertrude is never shown to articulate that struggle, so that the play, rather than being *about* that struggle, uses the struggle itself to engage with the preoccupations of the tragedy, especially the working out of the revenge trope through the psychic crises of the hero.

In this scene, Gertrude's attempts at a kind of maternal intimacy with Hamlet are confined to brief exchanges, circumscribed by Claudius's longer speeches in which he takes control of both the substance of discussion between mother and son and of the pacing of the scene, interrupting dialogue between Hamlet and his mother with his own extended responses.[26] In this way a disturbing dynamic is set up which reveals Gertrude's position as doubly complex. Her politically consolidating position as queen, so clearly described in Claudius's opening speech, and Hamlet's obvious antipathy to it, makes it necessary for her to reconcile the demands of both family and state: 'Good Hamlet, cast thy nighted colour off / And let thine eye look like a friend on Denmark' (1.2.68–69).

Throughout the scene, maternal solicitude sits uneasily alongside the demands of Gertrude's role as 'imperial jointress', which is again complicated by the fact that she is Claudius's wife. Her plea, 'Let not thy mother lose her prayers, Hamlet. / I pray thee stay with us' (118–19) combines the royal pronoun with the singular emotions of a parent; the plural pronoun itself referring to the married couple, Claudius and Gertrude, as well as to Denmark.

It is difficult for an audience to read Gertrude here, beyond this. As a character, her speech offers no more clues; as a figure she is overburdened with the competing typological demands of queen, wife, widow and mother. It is left to Hamlet to construct a single narrative line for the audience, developed during the soliloquy that follows the exit of the court (and Gertrude) from the stage. Without the complicating stage presence of his mother, her son can recast her in simpler terms by referring to conventional and familiar images of the remarried widow:

> Must I remember? Why she would hang on him
> As if increase of appetite had grown
> By what it fed on; and yet within a month –
> Let me not think on't; frailty thy name is woman –
> A little month, or ere those shoes were old
> With which she followed my poor father's body
> Like Niobe, all tears, why she, even she –
> O god, a beast that wants discourse of reason
> Would have mourned longer – married with my uncle,
> My father's brother, but no more like my father
> Than I to Hercules. Within a month,
> Ere yet the salt of most unrighteous tears
> Had left the flushing in her galled eyes,
> She married. O, most wicked speed, to post
> With such dexterity to incestuous sheets. (1.2.143–7)

The ideas informing this speech, the hints about untrammelled lustiness, false tears, deception and 'frailty', are redolent of conventional antifeminism, offering no reference to the queen's complex situation in the scene that has just passed. Hamlet's speech constructs an account of the queen as worthy of blame, and sets her against a version of her earlier self where his father's love and protection kept her chaste.[27] But this speech is also an articulation of profound and complex grief. Hamlet's personal misery finds expression in traditional typology here, signalling the establishment of a conventional pattern of revenge. These elements combine to create a dramatic structure which brings together metaphysics and dramaturgy similar to that identified by Dollimore in Shakespeare's *Troilus and Cressida*: 'the disintegrating effects of grief are resisted . . . through . . . a commitment to revenge – a vengeful re-engagement with the society and those responsible for that grief . . . [I]t is a society which has fallen into radical disharmony'.[28]

Hamlet's commitment to revenge, and his articulation of grief, once avowed on stage, colours an audience's subsequent response to Gertrude in ensuing scenes of the play. The typologising of his mother contributes to the revenge schema, but an audience is aware of a simultaneous narrative – that the Gertrude he describes is different from the Gertrude who has just left the stage – so that there are two competing readings of her: the audience's and her son's. This is reinforced in a tension between what she says and how she appears on the stage. She is consistently presented as companion to the king, their entrances always part of a court ceremony usually heralded by a flourish; thus she is primarily visible as an adjunct to the functioning of state and public matters. But there is always a gap between the political power exhibited by the full representation of the court and the personal subject matter that is Gertrude's only topic when she speaks. Her brief exchanges with Polonius and with Rosencrantz and Guildenstern demonstrate her personal concern to discover what it is that is hurting her son. In contrast, Claudius, surrounded by his court, appears only to pay lip service to such things. There is always a sense in which his enquiries, even when they allude to the personal, are political. He ensures that what should be intimate matters are inappropriately discussed publicly, as in his ceremonial welcome to Rosencrantz and Guildenstern in which he discusses Hamlet's 'transformation' (2.2). Gertrude's maternal solicitude is thus doubly contextualised; first because her personal anxieties are expressed only as public (or semi-public, if we are to consider them as articulated *sotto voce* or as asides), and secondly because she is, as Claudius's wife, linked in with both the consequences of fratricide and treason, and simultaneously, as Hamlet's mother, associated with her son's desire for revenge. Circumscribing all this is a sense of her powerlessness, both in her lack of knowledge of the circumstances of her late husband's death and in her inability to speak personally and privately to her son. It is impossible for her to break away from Claudius so that she can discover for herself, rather than through political agents, the cause of Hamlet's malady.

Gertrude's relentlessly public function as queen disallows her personal role as mother; thus she is forced to delegate, ordering servants to lead Rosencrantz and Guildenstern off stage 'to visit / My too much changèd son' (2.2.36), or seeing off her husband and Polonius to spy upon her son in a moment of private meditation (2.2.159–68).

Both queenliness and motherhood become conditions of abjection in Gertrude, both in the sense that this describes 'a state of misery and degradation' which builds upon the meaning of 'abject' as 'degraded, self-abasing', and in Kristeva's development of the term: 'I endure it, for I imagine that such is the desire of the other'.[29] This is clear in the 'closet scene' (3.4) where Gertrude, on stage for the first time without her husband, summons her son to her chambers, momentarily acquiring a kind of dramatic and rhetorical authority that is emphasised by Hamlet's call, 'Mother, Mother, Mother'.[30] His naming of her tantalisingly evokes the conventional comforts of maternal authority and filial intimacy, but the effect is immediately undercut when Gertrude's first words, 'Hamlet, thou hast thy father much offended', indicate a retreat from motherhood, placing herself foremost as a wife and, insofar as she is referring to the public play performance that disturbed Claudius, as queen. The stichomythia which characterise the ensuing exchange between mother and son offer a discomfiting mirroring of utterance between them so that meaning is constructed through a rhetorical patterning that culminates in a telling revelation of the incompatibility between the meanings that Gertrude embodies:

> Hamlet: Now, Mother, what's the matter?
> Queen: Hamlet, thou hast thy father much offended.
> Hamlet: Mother, you have my father much offended.
> Queen: Come, come, you answer with an idle tongue.
> Hamlet: Go, go, you question with a wicked tongue.
> Queen: Why, how now, Hamlet?
> Hamlet: What's the matter now?
> Queen: Have you forgot me?
> Hamlet: No, by the rood, not so!
> You are the Queen, your husband's brother's wife,
> And, would it were not so, you are my mother. (3.4.9–17)

Gertrude's wifely and queenly recourse to husband and king, 'Nay, then I'll set those to you that can speak', is redundant in this personal space where her son insists upon the primacy of her identity as his mother and in doing so takes both rhetorical and physical control of the scene: 'Come, come, and sit you down. You shall not budge' (3.4.18). Q1 is unique in a description given by Hamlet's mother of his behaviour in the closet scene – 'But then he throwes and tosses me about, / As one forgetting that I was his mother' – though whether this should be read as a kind of retrospective stage direction, or as the reformed Gertred exaggerating her account of Hamlet's madness to convince the king is difficult to ascertain.[31] In all versions Hamlet sets her before a 'glass' in which she is told to see herself in terms of what Kristeva calls 'the shame of compromise, of being in the middle of treachery'; she is talked at, more or less, until she is forced to admit to her own repugnance. It is at this point that Polonius is killed, so that the remaining action takes place in the presence of the dead body of Claudius's closest adviser. This visible reminder that Claudius is thus diminished underpins the change in the relationship between Hamlet and his mother that is being worked through here.[32] In Q1, she can only interject into her son's accusations with pleas to him to 'speak no more', though both other extant texts allow her to attempt an assertion of self, 'What have I done that thou dar'st wag thy tongue / In noise so rude against me?', which quickly breaks down before the torrent of her son's abuse:

> O Hamlet, speak no more,
> Thou turn'st mine eyes into my very soul,
> And there I see such black and grained spots
> As will not leave their tinct. (3.4.89–92)

Her son's immediate response is to refigure Gertrude in terms of bestiality and filth, her femininity only significant as a kind of malign debasement, which threatens to contaminate all that comes close:

> Nay, but to live
> In the rank sweat of an enseamed bed,
> Stewed in corruption, honeying and making love
> Over the nasty sty . . . (3.4.92–5)

Here, to continue to use Kristeva's discussion of abjection, the feminine, 'precisely on account of its power, does not succeed in differentiating itself as *other* but threatens *one's own and clean self*, which is the underpinning of any organisation constituted by exclusions and hierarchies' [original italics].[33]

In this scene, Hamlet and his mother engage in a kind of transformative ritual, which, as it plays out, enables Hamlet to proceed in his movement towards revenge.[34] The abjection of the maternal here provokes Gertrude's capitulation, which in turn brings about a release of intense emotion in Hamlet. The seated mother figure, undermined and rendered more or less speechless, becomes the locus of all that is literally rotten in the state of Denmark, her private room a place where Hamlet is able to express freely the grief that cannot properly be articulated in public. In this scene the mother conjoins the idealist and realist modes of mimesis described by Dollimore. Gertrude is a mother and queen whose overdetermined symbolic function is played out alongside a representation of familial intimacy that appeals to an understanding of the personal, emotional dynamics of the mother–son relationship. This dynamic gains ground as the scene proceeds, and the exchanges between mother and son become more intimate, particularly after the intervention of the Ghost: 'How is it with you, lady? / Alas, how is't with you?' (3.4.106–7). But it also increases in verbal violence until Gertrude can no longer contain her conflicting roles. Her broken, abject cry, 'O Hamlet, thou hast cleft my heart in twain!', is in clear contrast to his overwhelming control of her, 'I must be cruel only to be kind'.[35] Reading the scene from the perspective of psychoanalysis, Adelman notes that 'female sexuality in Hamlet is always maternal sexuality' and that only when its threat has been removed and she has thrown away 'the worser part' can the mother and son refigure their relationship (148).[36]

But in throwing off her partnership with Claudius, Gertrude is simultaneously separating herself from the political and dynastic role that went with it. 'Denmark' worked doubly as metonymy for the king and the state in the first scene of the play (1.2.69) and in relinquishing the worser part Gertrude is also repudiating the 'something rotten' (1.4.67) at its core. Assured of his mother's reform, Hamlet is able to restore her in his imagination (and in the play) as an ideal of mother love and, ultimately, maternal sacrifice. Having separated her from the rotten state, he can excise the rot, personified by Rosencrantz and Guildenstern, those courtier 'sponges' that soak up 'the king's countenance, his rewards, his authorities' (4.2.14–15) and dispose of it away from Denmark. Thus a purifying action on a wider scale which will culminate in the bloody revenge at the end of the play begins here with Hamlet's killing of the corrupt old statesman and his separation of Gertrude from her public and sexual functions as Claudius's wife. Hamlet, in reasserting and reformulating his relationship with his mother, is able to remake himself in new terms as an avenging son. Gertrude, in all versions of the play, is stripped of competing allegiances and reworked in terms that recreate a traditional and unproblematic ideal.

Gertrude is forced to the point where she has to make a personal choice between conflicting demands of husband, state and son upon her role as a mother. In *Coriolanus* the maternal is configured to a similar model, in that the play acknowledges competing ideological constructions of maternity, and tests them in a similar narrative shift towards consideration of the mother's influence upon the character and motivation of her son. But whereas in *Hamlet* there is a clarification and renegotiation of the mother's role in the drive towards a satisfactory working out of the revenge plot, *Coriolanus* creates tragedy by exposing disjunctions between conflicting meanings of motherhood. It concludes by raising political questions about the relations between state and subject by reference to the depiction of the relationship between the hero and his mother.

In a recent edition of *Coriolanus* Lee Bliss shows that 'for much of the play's history [Volumnia] has been seen as an ideal'. Bliss cites Sir William Cornwallis, who wrote in 1601 of his regret at a contemporary lack of 'hardiness' in mothers, who in tougher times might have put their sons' glory before their safety.[37] Sir William's ideal positions the mother at the service of the state and sees her function in terms of its political value.[38] This ideal is also addressed by Coppelia Kahn, in a discussion of Plutarch's *The Sayings of Spartan Women*, where she comments that 'the implied reader is expected to shudder at but nonetheless admire' such women. She acknowledges contradictions in representations of mothers in wartime: 'the interaction between mothering and warmaking has a social and literary history that begins in ancient Greece: typically it is oppositional, hierarchical and complementary'.[39] In *Coriolanus*, Shakespeare revisits the idea of the 'hardy' patriotic mother that informed his portrait of Margaret of Anjou, but this time to explore the implications of such maternity for her child.

For the First Citizen there is not necessarily a direct link between fighting to please Volumnia and fighting for the country as he sets out alternative explanations for Coriolanus's valour: 'Though soft-conscienced men can be content to say it was for his country, he did it to please his mother and to be partly proud, which he is, even to the altitude of his virtue' (1.1.28–30). By placing 'country' and 'mother' in the same sentence, Shakespeare makes an association between them that distinguishes a patrician understanding of motherhood as associated with patriotism from the Citizen's plebeian reading of the two as separate and indeed unconnected. Volumnia is similarly subject to competing readings. To her patrician associates she is a 'noble lady' (3.2.70) whose dedication to the country she calls 'our Rome' (2.1.176) is at one with her dedication to her son. Her role is highly public and political: apart from the first scene in which she appears, her interlocutors are male, and her conversations take place in the civic arena. Sicinius the tribune, on the other hand, thinks that she is 'mad' (4.2.11), which, whether meaning furious or insane, suggests a mother out of the control of reason. The tension between these versions of Volumnia – the patriot mother and the mad mother – creates one of a series of disjunctions in which competing claims upon the maternal offer an organising framework for a dramatic dynamic which creates its tragedy out of incompatibilities and contradictions.

This dynamic is evident in the first scene in which Volumnia appears. It opens with an emblem of iconic femininity, the wife and the mother as one in domestic harmony: '*Enter* Volumnia *and* Virgilia, *mother and wife to Martius. They set them down on two low stools and sew*' (1.3). Needlework scenes had a conventional, emblematic value signifying 'virtue in temporal life', and tended to celebrate a commendable feminine withdrawal into private and domestic space. The necessary stance involved – seated, head bowed – is essentially modest; the idea of productive work is commendable in both Catholic and Protestant constructions of ideal femininity, and is associated with quietitude as the woman is absorbed in her work.[40] What an audience hears in this scene, however, conflicts with what it sees – the emblem and the rhetoric operating in an opposition that jars against convention and forces attention upon the disjunction it presents. Volumnia opens the scene by speaking in garrulous prose that in itself implies a kind of crudity (the only previous prose speakers in the play have been citizens) when set against the elegance of the pentameter spoken by the patricians and the tribunes in the preceding scenes, and that conflicts with the visual image of a high-class Roman matron. What she actually says furthers the disjunction between what she appears

Typology and subjectivity in 'Hamlet' and 'Coriolanus' 181

to be and what she speaks – a mother, presiding over a domestic activity, who repudiates the 'comeliness' of her 'tender-bodied' son, and celebrates instead his warlike manliness (1.3.3–5). But the most extreme dislocation happens when she shifts into verse to imagine her son in action. Amidst the rituals of domestic life – sewing, having female visitors to the home ('Madam, the Lady Valeria is come to visit you' (1.3.21)) – Volumnia realises rhetorically a scenario which has no place in such a setting:

> Methinks I see him stamp thus, and call thus:
> 'Come on you cowards! You were got in fear,
> Though you were born in Rome.' His bloody brow
> With his mailed hand then wiping, forth he goes,
> Like to a harvestman that's tasked to mow
> Or all or lose his hire. (1.3.27–32)

Both visual and rhetorical narratives are disrupted as Volumnia not only breaks decorum to imitate her son's gestures and battle cry, but also shatters the visual composition of the sewing scene, physically stamping as she assumes the imagined actions of her battling son. The effect is a queasy merging of mother, son and wife ('If my son were my husband') as Volumnia's absorption in her role implies a connection so intimate with his masculine, martial life that her son's actual wife is reduced to the status of spectator, only able to react in fright and horror to the story that her mother-in-law acts out before her (1.3.2).[41] For Lee Bliss this suggests that Volumnia has a 'curiously abstract' idea of her son, 'identical with the one function for which she bred him; hence the man and his reputation are interchangeable'.[42] Certainly her words suggest this. But the effect of her combined words and gestures, of her vocally and rhetorically becoming her son, suggests the opposite, a total absorption in his physical and emotional self: the desire to embody him.

There is a jarring bringing together of the domestic and the martial which is so extreme that its effect is darkly comic when Volumnia's most violent juxtapositioning of images tears through the unremarkable rituals of domestic hospitality:

> The breasts of Hecuba,
> When she did suckle Hector, looked not lovelier
> Than Hector's forehead when it spit forth blood
> At Grecian sword, contemning. Tell Valeria
> We are fit to bid her welcome. (1.3.35–9)[43]

Valeria's exclamation on entering – 'you are manifest housekeepers. What are you sewing here? A fine spot, in good faith. How does your little son?' (1.3.46–8) – disturbs at this point because it is an eruption of the ordinary into the extraordinary. But the return to domesticity is incomplete as the new guest brings a story of Volumnia's grandson killing a butterfly: 'When he caught it, he let it go again, and after it again, and over and over he comes, and up again, catched it again. Or whether his fall enraged him, or how 'twas, he did so set his teeth and tear it' (1.3.54–8). Volumnia's approval of the story, 'One on's father's moods', and Valeria's uncomplicated concurrence have an odd effect; the violence of the story about the little boy tearing apart the fragile butterfly (linked to the idea of the soul in classical mythology) is at odds with its passive reception.[44] The women go about what is ostensibly a life appropriate to Roman matrons; they prepare to visit a 'good lady that lies in' (1.3.70). And yet the violent rhetoric that appears as much a part of their world as their sewing and gossiping (in all senses) is disconcerting and at odds with assumptions about what domesticity and maternity comprise.

Volumnia is contrasted in the scene with her daughter-in-law, who presents a more familiar version of wifehood and maternity, anxious about her husband, affectionate and practical in relation to her young son. In terms of contemporary discourses about motherhood, Virgilia appears as an appropriately modest and industrious matron, which raises the problem of how an audience is supposed to read Volumnia against her. The figures of the patriotic hardy mother and the dangerous mad mother are situated, with their more conventional foil, along a continuum which is juxtaposed against a model of conventional domesticity, a celebration of ordinariness. Volumnia's worrying boast that her grandson would 'rather see the swords and hear a drum than look upon his schoolmaster' is at odds with prevailing early modern notions which stress education rather than martial prowess as a means by which a man might serve his country. Writing later in James's reign, Dorothy Leigh makes clear her own understanding of a maternal obligation to ensure that her children recieve an education as part of their training as good and useful citizens:

> I am further also to entreate you, that all your Children may bee taught to reade, beginning at foure yeeres old or before, and let them learne till ten, in which time they are not able to doe any good in the Commonwealth, but to learn how to serve GOD, their king and Country, by reading.[45]

This is not to make a crude point about the similarities between dramatic discourse and the very different form of the advice books, but rather to raise the question of Volumnia's representation and whether her maternity is to be understood – at this point in the play – as malevolent or heroic. An answer might be that in the breaking of decorum there is a kind of theatrical heroism about a character who evokes a thrill by a dangerous defiance of convention. But simultaneously, in the story, the mother who refutes maternity for a vicarious delight in slaughter signals tragedy. The tensions embodied by Volumnia – the widow who impersonates a butchering soldier, the high-born matron who speaks like a plebeian, the mother who repudiates conventional maternal feelings – seem impossible to contain or to reconcile. This construction of motherhood is one that refuses traditional meanings, and by doing so creates the conditions for a hero who is always driven away from the maternal.

There is another reading of Volumnia in the play, of course: that of her son. Just as Hamlet rhetorically constructs a version of his mother that seems at odds with what an audience sees, so, in opposite terms, does Coriolanus in this play. At their first encounter, his reaction is both affectionate and respectful; his exclamation 'O!' when he sees her implies his tender recognition (2.2.143). He imagines her praying on his behalf – 'You have, I know, petitioned all the gods / For my prosperity' – which is presumably understood with a certain amount of irony by an audience, given what they know. What is impossible to discern from the text, of course, is the intended tenor of Coriolanus's delivery of the line, which can imply either an uncomplicated appreciation of his mother's concern or a knowing acknowledgement of her political ambitions. Certainly, later in the scene, he understands and dismisses his mother's plans in a manner which suggests that he is aware of her motives: 'Know, good mother, / I had rather be their servant in my way / Than sway with them in theirs' (2.2.177–9) Whichever, his affectionate and informal treatment of both his wife and mother – 'Your hand, and yours' (2.2.168) – suggests that he appreciates them in terms of the traditional domestic roles which were implied at the beginning of the 'sewing scene' discussed above. He approves his wife's modesty ('My gracious silence' (2.1.148)) and certainly the spectacle here, the hero welcomed by the maid, the wife and the mother, situates Coriolanus – at this point in the play – in terms of an implied rich, domestic, personal world. There is an irony in the disjunction between what Coriolanus appears to understand by what he sees and what that means to him, and what an audience already knows about his mother's preference to 'rejoice in that absence wherein he won honour' (1.2.3) and thus what the three women signify.[46] Janet Adelman acknowledges the significance of the insufficiency of motherhood in her assertion that 'Coriolanus begins in the landscape of maternal deprivation' and there is a sense of that in this scene, where the rather traditional and ordinary domestic aspirations of the hero appear to be unmatched by an audience's experience of the play thus far.[47]

Such aspirations are only half realised, however. A sense of the unattainability of 'home' as a signifier of domestic contentment for Coriolanus permeates the text, as the hero is always precipitated away from the private into public action: 'Ere in our own house I do shade my head / The good patricians must be visited' (2.2.169–70). As in the first part of *Hamlet*, the mother is only available in public spaces. But unlike Gertrude, who constantly tried to solicit information about Hamlet's private state of mind, Volumnia seems not to desire – or to recognise the absence of – an intimate understanding of her son. The turning point in *Hamlet*, the point at which he can start to 'set it right', is the moment at which he is able to negotiate a new relationship with his mother in the intimacy of a private space. But Coriolanus is always driven back into the public arena. Home is merely the place for the briefest of unwilling retreats after the first fight with the plebeians – 'I prithee, noble friend, home to thy house' (3.1.236) – and a place which offers little sanctuary in the eyes of his enemies: 'We'll hear no more / pursue him to his house, and pluck him thence' (3.1.314–15).

At the heart of this play, as in *Hamlet*, there is a confrontation between mother and son, but here the house offers no opportunity for such a meeting, and Volumnia creates no space for intimacy within the family home. She sends her son back out into the city ('Go and be ruled' (3.2.91)) with the full force of patrician approbation behind her. The scene in which this happens offers almost the obverse of the 'closet scene' in *Hamlet*. In *Coriolanus* the mother refuses to offer either intimacy or sanctuary. Coriolanus has to force her attention – 'I talk of you' (3.2.14) – on a crowded stage where the mother's presence and thus her significance is visually foregrounded because she is the only woman present. This arrangement of figures on the stage – soldiers, patricians and the mother – signifies the potential for intimacy between mother and son, even as the dialogue makes clear that there will be no opportunity for such intimacy. Jonathan Dollimore says that 'what Volumnia signifies here is not motherhood so much as socialisation', and in her consistently public role, as well as what she says and does in this scene, this is certainly true.[48] But by dint of who she is, she also signifies motherhood, and it is again a tension between what she signifies as a mother and what she means in terms of this story that jars both for an audience and for Coriolanus, whose bewilderment at her determination to override his concerns for the sake of office is clear: 'Why force you this?' (3.2.53). What happens between mother and son here is a kind of contest of wills based, as Dollimore points out, upon a conflict between Volumnia's understanding of *virtus* 'not as essence but as political strategy' and her son's essentialism: an uneven contest because, as Dollimore says, 'it is she who has nurtured Coriolanus in his essentialist consciousness'.[49] Volumnia quickly gets the upper hand. As in *Hamlet*, this central confrontation with the mother is pivotal in determining the outcome of the plot, but here, rather than facilitating resolution, the scene, in Dollimore's words, 'generates both for and in Coriolanus the tensions which will break him'.[50] What Coriolanus finds particularly difficult is his mother's insistence upon a kind of duplicity. Her argument that policy requires him to 'dissemble' to the citizens is at odds with his own understanding of honour in terms of truthful representation: 'Would you have me / False to my nature? Rather say I play / The man I am' (3.2.15–7).

Volumnia uses the language of maternal familiarity to her son, but deploys it as an aspect of policy, in public and to public and political ends. She chides him, cajoles him, obliterates any distinction between Coriolanus's domestic life and public reputation – 'I am in this / Your wife, your son, these senators, the nobles' (3.2.66) – and infantilises him:

> I prithee now, sweet son, as thou hast said
> My praises made thee first a soldier, so
> To have my praise for this, perform a part,
> Thou hast not done before. (3.2.108–11)

Coriolanus is doubly diminished: Volumnia's words recall for an audience the childhood she evoked in the 'sewing scene', and at the same time reduce him in this scene to the status of a child. She maintains that infantilisation in a way that proffers the succour of continued attachment to the mother, but which also threatens rejection: 'Thy valiantness was mine, thou suck'st it from me, / But own thy pride thyself' (3.2.130–1). Volumnia both consoles and warns here, first asserting intimacy in the image of the baby at the breast, and then threatening separation by differentiating her qualities from his. There is a similar confusion in her celebration of his battle scars and her desire – and that of Rome – that they must be displayed: 'O, he is wounded; I thank the gods for it' (2.1.99). The degree of her intimacy with her son's body is revealed when she and Menenius enumerate her son's battle scars (2.1.119–29). Of course she is assessing their effectiveness in his application for a place in the Senate here; nevertheless the extent of her knowledge blurs the distinction between what she knows for political reasons and what is excessive maternal intimacy, a point exacerbated by the silent presence of his wife – who should know his body but says nothing – throughout the dialogue. In a reversal of the convention identified by Katherine Park that a good mother's body is made available for male scrutiny, Volumnia scrutinises her son, tracing the heroism that she has engendered by investigating the wounds on his bleeding body.

Volumnia uses the idea of 'play' repeatedly in her efforts to persuade Coriolanus, and he uses the word when referring to her for comments upon his actions.[51] She has, she implies, taught him his warrior qualities through play, just as she attempts to persuade a new performance from him in peacetime. She offers a double-edged performance of policy in this scene, demonstrating to Coriolanus how to persuade the citizens, while simultaneously persuading him to do as she wishes. As she teaches him to plead with his knee 'bussing the stones', assuring him that 'in such business / Action is eloquence, and the eyes of th'ignorant / more learnèd than the ears' (3.2.76–8), she is prefiguring her own actions before him at the end of the play, when she will be a more consistent and persuasive performer than he. In the practice and demonstration of policy in this scene, Volumnia is rehearsing the scenario that will destroy her son at the end of the play, even as she offers the advice which should create a new identity for him. Volumnia's gift to Coriolanus is also his destruction; her love has an integral greed to it, as Janet Adelman finds:

> A cannibalistic mother who denies food and yet feeds on the victories of her sweet son stands at the darkest centre of the play, where Coriolanus's oral vulnerability is fully defined. Here talion law reigns: the feeding infant himself will be devoured; the loving

mother becomes the devourer. In this dark world love itself is
primitive and dangerous [. . .] [T]o be loved is to be eaten.[52]

This engulfing maternity, which insists upon its pre-eminence
and appropriates even the child's physical actions – 'Go to them
with this bonnet in thy hand' – is inescapable in this scene, where
the patricians and the nobles likewise insist that Volumnia is right
in her demonstration that 'Action is eloquence' (3.2.77). In *Hamlet*,
the hero was able to transform the power of the maternal when
he made his mother recognise his difference from her and from
'Denmark'. She was forced to acknowledge his new, separate
authority with her abject, defeated question, 'what shall I do?'
(*Hamlet* 3.4.164). Coriolanus is instead forced to cede authority to
the combined demands of his mother and the state, when he
similarly asks, defeated, 'What must I do?'(3.237), in an acknowledgement that he has no separate individualised authority. His
efforts to return his mother to a more traditional relationship within
the intended family structure, 'Commend me to my wife' (3.3.136),
are inadequate in the face of his capitulation to her; even as he
tries to refigure the link between mother and son, his capitulation
is made clear.[53]

The emphasis upon play as both a way of constructing identity
and a way of pleasing mother builds upon the image of the small
boy mutilating a butterfly in 1.3.52–8 and links the child's play
with the man's violence in battle. The scenario, in which the child's
apparent independent action is circumscribed by the surveillance
of the watching mother (Valeria stands in for the maternal here),
offers an image of Coriolanus's predicament. On his victorious
return from Corioli the hero has, as Janet Adelman says, experienced a kind of rebirth – a renewal on his own terms: 'the assault
on Corioli is . . . a rebirth . . . the fantasy of self authorship is
complete when Coriolanus is given his new name, earned by his
own actions'.[54] But such self-authorship, such apparent inde-
pendence of action, is compromised in at least two ways. First, the
audience has seen Volumnia 'ghosting' her son's battle actions,
taking them on as her own, thus dramatically creating a link
between her son's martial attainments and her own victory.
Secondly, despite Coriolanus allocating his mother a traditional
role in his family when he returns following the battle, he cannot
sustain the authority over her that he initially claims. Volumnia is
always the champion of the city, embroiled in its civic and political
affairs, donating her maternal body and her maternal care to raising

her son as a champion for the city's defence. There is no escape from the mother's control in the Rome to which her maternity is bound.

Battle offers a temporary retreat away from Rome and Volumnia and into the world of play which so absorbed Coriolanus's son in his attack on the butterfly. The companionship of war offers a male environment where, for Coriolanus, the mother has no place, though the audience, having seen Volumnia's account of his actions, is aware of a kind of surveillance from a distance, so that his actions are circumscribed by our understanding of her approval. Coriolanus's deadly war games work as 'playing' does in Isobel Armstrong's formulation, in which it offers the opportunity for separation from the mother: 'A mode of release from, not a fetishistic encounter with the mother's body, not at the mercy of the mother's functions, but attentive to its experiences, moving from continuity to contiguity, to non-omnipotent relations and to the re-negotiation of boundaries'.[55] The problem for Coriolanus is that such a release is illusory. He returns from Corioli confident that his victory and renaming will relegate the maternal to its traditional role, but as he approaches Rome and his mother he is as subordinated as ever. The link is made clear by Adelman, who sees Volumnia and Rome increasingly closely identified while he remains in the city until 'Rome and his mother are finally one . . . [I]n exiling Coriolanus, Rome re-enacts the role of the mother who cast him out'. Ronald Knowles pursues the link between Volumnia and Rome back to the mythological beginnings of the city, so that the she-wolf that nursed Romulus and Remus is refigured in a construction of Rome in terms of maternal nurture and maternal demands.[56]

Adelman suggests that 'the union with Aufidius is for Coriolanus a union with an alter-ego; it represents a flight from the world of Rome and his mother towards a safe male world'.[57] But it is also, importantly, to an alternative home, to which Coriolanus is welcomed:

> Thou noble thing, more dances my rapt heart
> Than when I first my wedded mistress saw
> Bestride my threshold. (4.6.113–5)

Antium is a place in which wives are referred to with sufficient regularity to construct a sense of a traditional social world where marriage follows familiar rules; ordinariness is evoked both in

Aufidius's conventional assertion of his response to his wife quoted above (perhaps less conventional as a response to Coriolanus, however) and in the routine, easy, antifeminist humour that precedes Coriolanus's entrance into the city.[58] It is a world without mothers, where all the power – martial, social and domestic – is in the hands of men. When Coriolanus enters Antium he eschews the convention of describing the consequences of war in terms of 'mothers who lack sons' (2.1.152) that served him when he returned to Rome after the battle of Corioli. Repudiating his mother city (and thus the mother who lives there) – 'my birthplace hate I' (4.4.23) – he discovers instead a 'goodly' city where he finds wives rather than mothers:

> A goodly city is this Antium. City,
> Tis I that made thy widows. Many an heir
> Of these fair edifices 'fore my wars
> Have I heard groan and drop. Then know me not,
> Lest that thy wives with spits and boys with stones
> In puny battle slay me. (4.3.1–6)

Antium is a city where embraces are between men – 'Let me twine / mine arms about that body' (4.5.103–4) – and where passionate fantasies are of masculine, martial intimacy. It is a world where the comforts of home denied to him in his mother city – the welcoming threshold, the 'upper end'th'table' (4.5.187) – are presented by men, and where the deference a man should traditionally expect from his womenfolk is given by a man, according to Aufidius's servants: 'Our general himself makes a mistress of him, sanctifies himself with's hand, and turns up the white o'th'eye to his discourse' (4.5.188–90). The welcome here is personal, not political; the plans offered in Antium are not to do with policy or civic concerns, but with making war. In this martial world, where the commoners are comic rather than threatening, it is understood that war creates love between men because they need one another. There is no sense of the civilities of Rome, or the motherhood which embraces and embodies them.

Rome is itself threatened from within, as the tribunes attempt to represent the interests of the hungry civilians. It is another of the complexities of the play that, as Dollimore acknowledges, 'the plebeians are presented with both complexity and sympathy'.[59] The conniving of the tribunes throws the concerns of the commoners into sympathetic relief just as the patrician insistence upon the processes of power and policy reveals Coriolanus as a figure of integrity, despite his limitations. It is possible to discern another alignment of interests in the play, which posits both Coriolanus and the plebeians in tension with an overwhelming and controlling mother Rome. Diane Purkiss discovers a similar trope in Swetnam's *The Arraignment of Lewd, Idle, Froward and Unconstant Woman*, which she suggests seeks to define 'a youthful and essentially plebeian masculinity over and against the coercive discourses of morality as well as over and against femininity'.[60] Purkiss highlights Swetnam's distinction between male and female worlds:

> Is it not strange that men should be so foolish to doat on women who differ so farre in nature from men? For a man delights in armes & in heating the rattling drums, but a woman loves to hear sweet musicke on the lute ... a man rejoices to march among the murthered carcasses, but a woman to dance on a silken carpet.[61]

For Purkiss, this figures a 'self-constituted shift from the household of childhood ... in gender terms, their emergence from a feminised sphere into a masculine one'.[62] The problem that this play posits for both Coriolanus and the plebeians is that neither Volumnia nor mother Rome will allow such a shift. The mother and the city are as warlike as their men. The tragedy is thus born out of the impossibility of differentiation and separation; not only the man of integrity is destroyed, but the threat of war undermines the claims of the citizens. The celebrated scene in which Volumnia persuades her son not to attack Rome thus begins a process where policy confronts 'instinct' (5.3.34), and triumphs; the power games of the patricians win over the citizens.

Because Volumnia has shown how well she understands the politics of persuasion, of gestures like kneeling, of the rhetoric of policy, her actions in this scene, as Lee Bliss rightly points out, are open to contradictory interpretations.[63] The text does not allow for a reading of her motivation, and this is perhaps the point. To an audience, the mother's effect upon her son is evident in the running commentary he makes on the progress of his family towards him: 'My wife comes foremost, then the honoured mould / Wherein this trunk was framed, and in her hand / the grandchild to her blood' (5.3.22–4). As Adelman points out, the emphasis is upon Volumnia as genitrix: 'Coriolanus does not acknowledge the child as his and his wife's: he first imagines himself in his mother's womb and then imagines the child as an extension of his mother'.[64]

This collapsing of the hero's world into an overwhelming maternal presence has its affirmation in Volumnia's famous assertion to her son that 'thou shalt no sooner / March to assault thy country than to tread – / Trust to't, thou shalt not – on thy mother's womb / That brought thee to this world' (5.3.122–5). Perhaps because her speeches and her gestures in this scene are so closely reliant upon Plutarch, or perhaps because she is playing at policy for all she is worth, there is a sense of conventionality about Volumnia's persuasion. The scene can be read as a final confrontation between the hardy politic mother and the son struggling against instinct in an effort to be 'author of himself' (5.3.36). But, as Adelman puts it, Coriolanus 'ends fully subject to the place of origin'; all his actions circumscribed by the surveillance and control of an omnipresent mother.[65] Unlike Hamlet, who broke his mother's heart in two and then remade her so that he became her author and was able to authorise his own subsequent vengeful actions, Coriolanus struggles against a maternity which refuses to conform, despite his efforts to constrain it. That the struggle is lost is signalled by the uncontrolled hyperbole with which he reads his mother's greeting gesture: 'My mother bows, / As if Olympus to a molehill should / In supplication nod' (5.3.29–31). The disproportion in the image anticipates his final capitulation and abjection, as Adrian Poole points out:

> He transfers her gesture into one of the most memorably invidious comparisons in the play . . . this would be laughable if it were not so pathetic – to find a man wishing or needing to believe that such a vertiginous scale of comparison could possibly measure a human relationship.[66]

In *Hamlet*, Gertrude's dramatic meaning is constructed out of silence and a lack of movement because her role of queen always constrains her. Volumnia's dramatic meaning is created out of language and gesture, the expression of a tension between meaning and speaking. When she persuades her son to stop his assault she, who understands the politics of playing so well, is able to present herself in terms of the traditional silent suffering mother, even as she belies this image in favour of public speech and the ritual gestures of public courtesy:

> Should we be silent and not speak, our raiment
> And state of bodies would bewray what life
> We have led since thy exile. (5.3.94–6)

This is after, and in spite of, over eighty lines of speech: 'I am hushed until our city be afire, / And then I'll speak a little' (5.3.181–2). Typology is absorbed into Volumnia's rhetorical strategy; she dramatises herself in terms of traditional constructions of motherhood, creating a visual and verbal image of pathos which her son finds impossible to resist. Volumnia performs verbally and visually (by kneeling) the very terms of maternal vulnerability and acquiescence that Coriolanus has wishfully constructed for her throughout the play: at last he sees her as he has wanted her. The effect, signalled by the famous direction 'holds her by the hand, silent' (5.3.183), is the collapse of his attempt at self-authorship in the face of his mother's will.

In both plays discussed in this chapter it might be argued that children are in danger of paying a price for their mother's public function, however carefully the mothers fulfil that role: a danger thwarted in *Hamlet* and realised in *Coriolanus*. The tragic outcomes of both plays are presaged by a sense of imbalance, of things 'out of joint', that is generated by the mother's position: a tension between public and private; between political and domestic, between the demands of state and the needs of family. These tensions, and their developing meaning in plays from the early seventeenth century, are the subject of the next chapter.

Notes

1 T. S. Eliot, 'Coriolan II', in *Collected Poems 1909–1967* (London: Faber & Faber, 1974), ll. 50–1, p. 143.
2 See Jonathan Dollimore, *Radical Tragedy: Religion, Ideology and Power in the Drama of Shakespeare and his Contemporaries* (Brighton: Harvester Press, 1984), p. 71. Dollimore does not discuss *Hamlet*; nevertheless his compelling discussion of Jacobean revenge tragedy is clearly important in any subsequent work on plays covered by the definitions of the genre.
3 Janet Adelman, *Suffocating Mothers: Fantasies of Maternal Origin in Shakespeare's Plays* (London and New York: Routledge, 1992), p. 1.
4 *Hamlet*, 1.4.23–6. All references, unless otherwise stated, are to the edition of the play in *The Oxford Shakespeare*, eds. Stanley Wells and Gary Taylor (Oxford: Clarendon Press, 1988).
5 Deborah Willis, *Malevolent Nurture: Witch-hunting and Maternal Power in Early Modern England* (Ithaca and London: Cornell University Press, 1995), pp. 17–18.
6 Adelman, *Suffocating Mothers*, p. 11.
7 A. C. Bradley, *Shakespearean Tragedy* (London: Macmillan, 1904), p. 118.

8 *Hamlet*, 1.2.15–17. Claudius emphasises the political importance of the marriage by stressing that the court has 'freely gone / with this affair along, (ll. 14–15).
9 Bradley, *Shakespearean Tragedy*, p. 119.
10 T.S. Eliot, *The Sacred Wood: Essays on Poetry and Criticism* (London: Methuen, 1920, repr. 1972), pp. 96–7 and 101.
11 Eliot, *The Sacred Wood*, p. 98.
12 Adelman reads the disjunction that Eliot identifies psychoanalytically as symptomatic of 'the struggle . . . to free the masculine identity of both father and son from its origin in the contaminated maternal body'. Adelman, *Suffocating Mothers*, pp. 15 and 17.
13 Jacqueline Rose, 'Sexuality in the Reading of Shakespeare: *Hamlet* and *Measure for Measure*', in *Alternative Shakespeares*, vol. 1, ed. John Drakakis (London: Routledge, 1985), pp. 95–118.
14 Rose, 'Sexuality in the Reading of Shakespeare', p. 103.
15 Rose, 'Sexuality in the Reading of Shakespeare', p. 118.
16 Dorothea Kehler, 'The First Quarto of *Hamlet*: Reforming Widow Gertred', *Shakespeare Quarterly*, 46:4 (1995), 399.
17 Kehler, 'The First Quarto of *Hamlet*', p. 398.
18 Kehler, 'The First Quarto of *Hamlet*', p. 403.
19 Kehler, 'The First Quarto of *Hamlet*', p. 407.
20 See, for example, Lisa Jardine, *Still Harping on Daughters: Women and Drama in the Age of Shakespeare* (Brighton: Harvester, 1983), p. 128.
21 Jardine, Still Harping on Daughters, p. 72.
22 Dollimore, *Radical Tragedy*, p. 29.
23 Christine Buci-Glucksmann, *Baroque Reason: The Aesthetics of Modernity*, trans. Patrick Camiller (London: Sage, 1994).
24 Buci-Glucksmann, *Baroque Reason*, p. 71.
25 Adelman, *Suffocating Mothers*, p. 19.
26 See, for example, Claudius's interruption at l. 87, ' 'Tis sweet and commendable' or later at l. 121, ' 'Why, 'tis a loving and a fair reply'.
27 Adelman suggests that Gertrude's sexual and maternal meanings were thus 'contained' by her former husband's protective control. Adelman, *Suffocating Mothers*, p. 20.
28 Dollimore, *Radical Tragedy*, p. 40.
29 The definitions are from the *Oxford English Dictionary* online. The essay by Kristeva is *Powers of Horror: An Essay on Abjection*, trans. Leon S. Roudiez (New York: Columbia University Press, 1982). Quotation from p. 2.
30 The sense of this encounter taking place in a private space is also constructed through the furnishings indicated in the text: 'Come, come, and sit you down,' (3.4.19. The portraits of Old Hamlet and Claudius (if we take them to be wall-hung and not miniatures) indicate that the space is more personal. Catherine Richardson has said in conversation that portraits were usually to be found in chambers and parlours, functioning as part of a construction of the private self as

opposed to the public person. The visual effect of both portraits (if this is how they are presented in performance) would enhance Adelman's argument that whatever Hamlet's original intentions in approaching his mother in 3.4, 'his most immediate need [...] is to force her to acknowledge the difference between the two fathers'. Adelman, *Suffocating Mothers*, p. 22.

31 W. Shakespeare, *Hamlet*, First Quarto, 1603, Facsimile, Oford, Clarendon Press,1965, G3V.
32 Kristeva, *Powers of Horror*, p. 2.
33 Kristeva, *Powers of Horror*, p. 65. Here she cites Georges Bataille, who discusses the abject in connection with what she calls 'the logic of prohibition'. Kristeva develops Bataille's analysis to link it specifically to the production of mother as object.
34 See Adelman: 'the main psychological task that Hamlet seems to set himself is not to avenge his father's death but to re-make his mother'. Adelman, *Suffocating Mothers*, p. 31.
35 *Hamlet*, 3.4.158 and 3.4.179.
36 Adelman, *Suffocating Mothers*, pp. 27 and 32.
37 Lee Bliss, ed., *Coriolanus*, New Cambridge Shakespeare (Cambridge: Cambridge University Press, 2000), p. 48. All subsequent references to the play will be taken from this volume unless otherwise stated.
38 Volumnia was a popular example of ideal maternity for this reason in eighteenth-century and nineteenth-century England, but as Bliss points out, the play was often rewritten in production to ensure that she could be unproblematically celebrated. See Bliss, ed., *Coriolanus*, pp. 71–5.
39 Coppelia Kahn, *Roman Shakespeare: Warriors, Wounds and Women* (London: Routledge, 1997), pp. 145–6.
40 Martha Hester Fleischer, *Iconography of the English History Play* (Salzburg: Institut für Englische Sprache und Literatur, Universität Salzburg, 1974), p. 117.
41 Coppelia Kahn has noted: 'The play dislodges "mother" as a representational category... making it a contestable term that cannot be placed securely on either side of a male/female, public/private, warmaking/mothering binarism'. Kahn, *Warriors, Wounds and Women*, p. 147.
42 Bliss, ed., *Coriolanus*, introduction, p. 49.
43 Kahn offers a wonderful analysis of Volumnia's words here, particularly in her discussion of the site of Hector's wound, which means, Kahn says, that Volumnia nursed her son 'in contempt, as it were, of erotic options'. Kahn, *Warriors, Wounds and Women*, p. 151.
44 Marina Warner, *Fantastic Metamorphoses, Other Worlds* (Oxford: Oxford University Press, 2002), pp. 91–2.
45 Dorothy Leigh, 'The Mother's Blessing', excerpted in Suzanne Trill, Kate Chedgzoy and Melanie Osbourne, *Lay by Your Needles, Ladies,*

Typology and subjectivity in 'Hamlet' and 'Coriolanus' 195

Take the Pen: Writing Women in England 1500–1700 (London: Arnold, 1997), p. 110.
46 This scene of welcome is paralleled at the end of the play when the same trio visit him to plead for the safety of Rome. The visual trope of the three women recalls the visit of the three Marys to the tomb of Christ, and its typological reworking in medieval depictions of birth and death, where three women are traditionally shown to attend.
47 Adelman makes a link between the preoccupations of the play and the food shortages in England in 1607. Adelman, *Suffocating Mothers*, p. 147.
48 Dollimore, *Radical Tragedy*, p. 220.
49 Dollimore, *Radical Tragedy*, p. 218.
50 Dollimore, *Radical Tragedy*, p. 219.
51 Alexander Leggatt draws attention to the way in which Volumnia coaches her son in play-acting. See Alexander Leggatt, *Shakespeare's Political Drama* (London: Routledge, 1988), p. 193.
52 Adelman, *Suffocating Mothers*, p. 158. Adelman is here analogising from Menenius's characterisation of Rome as an unnatural mother who consumes her own in 3.1.296–9.
53 Coppelia Kahn notes that because Volumnia is so closely identified in the play with every aspect of her son's identity, 'any social recognition of Coriolanus as a man, warrior or civic leader also re-inscribes him as her nursling'. Kahn, *Warriors, Wounds and Women*, p. 154.
54 Adelman, *Suffocating Mothers*, p. 152.
55 Isobel Armstrong, 'So What's All This about the Mother's Body?: The Aesthetic, Gender and the Polis', *Women, A Cultural Review*, 4:2 (1993), 184. Armstrong is reading the idea of play through Winnicott here.
56 Adelman, *Suffocating Mothers*, p. 157. Also Ronald Knowles, *Shakespeare's Arguments with History* (Basingstoke: Palgrave, 2002), p. 155.
57 Adelman, *Suffocating Mothers*, p. 156.
58 *Coriolanus* 4.3.25–7: 'I have heard it said the fittest time to corrupt a man's wife is when she's fallen out with her husband'.
59 Dollimore, *Radical Tragedy*, p. 224.
60 In Clare Brant and Diane Purkiss, *Women, Texts and Histories 1575–1760* (London: Routledge, 1992), p. 82.
61 Brant and Purkiss, *Women, Texts and Histories*, p. 78.
62 Brant and Purkiss, *Women, Texts and Histories*, p. 77.
63 Bliss, *Coriolanus*, pp. 56–8.
64 Adelman, *Suffocating Mothers*, p. 161.
65 Adelman, *Suffocating Mothers*, p. 162.
66 Adrian Poole, introduction, *Coriolanus*, Harvester New Critical Introductions to Shakespeare (Hemel Hempstead: Harvester Wheatsheaf, 1988).

7

Dead mothers among the living

> let me go
> Perfect and undeformed to my tomb.[1]
> Heywood, *A Woman Killed with Kindness*

> deare child, reade here my love[2]
> Elizabeth Jocelin

When Elizabeth Grymeston, feeling herself to be at the end of her life, wrote her *Miscellanea* for her son Bernye, her purpose was to ensure that her maternal advice and guidance would continue to support Bernye after she died: 'I leave thee this portable *veni mecum* for thy Counsellor, in which thou mayest see the true portraiture of thy mothers minde'. She writes of herself as at a point of transition between life and death, 'a dead woman among the living', and she knows that this gives her words potency: 'being my last speeches, they will be better kept in the conservance of thy memory; which I desire thou wilt make a Register of heavenly Meditations'.[3] Her explicit purpose is to ensure that those 'last speeches' will continue to resonate beyond her physical life. Twenty years later, Elizabeth Jocelin's 'Legacie' to her unborn baby was imagined by its writer as a means by which her words would influence her child after her death: 'When thou seest men purchase land, and store up treasure for their unborne babes, wonder not at mee that I am carefull for thy salvation, being such an eternall portion: and not knowing whether I shall live to instruct thee'.[4]

Both mothers addressed the prospect of their own demise by making arrangements to continue their care for their children beyond their own lives by the perpetuation of their individual voices through the medium of their writings. Their texts connected their children's future lives back to their own – to the moment of motherly love that impelled the writing – at the same moment as their voices reach forward into the future, so that Elizabeth Jocelin was able to guide her unborn child as it grew and Elizabeth Grymeston could advise Bernye at those times in his life when she believed that he would need it most but when she would no longer be alive to give it: 'that thou mightest be fortunate in two houres of thy life time: in the houre of thy *marriage*, and at the houre of thy *death*' (original italics).[5]

The significance of a 'dead woman among the living' was well understood. In 1603 Elizabeth Caldwell, condemned to hang for trying to kill her husband, remained alive in prison awaiting the birth of her baby. During this wait for death she underwent what Lucinda Becker has called a 'transformation from repentant sinner into potential spiritual leader' and in doing so attained a kind of celebrity.[6] Although no doubt she was for many of her visitors an object of curiosity, and for others a soul to be saved, the sheer numbers (if Gilbert Dugdale, whose account of the story we have, is to be only half believed) suggest that her significance was powerful. Dugdale recounts that 'no fewer some daies then three hundred persons' visited her, to whom she gave 'good admonitions, wishing that her fall might be an example to them'.[7] Elizabeth continued her 'admonitions' beyond her death, a letter to her husband exhorting him to 'let my speeches finde acceptance, and doe not slightly esteeme what I write vnto you, but reade these lines againe, and againe, and lay them vp in your hart'.[8] Elizabeth, with Dugdale's apparent connivance, is ostensibly exhorting her husband to religious faith, but her language also seems to hint at his own shortcomings, reminding him 'what a case you haue liued' and warning that 'If you continue in your abhominations, and shut your eares against the worde of Exhortation, you cannot haue any hope of saluation'.[9] Elizabeth expressed the same views at the gallows, using the resonance of her imminent death to create an influential presence for herself in her husband's future life. Dugdale likewise understood and utilised the conventions that she had invoked, in his account of her.

The process of dying well meant behaving according to an ideal that constituted, according to Lucinda Becker, a 'strenuous and personal challenge for the early modern Englishwoman'.[10] This Becker finds particularly true for Protestant women, for whom dying 'represented a crossing point on a journey already begun'.[11] For Clare Gittings, Catholics and Protestants alike 'tended to emphasise the difference, rather than the continuum, between the soul and the body and between the two states of life and death'.[12] We have accounts of this most personal and lonely point in some women's lives because they were watched as they endured it, usually by people who loved them, or wished them well and celebrated their role as exemplars. Becker suggests that the deathbed was a 'semi public arena' that represents a shift from the 'private, domestic sphere' just as it becomes a stage for 'the transition from physicality to spirituality'.[13] In the cases of Grymeston and Jocelin and others who wrote as they approached, or anticipated, their deaths, or who were observed in the processes and anguish of dying, their voices and the examples they set were made meaningful for wider audiences through the publication of their writings or the recording of their words, whether this had been their explicit wish or not.[14] It is the very privacy of a mother's struggle with death that is the point. The pleasure of such accounts for a reader is associated not only with the satisfaction of a story of moral and religious rectitude and self-effacement but also with the idea of a good mother's love and care as transcendent and exemplary, and an understanding that her voice, speaking from a place of intensely personal and introspective struggle has meaning beyond individual experience and is therefore appropriate as a story for public consumption. More than that, there is a touching dynamism, a sense of continued movement, in the expressed desire of these women to reach out into the future with their words, which they hope will move forward through time with their children as they grow.

Advice books by mothers, published posthumously, flourished in the period, though Patricia Crawford's detailed analyses show that although the amount of women's writing that was published increased throughout the seventeenth century (especially in the second half), the nature of the work changes.[15] Chris Laoutaris cites Elizabeth Hoby Russell as the author of one of the first texts to identify itself explicitly as 'a lasting Legacie' deriving from the prayers and supplications of 'a tender mother', arguing that Hoby Russell 'both engages in, and in some sense initiates, a tradition of maternal legacies which grew in popularity from the early seventeenth century'.[16] In the main, these texts are a phenomenon of the early Jacobean period with the publication of several that focused particularly upon the maternal role. These were evidently popular: Valerie Wayne describes them as 'bestsellers'.[17] Grymeston's book ran to at least four editions between 1604 and 1618 and Jocelin's *Legacie* was, according to Betty Travitsky, reprinted seven times during the 1620s and 1630s.[18] Dorothy Leigh's *A Mother's Blessing* was even more consistently popular, first appearing in 1616 and running to sixteen editions. All of these appeared posthumously, though Patricia Crawford shows that Leigh, at least, clearly intended her work for publication. The writers' exemplary piety and humility (celebrated, for example, in the Approbation to Jocelin's work) and the pathos engendered by the notion of deceased motherhood surely contributed to the attraction of these books. They offered the reader the opportunity to engage, through reading, in an act of contemplative devotion enhanced by a sentimental appreciation of the circumstances of the writer.[19] The popularity of advice books influences Catherine Belsey's argument that an 'ideal of the affective nuclear family in early modern England' emerged out of the religious, political and economic upheavals of the period.[20] Belsey, who finds expression of this change in the cultural products of the period, focuses upon Jacobean funerary architecture and contemporary English drama for her discussion. She sees a Protestant valorisation of the family which imagines it as a nexus of affective ties and thus as contributing to a new interest in 'family values'. Belsey finds the idea of a loving mother at the centre of an affective family – as a modern audience might know her – expressed in the representations of family in some of Shakespeare's plays, notably *The Winter's Tale*. There is some consensus among historians and critics that the idea of the family was subject to a new kind of attention in Jacobean Protestant England and that the dramatic depiction of the loving mother was affected by shifts in the Jacobean understanding of the meaning of the family. However, it is becoming clear that this attention was complicated and that representations of the affectionate mother were neither new nor unproblematic for an early modern audience.

Protestantism had no special claim upon the assertion of family affections; in fact its emphasis upon the control of personal feeling, in so far as emotional expression should be directed towards God rather than to other people, tended to stress the need to restrain the expression of emotional attachment. For example, the metaphor of indulgent maternal nursing or 'nusling' as a means of expressing the malign effects of Catholic heresy from the early sixteenth century onward, discussed earlier, suggested a Protestant antipathy – at least in theory – to overt demonstrations of maternal affection. Moreover, celebrating the affective family was not a new, nor an especially Protestant, development. Grymeston, a Catholic, had no problems expressing the strength of her attachment to her child:

> My dearest sonne, there is nothing so strong as the force of love; there is nothing so forcible as the love of an affectionate mother to hir naturall childe: there is no mother can either more affectionately shew hir nature, or more naturally manifest hir affection, than in advising hir children out of hir owne experience, to eschue evill and encline them to do that which is good.[21]

Betty Travitsky points out that Grymeston's work is characterised by reference to both canonical and contemporary Catholic writers.[22] Grymeston, therefore, self-consciously places herself within a religious tradition which, it seems, can comfortably accommodate emphatic expressions of maternal affection and subjective experience into a wider discussion about spiritual concerns. For example, she associates the expression of her love for Bernye with her last illness in a way which suggests more than just the routine deployment of a rhetorical gesture: 'Thou seest my love hath carried me beyond the list I resolved on, and my aking head and trembling hand haue rather a will to offer, than abilitie to afford further discourse'. Her insistence upon the mother's love which informs her work suggests that she perceived no problem in situating a passionate expression of her personal affection for her son within the discourses of Catholicism.[23] For Grymeston, maternal love provided the impetus for a discourse which, she hoped, would lead to the betterment of Bernye's spiritual prospects.

While Grymeston's acknowledgement of a mother's responsibility to act as a spiritual and moral mentor to her children was in sympathy with contemporary Protestant discourses her approach to the demonstration of affection is very different from that of the Puritan minister William Gouge, whose later (1622) conduct book promotes family love as a manifestation of religious and moral rectitude. In one of his many somewhat disconcerting analogies, Gouge appears to understand familial affection as the consequence of respect and duty: 'If the worlds proverbe holds true *(love me and love my dog)* how much more true is this Christian rule, *love me and love my child:* or *love me and love mine husband:* or *love me and love my wife*'.[24] Gouge demonstrates a generally disapproving preoccupation with the social manifestations of personal feelings, urging, for example, the wife to affect modesty in both gesture and speech, so that her behaviour does not cause confusion to onlookers: 'lightness ... in a wife, is not so much a mutuall familiarity with her husband by his good liking, as a wanton dallying with others to his griefe and disgrace'.[25] He is similarly insistent upon the need to control the physical and verbal expression of affection within the family, notably demonstrations of parental love, which he sees as potentially bestial: 'Is this not mere Apish kindnesse? For Apes kill their young ones with hugging'. 'This is no love', he says, 'but plaine dotage'. For Gouge such demonstrations can be dangerous: 'But what may be said of those that are so hellishly enamoured with their children as to commit incest or buggery with them?'[26] Thus an understanding of affective family relations in the early modern period must be highly qualified. Puritan affection is, according to Gouge, ideally expressed through godliness and restraint and through a proper sense of priorities which are exemplified, he says, in the proverb 'better be unfed than untaught'.[27] Such calls for restraint, from the address to parents in the sixteenth-century moral play *Nice Wanton* discussed earlier in this book, to Gouge's polemic above, suggest that the affectionate family unit was widely accepted as the norm in the sixteenth century and indeed earlier, and that late Protestant attention to the family demonstrates an attempt to *control* that unit, to codify its significance, to celebrate familial affection, but within the constraints of a particular moral and spiritual view.[28] As Ann Rosalind Jones puts it, 'the Protestant definition of marriage gave new importance to family relations, but it shaped those relations according to a newly elaborated theory of patriarchalism' as much as, in Belsey's terms, 'a culture that chooses to ground the family on romantic love'.[29] Indeed Christina Luckyj, discussing Dorothy Leigh's *The Mothers Blessing*, warns of 'the danger of essentialising [the] maternal voice and overlooking its political and social construction'. Luckyj is arguing that there is in fact 'a *struggle* over the construction of motherhood in contemporary English Puritan ideology'.[30] Writing of conditions at the end of the period covered by this book, Luckyj contends that some English Puritans sought to reappropriate the idea of the church as mother, frustrated by King James's overtures to Jesuits and others. She links this move to the 'popular mothers' advice books', arguing that, as a response to the king's 'paternal negligence', such texts 'authorised the good mother, frequently figured as the true church and bride of Christ, to use her own powers of persuasion'.[31]

So, for Luckyj, the popular representation of motherhood was innately political, and discourses that address motherhood and families must be read in that context. Certainly a new focus on family relations was expressed in the interest in the duties and roles of family members in the conduct books that proliferated in the period, of which Gouge's *Of Domesticall Duties*, first published in 1622, is a late example, suggesting concern with the regulation of the family unit in the later phase of the Protestant state.[32] This interest in the control of social roles was also manifest in the operation of law as it related to maternity. Unmarried mothers came under increasingly tough legislation at the end of the sixteenth and beginning of the seventeenth centuries. The punishment for mothering a bastard in 1576 was whipping; in 1610 this was changed to imprisonment and whipping, though in 1593 the Commons had rejected a proposal that the fathers of illegitimate children should be punished.[33] At the same time there was increasing pressure for the laws governing infanticide to be tightened (most women committing this offence seem to have been unmarried young women or widows disposing of illegitimate offspring) and in 1623 an act 'to prevent the destroying and murdering of bastard children' was passed.[34]

The popularity of written works from dead mothers is in contrast to the reception of publications by more robust, living women who were less interested in piety than practical parenting. Elizabeth Clinton's 1622 treatise in support of breastfeeding only ran to one edition, perhaps an indication of the comparative unpopularity of this work.[35] As a living and forthright writer, her work was possibly less ideologically and emotionally satisfying, while the notion of an advice book written by a woman on a subject which was being thoroughly covered by the authoritatively male writers of conduct books and obstetric manuals was perhaps somewhat unsettling for the buyers of such works, whoever they were.[36]

The high point of the production of advice books coincided not with a theatrical celebration of the affective family, but rather with a focus in the theatre upon the plight of abused, lost, dead and dying mothers. The transformation of the Griselda story into a wife-taming play which offers the visual thrill of the heroine's humiliation offers one example. In another kind of reworking, the domestic tragedies discussed earlier gave Thomas Heywood the structure for his Jacobean fiction, *A Woman Killed with Kindness*, which offers as its climactic spectacle a mother starving herself to death before her family (and the audience) to atone for an adulterous affair.[37] When dramatised mothers die, or seem to die, their meaning intensifies. Like Grymeston and Jocelin and Caldwell they become significant outside of their own personal story and continue to impact upon the experience both of those still living within the dramatised story in which they feature and of the audience. Dramatic discourses that address dying or dead mothers work in an analogous way to the voices of contemporary mother writers. Lucinda Becker shows that early modern mothers were often described by those who wrote their stories in terms of their ability not only to see ahead prophetically to their own demise, as did Elizabeth Jocelin, but also to return to the living after death as ghosts or in dreams or as a continued influence.[38] Jocelin ordered her shroud in advance of her confinement. Her touching work combines cultural sophistication (a sense of the symbolic weight of a mother's death; familiarity with the conventions required of a 'Legacie') with intense emotion: love for her husband, concern for her child, fear for herself, religious fervour and a need to reach somehow into an uncertain future.

Like the authors of mothers' legacies, Jacobean dramatised mothers demonstrate an awareness of their own symbolic importance. They function not only to draw attention to the emblematic status of martyred, threatened or abused motherhood in their individual narratives, but also to use that status to reinforce a moral point and to speak out beyond the world of the play. In *A Woman Killed with Kindness*, for example, the adulterous Anne Frankford turns to the audience to exhort them to read her moral meaning:

> Oh, women, women, you that have yet kept
> Your holy matrimonial vow unstained,
> Make me your instance.[39]

Anne has been discovered *in flagrante* in her nightclothes, her attire visually reinforcing the discovery and the significance of her sin. In such scenes, the mother figure functions in these plays as a 'speaking picture' in the Renaissance sense of the term as defined by Michael Bath: what she says, and how she appears, combine at crucial moments to create meaning which resonates beyond the narrative of the play itself.[40] Such scenes engage with the discourses that inform the conduct books and advice books which see motherhood as exemplary, sacrificial and iconic, as does the 'new interest in the depiction of emotional relationships' resulting in a version of 'mimesis' that Belsey discerns in tombs of the period and in contemporary dramatisations of motherhood.[41]

In *The Winter's Tale* the tensions between an idealised reading of motherhood and the material experience of it are explored in the context of a folk tale where the symbolic operates alongside the mundane. Hermione's body, pregnant, lactating, maternal, is one of the dominant images of the play, certainly in terms of the way that it is rhetorically constructed and equally so, we must assume, as it was originally seen in performance. As has often been noted, *The Winter's Tale* has much in common with the Griselda story: a blameless breastfeeding mother is lost to her family through the cruelties of an aberrant husband, and is reinstated only when her children are themselves old enough to be married. Just as the Jacobean version of the Griselda tale offers the old story alongside the contemporary pleasures of a wife-taming play, Shakespeare's wronged mother is more than the tale of a mother lost and found. For many critics, this is a play which, along with other late plays of Shakespeare's, appears to engage with a new shift in representations of authority that takes its lead from the Jacobean court. According to Suzanne Penuel:

> Especially after the accession of James 1 in 1603, what Jonathan Crewe has termed the 'repaternalization' [sic] of culture and politics became a high priority for both king and court. Scholars including Janet Adelman, Peter Erikson, Coppelia Kahn and Valerie Traub have claimed that [Shakespeare's late romances] participate in a conservative reestablishment of the father as the linchpin of society, burying the mother and validating patriarchy.[42]

Such criticism points out that *The Winter's Tale* addresses the troubled dynamics of its central family by exposing a male desire for an alternative, masculinised space which is imagined by the male characters as untroubled by the complicating presence of the maternal.[43] What characterises this space, as in *Coriolanus*, is that it functions as an arena for play. In *The Winter's Tale* this is recuperated through nostalgic recollection. At the beginning of the play Polixenes recalls his uncomplicated boyhood with Leontes:

> We were as twinn'd lambs that did frisk i'th'sun,
> And bleat the one at th'other: what we chang'd
> Was innocence for innocence: we knew not
> The doctrine of ill-doing, nor dream'd
> That any did. (1.2.67–71)

Polixenes sentimentally invokes a flawed and incomplete ideal, made clear by Hermione's wry response, 'by this we gather / You have tripp'd since (1.2.75–6), which provokes a confirmation that it is indeed the feminine that has contaminated such 'unfledg'd' innocence. Polixenes recalls a world where maternal influence for the good is missing; where he and his friend revelled in boyish ignorance as much as innocence. As Stephen Orgel notes, 'The return to childhood here is also a retreat from sexuality'.[44] Frivolous though this intercourse is, it exposes an inadequate ideal, and thus the inadequacies of those who imagine it to be sufficient. It is an ideal which Leontes, struck by jealousy, tries to recreate in his relations with his son, taking the tone of childish banter: 'Why, that's my bawcock. What! Hast smutch'd thy nose?' (1.2.212). Such playfulness is the corollary to a serious concern that the father is properly replicated in the son, untainted by the corruption of adultery: 'art thou my boy?' (1.2.118). Leontes seeks assurance that a clean, masculine honesty can be perpetuated, despite the necessity of a mother to the production of a son. Playing offers a way back to the pristine boyish world that Polixenes had described and in which he sees his son: 'Go play, Mamillius; thou'rt an honest man' (1.2.211).[45]

Donna C. Woodford argues that *The Winter's Tale* 'provides a fantasy of male control over reproduction and nurture without the painful, permanent loss of wife and child suffered by Macduff, or the paternal guilt placed upon Pandosto' [in Shakespeare's source].[46] She sees this extending across the play to the marriage of Florizel and Perdita, which, she argues, 'unites two children who have been reared exclusively by men without the tainting influence of their mothers or other women. The heirs of the two kingdoms are copies of their fathers, untainted by their mothers' milk, while Mamillius, the child in whom Hermione had "too much blood" is effectively sacrificed for not being an uncorrupted copy of his father'.[47] Leontes prefers an idea of his son as his own flesh, referring to him as 'my collop' (1.1.137). Such a fantasy links with the classical myth of heroic birth, where, says Park, 'although the mother is not altogether absent, she functions primarily as a receptacle and incubator, living only long enough to receive her husband's seed and bring her son to term, in line with theories of kinship and generation that minimised mothers' contribution to their children'.[48]

The Winter's Tale exposes that fantasy and dramatises its inadequacy. Leontes and Polixenes nostalgically recall events from outside the dramatised present. Their fantasy offers an imagined contrast to what is insisted upon in the play: the physical, moral and emotional importance of maternity to the construction of the successful family and by analogy, a robust state. In Act 1 Scene 2 the visually striking figure of the pregnant Hermione signifies both the sexual and emotional link between husband and wife, and the physical and spiritual link between parents and children. Her success in persuading Polixenes to stay is indicative of her value as mediatrix between the king and his friend, registered in terms of physical gesture. The scene stages a visual history of the royal family, Polixenes figuring Leontes' princely past and political present and Mamillius signifying the royal future. This history coheres through the pregnant figure of Hermione, who functions as the dynamic, fruitful heart of the family and the court.

For jealous Leontes, Hermione's function is divisive, her pregnant body evidence of corruption. He imagines this in intensely physical and material terms as a too-ready exchange of blood: the friendly gestures between Hermione and Polixenes are rhetorised as 'mingling bloods' (1.2.109) just as he later fears that his wife has 'too much blood' in his son (2.1.58). Katharine Hodgkin has discussed the notion of excess of blood as a contemporary metaphor for 'a commitment to the flesh and to fleshly desires' and Leontes appears to discover this.[49] His wife's affectionate behaviour to her son and to her husband's friend demonstrates for him her depravity rather than her exemplary wifely and motherly love. As Gouge was later to warn, demonstrations of family affection are potentially dangerous both because they may mislead (as Leontes is misled) and because of their potential to corrupt (as Leontes fears they have). The play maintains a resolute dual focus upon the material reality of the mother's body and upon the iconicity of that body, and thus creates a dynamic that challenges Leontes' tendency to see the fleshly and material as separate from – or dangerous to – what is moral and spiritual. Hermione's pregnant body is referred to with anticipation and approval by her waiting-women: 'The queen your mother rounds apace' (2.1.16); 'She is spread of late / Into a goodly bulk' (2.1.20). But for Leontes her pregnancy implies disease: "tis Polixenes / Has made thee swell thus' (2.1.62). When he invites his court to read the meaning of his wife's pregnant body according to his own interpretation, his isolation, as the only character reading her this way, is clear:

> Look on her, mark her well: be but about
> To say 'she is a goodly lady,' and
> The justice of your hearts will thereto add
> 'Tis pity she's not honest, honourable. (2.1.65–8)[50]

Katherine Park shows how a contemporary appreciation of the physiology of the mother's body had the effect of foregrounding not only 'indelible corporeal links between a mother and her children' but also a sense of the frailty of the process of generation, by exposing 'the agonisingly fragile bodies on which the lineage depended'.[51] The way in which the play rhetorically redirects attention back Hermione's body in this scene reinforces a sense of that frailty and all that is at stake when that frail body is endangered. The audience, like the court, 'knows better' than Leontes, so that his reading of her is understood as abuse. The authority of the patriarch, however sincere his belief, is undermined by a common appreciation of the meaning of the mother and of her place at the centre of the family, so that the deployment of that familiar dramatic trope, the forced separation of mother and child, transforms Hermione's pregnant body to a signifier of sacrifice and suffering as her young son Mamillius is removed from her and from the stage:

> Give me the boy: I am glad you did not nurse him:
> Though he does bear some signs of me, yet you
> Have too much blood in him. (2.1.53–6)

This concern about too much blood, about the threat posed for Leontes by Hermione's physical link to her child, is exposed as a mistake. The truth, as the audience recognises it, is that blood is emblematic of love. The conventional early modern relation between blood and milk is recalled in Hermione's later accusation that Perdita has been taken from her, 'the innocent milk in its most innocent mouth' (3.2.100). The two images of separation of mother and child that the blood/milk analogy figures in this play (Hermione and Mamillius; Hermione and Perdita) intensify the impact of the understanding of maternal blood as nourishment, in its transformation into mother's milk, by reference to its sacrificial significance. Nursing as a kind of willing, loving bleeding was formally symbolised in the popular emblem of the pelican wounding her breast in order to nourish her young with her blood, a practice fabulously attributed to the bird and appropriated by Elizabeth I as a metaphor for her relationship with her subjects.[52] An emphatically practical and literal corollary to such an image is offered by Gouge's argument that 'soreness' should not prevent a mother nursing: 'A mother with enduring a little more paine may safely give the childe sucke. Many mothers have given their children sucke when bloud hath runne by the mouth of the childe'.[53]

The link between motherhood and suffering that creates a figure flexible enough to model the complexities of social corruption, religious controversy or civil war has been a recurring motif in this book. The difference in *The Winter's Tale* (and a difference it shares with the Jacobean *Grissil*) is that suffering makes the mother iconic in a new way because the mother figure was liable to be read by an audience in the light of new pressures. Alongside Luckyj's description of the battle for the mother metaphor between Puritan groups who were unhappy with the king's overtures to Catholics must be set the more general tenet of Jacobean ideology that promoted a new model for the understanding of the relations between subject and state. This repudiated the Elizabethan version, as James himself explained: 'It is casten up by divers, that employ their pens upon Apologies for rebellions and treasons, that everie man is borne to carrie such a naturall zeale and dutie to his common wealthe, as to his Mother'.[54] As is recorded by critics such as Gloria Olchowy, 'James I, unlike Elizabeth, did not find the power associated with mothers in the inherited ideologies amenable to his patriarchal view of monarchical rule.'[55] His preference was to promote himself in paternalistic terms (as in the *Basilicon Doron*) as a 'loving nourish [nurse] father, offering his subjects 'nourish milk'.[56] The affective tenor of this is perhaps modified by Claire McEachern's reading that, for James, 'it is not feeling for the mother which should determine civic identity, but duty to the father – not love, but law'. This then offers a model for '"the reciproke and mutuall dutie between a free king and his naturall people"'.[57] Both approaches resonate with Victoria Kahn's point that 'domestic order is the font of political order, and the passions that help to constitute domestic order have a role to play in the political realm as well'. For Kahn, emotional engagement between subject and sovereign is key to this new model, as promulgated in conduct books: 'Like the husband, the sovereign declares his love for his subject; like the wife, the subject is expected to be fearful and obedient. In both cases, passion is part of the "conscionable performance" of one's duty'.[58]

It has been widely argued that the promotion of a new model that valorised the benign authority of a paternal king had an effect upon dramatic representations of motherhood. The corollary to this new emphasis upon paternalism, though, appears to be a sense of loss, at least in some quarters, for the maternal tenor of the previous reign. Sir John Harington seems still to be missing Queen Elizabeth when he commented three years after her death, 'we did all love her, for she said she loved us'. And the Venetian ambassador remarked in 1607 that James 'did not caress the people, nor make them good cheer as the late queen did, whereby she won their loves'.[59] There appears to be a kind of mourning here; a desire to rediscover the mother, which may make sense of the conflicts about her meaning that Luckyj outlines. The effect of this nostalgia, as much as that of James's new paternalism, may be why mothers in these later plays become rather more remote and perfect. The mother is increasingly idealised as a figure whose meanings are domestic and associated with the safety and success of the family and the household, or their analogues. She remains crucial to the successful functioning of the state, but becomes intensely private in her contribution to it. The links between maternity, the family and household, mediating the public and the private, and a new attention to the experience of the child, combine with established models to offer a version of the mother figure whose suffering ensures the continuity and safety of the domestic family, whose sacrifice is understood in terms of a motherly love that is governed by morality and duty and expressed through pain. It is on these terms, rather than because of a discovery of affective family relations, that Hermione represents an ideal that is easily linked to polemical versions of the Jacobean Protestant mother.

Hermione is aware of this visual and symbolic meaning, and understands how to manipulate that meaning. She knows, for example, that part of her role is to negotiate between private life, interior thoughts and public meaning:

> I am not prone to weeping, as our sex
> Commonly are; the want of which vain dew
> Perchance shall dry your pities: but I have
> That honourable grief lodg'd here which burns
> Worse than tears drown: beseech you all, my lords,
> With thoughts so qualified as your charities
> Shall best instruct you, measure me. (2.1.118–14)

Hermione makes her 'honourable' private grief available to her audience (on and off the stage) at the same time as she dismisses 'vain' public displays of tears. She self-consciously figures her suffering, constructing herself rhetorically as the icon that she will literally become. The private and intimate affections of the mother, so celebrated in Protestant ideology, can only be made available to the world by a shift which recreates the mother as iconic, which separates her from the 'vain' passions that would debase her significance. At a time when, according to Betty Travitsky, women were encouraged to record their most private moments in diaries 'for the sake of religious discipline', and 'monuments to dutiful motherhood' in the form of maternal testimony were being published posthumously, this complex relation between an intensely private inner life and public testament to it offered a kind of double-take on motherhood as simultaneously private, intimate and instinctive, and public, iconic and idealised.[60] Philippe Aries says that 'it is no accident that in England, the birthplace of privacy, diaries were widely kept from the late 1500s' and it is significant that this should be so at a time when, as Belsey says, the personal and domestic experience of individuals became the focus of public discussion and the subject of dramatic representation.[61] Diaries and testimonials by their nature interrogate the meanings of individual lives even as they endow them with significance, whether intended only for personal use or for an audience. In the advice books and posthumously published works by early seventeenth-century mothers and their editors there is a sense of negotiation between the realities of private intimacy and the public meanings generated by an ideal of private intimacy for which the dead mother becomes an emblem.

The presentation of the statue of Hermione in the final scene of *The Winter's Tale* is informed by that tense interplay between private life and public meaning, between the fleshly and the monumental. Chris Laoutaris writes of memorial statues to motherhood, at least some of which were designed and the written content negotiated by mothers themselves, in terms of a tension between the static and the dynamic: 'Forever frozen in the dynamic act of nurturing, the motherly effigy "spoke" of the importance of the deceased's private "domestical" virtue'.[62] This sense of arrested movement has been identified, too, by Theresa Krier, in a reading of *The Winter's Tale* that sees Hermione at the start of the play 'in a continually improvised choreography in which her literal, embodied movements figure forth her desire' and which are translated into her 'statue'.[63] For Laoutaris, a 'feminised language of death circulated through the unique postures of the maternal body, was finding its way on to the stage'.[64] Belsey imagines this scene as if enacted before Hermione's tomb, and that the figure which descends represents the literal coming to life of a stone effigy, so that 'the family is saved by a miracle, an impossibility in nature'.⁶⁵ Certainly the impossible congruence of stone and flesh, between ideal and real, apparently happens; a trick, perhaps, but nevertheless an event of wonder to Leontes and his companions and a stunning spectacle for a theatre audience. It is Hermione's apparently bloodless effigy which, paradoxically, shifts Leontes into a desire for the return of the fleshly version of his wife and when he is permitted to touch her, the experience is for him entirely at the level of physical desire: 'O, she's warm! / If this be magic, let it be an art / Lawful as eatin'' (5.3.109–111).

Hermione, though, remains at the cusp between revered icon and embraceable body, an image of ambiguous 'picture-flesh'.⁶⁶ When she speaks she shifts between the supernatural and the mundane: the eternal ideal mother and the solicitous everyday mother; between the gods and her child:

> You gods, look down,
> And from your sacred vials pour your graces
> Upon my daughter's head! Tell me, mine own,
> Where hast thou been preserv'd? where liv'd? how found? (5.3.121–4)

Hermione's determination to see her daughter celebrates the affective tie between mother and child in all its poignant ordinariness but also acknowledges a disturbing supernatural power: the link to the Delphic oracle; the power to enter the dreams of others. Warner, like Belsey, imagines Hermione displayed 'in the form of a masterpiece of realistic statuary such as might have stood in a pilgrimage church'. However, the context of Warner's discussion makes the image more challenging. Warner is contemplating the ancient mummified body of Saint Caterina de Vigri and pondering 'the ambiguous, terrible and enthralling borderland between animation and lifelessness'.⁶⁷ Hermione's address to Perdita at the end of the play seems to confirm that ambiguity: 'Thou shalt hear that I . . . have preserv'd / Myself to see the issue' (5.3.125–8).⁶⁸ The idea of preservation jars a little here, resonating as it does of rituals associated with death as much as with the continuity of life and furthering a sense of uncertainty as to what Hermione actually *is* at this point. What she says is that she has 'preserved herself' against a future as a mother that would otherwise have been denied her.⁶⁹ This sense of the mother's agency in matters of her own life, death and preservation is represented differently in an example given by Laoutaris: a dedication to Elizabeth Crashawe, who died in childbirth in 1620: 'This rare blest wife. Her Infant Birthright gave / And (loving mother) digged herself a grave. / A Phaenix sure she was'.[70] Like the writers of the mothers, advice books and those mothers who, according to Laoutaris, negotiated the ways in which they would be memorialised, Hermione has preserved herself for a future where she remains accessible to protect and instruct her 'own'. In a dramatised world where patriarchy moves to minimise the mother's influence, her continued presence attests to an importance that is both absolutely grounded in the body and much more than merely corporeal. (Park shows that the intimacy of close scrutiny made possible in autopsies gave rise to a paradoxical understanding of motherhood as a spiritual state.[71]) The mother figures the divine and the worldly; she is both spirit and flesh. The 'new interest' in mimesis that Belsey finds in memorials allows the details of material actuality, the evidence of an individual life, to emphasise the spiritual triumph of the individual, particularly in their continued influence, through memory and legacy, upon the living.[72]

If *The Winter's Tale* offers a visually enthralling reading of the possibility of the convergence of mythic and actual motherhood that complies with a Protestant ideal, Webster's *Duchess of Malfi* gives an equally spectacular account of that ideal blown apart, at one level, by the demands of a material, Catholic culture. Mary Beth Rose cites *The Duchess of Malfi* as a play that offers one of those 'dramatic stories centred on mothers [which is] clearly one of the outstanding female roles', and sees the Duchess as a figure whose motherhood is 'central to her identity as a hero'.[73] That the story of the Duchess is about a woman who has married beneath her, is persecuted for it and who is also a mother enables Webster to construct his protagonist as heroic and to set her heroism against the corrupt Catholic world that she inhabits. Belsey has shown how Webster's play 'celebrates the family, identifying it as a private realm of warmth and fruitfulness separate from the turbulent world of politics, though vulnerable to it'.[74] A sense of privacy and separation are important to the heroic construction of the mother, placing her at the centre of a domestic world where all look inward and crave to be secure. To achieve this, Webster adjusted his sources, deflecting responsibility for the young Duke of Malfi away from the Duchess and towards her brothers, whose manipulation of the boy alienates the audience further from them.[75] Ferdinand's command to Bosola, 'Write to . . . my young nephew / She had by her first husband, and acquaint him / With's mother's honesty'

(3.3.68–70), is understood as malice rather than as a legitimate desire to protect his nephew's right and works to establish the Duchess's goodness through her rejection of her brothers' values and her resistance to their attempts to reform her.

Eileen Allman says that 'Ferdinand and the Cardinal determine the play's action, but the Duchess determines its meaning'.[76] This is clear in Dorinda Robbins's analysis of the first account that an audience hears of the Duchess (1.2.123–5), where Antonio cuts off all 'lascivious' associations and 'defines the Duchess in spiritual terms as a model of heavenly virtue: "Her Days are practic'd in such noble virtue, / That, sure her nights, nay more, her very sleeps, / Are more in Heaven, than other ladies shrifts"[TH]'. As Robbins says, '[Antonio] tries to re-contain her as a silent object rather than a sexually enticing subject'.[77] Antonio's version of his wife recalls Elizabeth Jocelin's husband's account of his role as 'an impartiall witnesse of her vertues and an happy partner of those blessings both transitory and spirituall, wherewith shee was endowed'.[78]

The irony that Webster builds into his narrative, of course, is that the Duchess's domestic world is, as Eileen Allman points out, illicit: what might be celebrated as privacy is in fact necessary secrecy and in order to create this world the Duchess has to compromise her public and political role. Allman sees this as a choice made willingly: 'Her secrecy reveals how well she understands the coercive force behind her brothers' construction of her roles as Duchess and sister, but she chooses to live as if the discourses that empower her as ruler and wife and mother supercede this'.[79] The impossibility of sustaining such a separation of roles is clear when the Duchess is discovered by her brother at a reunion with Antonio and their children at the shrine of Loretto. The shrine – the mystically relocated childhood home of Jesus – functions to signify the gap between the corrupt world in which the play is situated and the ideal life that the Duchess and her new family aspire to. It becomes a place where the impossibility of such an ideal, in the face of political and patriarchal interests, is exposed. Allman confirms this: 'Whatever the Duchess's motive for pilgrimage, she stands on that sacred ground as a mother whom tyranny has deprived of shelter, her family a replica of the holy family at Christianity's heart'.[80]

The play dramatises the mother's determination to pull away from her economic, social function as an emblem of the dynasties (her brothers', her dead husband's) with which she is associated to become a wife and mother, according to a contemporary understanding of the significance of that role as intimate, domestic and private. The problem for the Duchess is that she is operating in a world that sees the mother, and especially the mother's body, as political, and that does not allow for true privacy or for a real disassociation from the wider world. When she woos Antonio, she tries to distinguish between her public meaning and her private self by reference to the difference between icon and flesh – 'This is flesh and blood, sir, / 'Tis not the figure cut in alabaster / Kneels at my husband's tomb, (1.2.369–71) – but it is impossible to effect this separation of meanings in the politicised world of the play. There is no demarcation between public and private spaces; even the Duchess's most private space, her bed chamber, is infiltrated by her brother. And it has been well noted by critics such as Lisa Hopkins that the Duchess's body is similarly infiltrated, scrutinised and its material reality minutely recorded and given meaning:

> I observe our Duchess
> Is sick a-days, she pukes, her stomach seethes,
> The fins of her eyelids look most teeming blue,
> She wanes i'th' cheek, and waxes fat i'th' flank;
> And, contrary to our Italian fashion
> Wears a loose-bodied gown: there's somewhat in't. (1.2.66–72)[81]

Bosola the spy is detailed to discover and elucidate those meanings, to identify 'the young springal cutting a caper in her belly' (1.2.155), describing the pregnancy in terms that isolate the child leaping in the womb from its mother and from her family, as though she is incubating something that is independent from her and from the social world into which it will be born. As in *The Winter's Tale*, the mother's body offers opposing meanings. Antonio celebrates his wife's fecundity as a blessing, 'She's an excellent / Feeder of pedigrees' (3.1.4–5), but Ferdinand reads corruption, 'infected' and 'attainted' blood and a curse in the same body: 'Damn her! That body of hers, / While that my blood ran pure in't was more worth / Than that which thou wouldst comfort, call'd a soul' (1.6.119–21).

As the machinations of patriarchy and politics encroach upon and consume the Duchess's private life, she reasserts an authority that gains resonance from the moral identity she has established as a good mother. She is 'Duchess of Malfi still', but also a mother whose last thoughts are for her children: 'I pray thee look thou givst my little boy / Some syrup for his cold, and let the girl / Say her prayers, ere she sleep' (4.2.200–3). This assumption of political and moral rectitude renders her, like Hermione, heroic for an audience whose sympathies have been constructed by reference to a model of motherhood based on the ideal of family and the emotional tug of that idea. For Eileen Allman, this is a process of 'degendering authority' which means, she says, 'severing the automatic connection between dominance and maleness not only in the tyrant but also in the subject'. This 'allows men and women both, by asserting obedience to a higher authority, to assume, recognise and obey that authority in themselves and in one-another'.[82] In the case of both plays discussed in this chapter the ideology that insists upon the nuclear family as a microsmic version of the state provides the authority. Motherhood is fundamental to a social and political fabric which cannot hold without it. When the mother is lost, not only the families but the societies of both plays disintegrate. Mamillius dies, the court of Leontes falls into disarray and the social world of Webster's play implodes, as Jacqueline Pearson notes: 'The society of the play, deprived of the Duchess's healing presence, falls apart into melancholy, apathy, madness and murder'.[83]

The Duchess's slow shift from flesh and blood to alabaster has been widely discussed. Cariola, her servant, notes that before her death the Duchess in her grief has begun to resemble 'some revered monument / Whose ruins are even pitied' (4.2.34–5). Michael Neill has described 'her metamorphosis into the effigy of pious womanhood whose cold embrace she had sought to escape in the wooing scene . . . a metamorphosis which will be symbolically completed at the point of death where she self-consciously mimics the alabaster figure's kneeling posture'.[84] Chris Laoutaris writes of the way that contemporary memorials 'echoed the visual culture of the age' by dramatising their subject: 'The dying woman could gain a voice and even, as the funerary sermons indicate, an audience, by playing out the drama and trauma of their own fatal maternity'.[85] The Jacobean theatre, as Dympna Callaghan points out, offered a similar pleasure in what she sees as a celebration of dead good mothers who, 'once dead, become an example of absolute, unquestionable perfection'.[86] Michael Neill shows in his discussion of *The Duchess of Malfi* and other Jacobean plays that the visual representation of tombs and of tomb sculpture acts only as 'a theatrical cipher' for the 'true monument' which is motherly and wifely perfection: 'The Duchess's tomb, surrounded as it is by ruins that express the frailty of mere worldly greatness, stands for the individual renown earned by a woman whose unbreakable "integrity of life" is celebrated in the play's final couplet'.[87] As the Duchess of Malfi comes closer to her death, her transformation into an icon is realised in the way in which her flesh appears to become stone. As she dies, she becomes integral to the tomb that is the material monument to her fame. The immortality of what she stands for, the persistence of meaning is realised by the poignant call of her voice from her tomb.

Both Hermione and the Duchess of Malfi transcend the demands of patriarchy but simultaneously reaffirm the values that are inscribed in a paternalistic Jacobean version of Protestantism that celebrates motherhood in terms of intimacy, suffering and sacrifice. Laoutaris, writing of memorial texts, suggests that 'what these texts had in common was the way in which they allowed their female authors to secure a posthumous voice – a lasting memory – by subordinating the masculine machinery of inheritance to the biological and spiritual imperatives of the maternal bond'.[88] Becker quotes Elizabeth Jocelin's editor, who likens her *Legacie* to a twin sister for the daughter that she died bearing, 'issuing from the same Parent and seeing the light at about the same time'.[89] Jocelin's writing and that of other mothers discussed here projected into the future vital, dynamic, loving maternal voices to keep company with their children. The mimetic monuments to individual mothers that emerged from the same cultural moment allowed onlookers to realise imaginatively the living mother whose lifelike statue fixes her in time even as it acknowledges her continued potency, as though she might at any moment 'summon all her strength to breathe and move . . . to praise and bless' those who contemplate her likeness.[90] Hermione's statue and the Duchess of Malfi's tomb offer the consoling fantasy of motherhood as transcendent, as defiant, as eternal; of the mother who never really leaves.

Notes

1   Thomas Heywood, *A Woman Killed with Kindness*, in *Renaissance Drama: An Anthology of Plays and Entertainments*, ed. Arthur F. Kinney (Oxford: Blackwell, 1999), p. 65, ll. 95–6.
2   Elizabeth Jocelin, from *The Mother's Legacie to her Unborn Child* (London, 1624), quoted in Betty Travitsky, *The Paradise of Women: Writings by Englishwomen of the Renaissance* (New York and Oxford: Columbia University Press, 1989), p. 61. The full text is published in facsimile in Betty Travitsky, ed., *Mother's Advice Books*, in *The Early Modern Englishwoman: A Facsimile Library of Essential Works*, series 1, part 2, vol. 8 (Aldershot: Ashgate, 2001).

3   Elizabeth Grymeston, *Miscellanea Meditations Memoratives* (London, 1604), repr. in Travitsky, ed., *Mother's Advice Books*, The Epistle, sig. A2.
4   Jocelin, *The Mother's Legacie to her Unborn Child*, in Travitsky, ed., *Mother's Advice Books*, p. 9.
5   Travitsky, ed., *Mother's Advice Books*, The Epistle, sig. A3.
6   Lucinda M. Becker, *Death and the Early Modern Englishwoman* (Aldershot: Ashgate, 2003), p. 93.
7   Gilbert Dugdale, *A true discourse of the practises of Elizabeth Caldwell, Ma: Ieffrey Bownd, Isabell Hill widow, and George Ferneley, on the parson of Ma: Thomas Caldwell, in the County of Chester, to have murdered and poisoned him, with diuerse others*. (London: James Roberts, 1604).
8   Dugdale, *A true discourse of the practises of Elizabeth Caldwell*, p. 8. It is clear from Dugdale's account that there were unsuccessful efforts to obtain a reprieve for Elizabeth. Because she was a 'gentlewoman' her situation attracted attention from people in high places. 'Ladie Marie Cholmsly', to whom Dugdale dedicates his account, was one of her supporters.
9   Dugdale, *A true discourse of the practises of Elizabeth Caldwell*, p. 9.
10 Becker, *Death and the Early Modern Englishwoman*, p. 17.
11 Becker, *Death and the Early Modern Englishwoman*, p. 169.
12 Clare Gittings, *Death, Burial and the Individual in Early Modern England* (London and Sidney: Croom Helm, 2001), p. 13.
13 Becker, *Death and the Early Modern Englishwoman*, p. 6.
14 Betty Travitsky reminds us that Elizabeth Jocelin, for example, wished for her advice to be kept private. Travitsky, ed., *Mother's Advice Books*, p. xii.
15 Patricia Crawford, 'The Sucking Child', *Continuity and Change* 1 (1986), 23–54.
16 Chris Laoutaris, 'Speaking Stones: Memory and Maternity in Shakespeare's *Antony and Cleopatra*', in Kathryn M. Moncrieff and Kathryn E. McPherson, eds, *Performing Maternity in Early Modern England* (Aldershot: Ashgate, 2007), p. 155, quoting Elizabeth Hoby Russell, *A Way of Reconciliation of a good and learned man*, from *The Early Modern English Woman: A Facsimile of Essential Works*, series 1, Printed Writings 1500–1640, part 2, vol. 12, *Protestant Translators: Anne Lock Prowse and Elizabeth Russell*, ed. Elaine V. Beilin (Aldershot: Ashgate, 2001), sigs. A2-A3.
17 Valerie Wayne, 'Advice for Women from Mothers and Patriarchs', in *Women and Literature in Britain 1500–1700*, ed. Helen Wilcox (Cambridge: Cambridge University Press, 1996), p. 56.
18 Travitsky, *The Early Modern Englishwoman*, p. xii.
19 Suzanne Trill, writing on memorials to women, points out that each memorial 'claims that the woman concerned was an exception to her "sexe" emphasising in each case the extraordinariness of each woman', quoted by Becker, *Death and the Early Modern Englishwoman*, p. 120.

20 Catherine Belsey, *Shakespeare and the Loss of Eden* (Basingstoke: Macmillan, 1999), pp. xiv and xvi.
21 Quoted in Elaine Beilin, *Redeeming Eve: Women Writers of the English Renaissance* (Princeton and Oxford: Princeton University Press, 1987), p. 268. Facsimile in full in Travitsky, ed., *Mother's Advice Books*, The Epistle, sig. A2.
22 Travitsky in *Mother's Advice Books*, p. x.
23 Quoted by Beilin, *Redeeming Eve*, p. 268.
24 William Gouge, *Of Domesticall Duties, Eight Treatises* (London: printed by John Haviland for William Blayden, 1622), *The Sixth Treatise: The Duties of a Parent*, p. 581.
25 Quoted in Suzanne Trill, Kate Chedgzoy and Melanie Osbourne, eds, *Lay By Your Needles Ladies, Take the Pen: Writing Women in England, 1500–1700* (London: Arnold, 1997), p. 114. Hilda Smith identifies a change in attitudes to women over the Jacobean period: 'In the seventeenth century, tracts concerning women's nature took on a scurrilous tone during the early reign of James I and evinced Puritan overtones later on in the 1620s'. See Hilda L. Smith, 'Humanist Education and the Renaissance Concept of Woman' in Helen Wilcox, (ed.), *Women and Literature in Britain 1500–1700* (Cambridge: Cambridge University Press, 1996), p. 12.
26 Gouge, *Of Domesticall Duties*, p. 500.
27 Gouge, *Of Domesticall Duties*, p. 529.
28 Gouge admits that there was some resistance to his preaching on the necessary subordination of women, manifest by the 'squirming' and 'murmuring' amongst the female members of his congregation. See Tristan Marshall's review of Comensoli in *Renaissance Forum*, 4:1. www.hull.ac.uk/renforum/v4no1/marshall.htm, accessed 10 June 2009.
29 Ann Rosalind Jones, 'Nets and Bridles: Early Modern Conduct Books and Sixteenth-Century Women's Lyrics', in *The Ideology of Conflict*, eds. Nancy Armstrong and Leonard Tennenhouse (London and New York: Methuen, 1987), p. 59. Belsey, *Shakespeare and the Loss of Eden*, p. 127.

Section 4
30 Christine Luckyj, 'Disciplining the Mother in Seventeenth-Century English Puritanism', in Moncrief and McPherson, eds, *Performing Maternity in Early Modern England*, pp. 101–2.
31 Luckyj, 'Disciplining the Mother', p. 103.
32 See Wayne, 'Advice for Women from Mothers and Patriarchs', pp. 56–79.
33 Keith Wrightson, 'Infanticide in Early Seventeenth Century England', *Local Population Studies* 15 (1975), 10–21. Also Keith Thomas, 'The Puritans and Adultery', in Keith Thomas and Donald Pennington, eds, *Puritans and Revolutionaries* (Oxford: Clarendon Press, 1978), pp. 257–82.

34 C. Damme, 'The Worth of an Infant under Law', *Medical History* 22:1 (1978) 1–24.
35 See Patricia Crawford, 'The Sucking Child', p. 222, also Appendix I.
36 Elizabeth Clinton, Countess of Lincoln, *The Countess of Lincoln's Nursery* (Oxford: Harleian Misc, 1622), vol. 4, p. 25.
37 Thomas Heywood, *A Woman Killed with Kindness*, in *Renaissance Drama: An Anthology of Plays and Entertainments*, ed. Arthur F. Kinney (Oxford: Blackwell, 1999), pp. 287–326.
38 Becker, *Death and the Early Modern Englishwoman*, p. 33.
39 *A Woman Killed with Kindness*, ed. Kinney, p. 318, ll. 137–9.
40 Michael Bath, *Speaking Pictures: English Emblem Books and Renaissance Culture* (London: Longman, 1994), pp. 53–6.
41 Belsey, *Shakespeare and the Loss of Eden*, p. 13.
42 Suzanne Penuel, 'Male Mothering and *The Tempest*', in Moncrief and McPherson, eds, *Performing Maternity in Early Modern England*, p. 115.
43 See Corinne S. Abate, *Privacy, Domesticity and Women in Early Modern England* (Aldershot: Ashgate, 2003), p. 2.
44 See Stephen Orgel, ed., *The Winter's Tale*, The Oxford Shakespeare Series (Oxford: Clarendon Press, 1996), p. 23.
45 The link between this nostalgia for a boyish, untainted past, the desire for the uncomplicated replication of the father in the son, and the dangers of maternal corruption are brought together in Leontes' response to Hermione's concern that Leontes appears moved (1.2.149): 'Looking on the lines / Of my boy's face, methought I did recoil / Twenty-three years, and saw myself unbreech'd, / In my green velvet coat; my dagger muzzl'd / Lest it should bite its master, and so prove, / As ornaments oft do, too dangerous' (1.2.153–8).
46 Donna C. Woodford, 'Nursing and Influence in *Pandosto* and *The Winter's Tale*', in Moncrieff and McPherson, eds, *Performing Maternity in Early Modern England*, p. 188.
47 Woodford, 'Nursing and Influence in *Pandosto* and *The Winter's Tale*', pp. 192–3.
48 Katherine Park, *Secrets of Women: Gender, Generation and the Origins of Human Dissection* (New York: Zone Books, 2006), p. 154.
49 Katharine Hodgkin, 'Dionys Fitzherbert and the Anatomy of Madness', in *Voicing Women: Gender and Sexuality in Early Modern Writing*, eds Kate Chedgzoy, Melanie Hansen and Suzanne Trill (Edinburgh: Edinburgh University Press, 1998), p. 78.
50 Leontes denigrates Hermione's 'without-door form' as out of keeping with her real nature.
51 Park, *Secrets of Women*, p. 131.
52 The 'pelican in her piety' was popular as a symbol of charity or of Christ the Redeemer. The emblem features (along with sea monsters, which were to become William Gouge's favoured symbol of the ideal nursing mother) on a jacket reputed to be designed for Elizabeth I at

the Victoria and Albert Museum in London. See Rosemary Freeman, *English Emblem Books* (New York: Octagon Books, 1966), p. 95.
53 Gouge, *Of Domesticall Duties*, p. 517. Gouge admits that there are limits to how much a mother should endure and that God requires 'mercy and not sacrifice'.
54 King James, Edinburgh, 1598, in Claire McEachern, *The Poetics of English Nationhood 1590–1612* (Cambridge: Cambridge University Press, 1996), p. 22.
55 Gloria Olchowy quoting Erasmus in 'Murder as Birth in *Macbeth*', in Moncrief and McPherson, eds, *Performing Maternity in Early Modern England*, p. 201.
56 In Suzanne Penuel, 'Male Mothering and *The Tempest*' p. 127.
57 McEachern, The Poetics of English Nationhood, p. 22.
58 Victoria Kahn, '"The Duty to Love": Passion and Obligation in Early Modern Political Theory', *Representations*, 68 (1999), 87.
59 Christopher Durston, *James I* (London: Routledge, 1993), p. 12.
60 Lady Margaret Hoby wrote her diary as part of a programme of religious discipline, according to Betty Travitsky in *The Paradise of Women*, p. 85.
61 Aries and Duby, *History of Private Life* vol. III, p. 5.
62 Laoutaris, 'Speaking Stones', p. 152.
63 Theresa M. Krier, *Birth Passages: Maternity and Nostalgia, Antiquity to Shakespeare* (Ithaca: Cornell University Press, 2001), p. 238.
64 Laoutaris, 'Speaking Stones', p. 155.
65 Belsey, *Shakespeare and the Loss of Eden*, p. 112.
66 From Marina Warner, *Fantastic Metamorphoses, Other Worlds* (Oxford: Oxford University Press, 2002), p. 169.
67 Marina Warner *Phantasmagoria* (Oxford: Oxford University Press, 2006), pp. 3 and 28.
68 All quotations from the play are taken from The Arden Shakespeare, *The Winter's Tale*, ed. J. H. P. Pafford (London and New York: Routledge, 1989).
69 Gouge stresses that parenting should last for the life of the child, and has advice upon last words and the importance of wills in ensuring that the parents' influence is felt long after the physical death of the parent.
70 Laoutaris, 'Speaking Stones', pp. 160–1.
71 Park, *Secrets of Women*, p. 131.
72 Stephen Orgel points out that the play responds to the fact that 'there was a royal family at the centre of English society for the first time since the death of Henry VII'. Orgel discusses James's arrangements for a new tomb for his mother, asserting that James clearly understood 'the power of art to memorialise, reconcile and restore'. See Orgel's introduction to the Oxford Shakespeare edition of *The Winter's Tale* (Oxford: Clarendon Press, 1996), pp. 15 and 55.
73 Orgel, ed., *The Winter's Tale*, pp. 296 and 313.

74 Catherine Belsey, *The Subject of Tragedy* (London and New York: Methuen, 1985), p. 198. Belsey refers in particular to Act 3 Scene 1, in the Duchess's bedchamber, where the dramatist takes time to establish a sense of intimacy between Antonio, Cariola and the Duchess and thus renders the effect of Ferdinand's unexpected entrance (l. 69) even more shocking.
75 See also Robert Ornstein in *The Moral Vision of Jacobean Tragedy* (Madison and Milwaukee: University of Wisconsin Press, 1965), p. 141.
76 Eileen Allman, *Jacobean Revenge Tragedy and the Politics of Virtue* (London: Associated University Presses, 1999), p. 148. All references to *The Duchess of Malfi* are taken from the New Mermaid edition, ed. Elizabeth M. Brennan (London and Tonbridge: Ernest Benn Ltd., 1973), unless otherwise stated.
77 Dorinda Robbins, University of Kent, unpub. essay, 2002.
78 Elizabeth Jocelin in Travitsky, ed., *Mother's Advice Books*, Approbation, sig. A3.
79 Allman, *Jacobean Revenge Tragedy*, p. 176.
80 Allman, *Jacobean Revenge Tragedy*, p. 153.
81 See 1.4, ll. 23 and 26. Lisa Hopkins describes Bosola's fascination with 'specifically female mysteries' and quotes Celia Daileader on Bosola's '"violent fantasy of visual penetration"'. Lisa Hopkins, 'With the Skin Side Inside: The Interiors of *The Duchess of Malfi*', in Abate, *Privacy, Domesticity and Women*, p. 23.
82 Allman, *Jacobean Revenge Tragedy*, p. 20.
83 Jacqueline Pearson, *Tragedy and Tragicomedy in the Plays of John Webster* (Manchester: Manchester University Press, 1980), p. 61.
84 Michael Neill, *Issues of Death: Mortality and Identity in English Renaissance Tragedy* (Oxford: Clarendon Press, 1997), p. 340.
85 Laoutaris, 'Speaking Stones', p. 161.
86 Dympna Callaghan, *Women and Gender in Renaissance Tragedy* (Hemel Hempstead: Harvester Wheatsheaf, 1989), p. 153.
87 Neill, *Issues of Death*, pp. 352 and 332.
88 Laoutaris, 'Speaking Stones', p. 155, quoting Elizabeth Hoby Russell, *A Way of Reconciliation of a good and learned man*, from *The Early Modern English Woman: A Facsimile of Essential Works*, series 1, Printed Writings 1500–1640, part 2, vol. 12, *Protestant Translators: Anne Lock Prowse and Elizabeth Russell*, ed. Elaine V. Beilin (Aldershot: Ashgate 2001), sigs. A2-A3.
89 Becker, *Death and the Early Modern Englishwoman*, p. 193.
90 Krier describing Hermione, *Birth Passages*, p. 248.

8

Conclusion

Hir pondrous speech, hir passion and hir paine,
Hir pleasing stile shall be admir'd like where.
The fruitful flowing of hir loftie braine
Doth now bewray a mothers matchlesse care¹
        Preface to Elizabeth Grymestone's *Miscellanea*
        Meditations Memoratives

The critic Jean Howard has warned against the assumption 'that theatrical representations have an ideological significance which is fixed and unchanging or which is unaffected by the conditions in which the representations are produced and consumed'.² This book has argued for the importance of motherhood in the drama of early modern England and has attested to the mother's value both as a signifier of unchanging values and as a figure whose representation readily responds to the demands of ideological and political change. The approach has been thematic: to discover how far genre and convention influence representation; and teleological: to test the potential of the mother figure to change over time in response to shifts in cultural and social values. While the aim was never to describe a steady change over the hundred years from the first quarter of the sixteenth century, this book has argued that the religious conflict of the English Reformation and its attendant issues of national identity created a complex series of dramatic possibilities for the mother figure which allowed her to function as a religious and political emblem that developed in complexity and dramatic value in the period. Elizabethan and Jacobean dramatisations of motherhood accommodated significant shifts in emphasis as English culture responded to the availability of classical and European texts and to increasing pressure from Protestant and later Puritan ideas as they gradually became mainstream. The period covered by this book ends at a time when for a number of possible reasons the mother figure appears to become less popular as a subject of dramatic interest.

Patrick Collinson has argued that there was a significant shift from early radicalism to later conservatism in Protestant discourse, and that this discourse became less popular as time passed:

> In some senses English Protestantism regressed, becoming less, not more, popular as we proceed from the mid sixteenth century to the early seventeenth, and from a time when the Reformation was associated with novelty, youth, insubordination and iconoclasm (when indeed it was still a protest) to the period of its middle age, when it was more obviously associated with the maintenance of the status quo than with subversion, with middle aged if not middle class preoccupations and when its attack on traditional culture met with widespread and popular resistance.[3]

Collinson links this with an 'inwardly and outwardly more repressive' approach that abhorred the emblematic, quoting a popular Puritan text from the Homilies: 'the seeking out of images is the beginning of whoredom'.[4] This perhaps prompted a turning away from the figurative usage of the mother and a shift towards a focus upon her personal value and meaning for her family. Elaine Beilin finds a similar conservatism in later early modern discourses including conduct literature and advice books written by women. She sees in *The Countess of Lincoln's Nursery* and *The Mother's Counsell* (entered in 1623) a return of focus to the domestic sphere that signals a regressive trend in women's writing:

> In those hundred years [between 1524 and 1623] appeared more translations, varied female personae and experiments with genre, style and voice as women steadily strove to establish a legitimate place for their own literary experience. If this constitutes a literary renaissance for women, it does not conform to that of masculine culture, nor does it extend much beyond the death of James I.[5]

Ann Rosalind Jones suggests that a backlash against women's religious testifying forced a retreat away from a public role. And Valerie Wayne contends that women writers became increasingly tentative and conservative, citing writers like Elizabeth Jocelin, of whom she observes, 'her admonitions show little change from Vives 100 years earlier'.[6]

In the theatre a similar new conservatism in the representation of women was noted by Juliet Dusinberre, who in 1975 wrote a more optimistic account of the representation of women in early modern drama than most critics have since allowed. Dusinberre discerned a positive response in the drama to the Puritan celebration of the wife/mother's status as 'helpmeet' and thought that this confirmed an enhanced status for Puritan women that was reflected in the drama. Yet she charts a change in attitude to the representation of women on the stage in the later Jacobean period – a shift she links to a gradual Puritan desertion of the theatre in response to religious and political difference with the Stuarts.[7] It is significant that, as one of the earliest and most persuasive advocates of the argument that the representation of women became increasingly liberal, Dusinberre acknowledges that that liberality was not sustained.

The argument that change was affected by politics is substantiated in a different context by Margot Heinemann, who refers to Glynn Wickham's suggestion that decadence in drama was attributable to 'the operation of censorship that prevented the serious treatment of political, moral and religious issues', thereby closing down the opportunity to figure political concerns through theatrical representation.[8] For Heinemann, the Jacobean theatre found itself operating in the face of developing tensions between court and city on 'the aristocratic and intellectual side of the revolt against the corruption and oppression of Stuart absolutism' and expressed those tensions through changes in the drama itself.[9] Jerzy Limon presses this further by suggesting that in the late Jacobean period, 'for the first time, dramatic texts were disseminated on a wide scale for basically political purposes'.[10] The mother figure, it has been widely argued, found little function in this increasingly politicised drama influenced by a monarch who had rejected the mother/state analogy for a more congenial model of benign paternalism.

However, it was inevitable that motherhood retained its potency at the heart of political and religious conflict in other discourses and cultural products. In a fascinating study, Christina Luckyj discusses two texts published in 1627 that purport to express a mother's voice: *The Answere of a Mother unto hir seduced sonnes letter* and an expanded version entitled *A Mothers Teares over hir seduced sonne*. She argues that both texts use motherhood to figure and articulate the conflict felt by a growing number of Puritans who 'identified with their national Church even as they felt themselves increasingly excluded from and opposed to its growing anti-Calvinist tendencies'.[11] As Luckyj shows, both texts take trouble to link themselves to published texts authored by women, quoting *A Mothers Teares*: 'There are two bookes that goe under a mothers name; A Mothers Blessing; A Mothers Legacie: now thou seest a Mothers Teares'. Although, Luckyj, according to 'real mothers' advice books are being appropriated both for their commercial value and their more straightforward English Puritanism', she warns that 'They are not being invoked as straightforward exemplars of maternal authority', which might link the grieving mother somewhat too closely to traditional Catholic analogy.[12] Instead *A Mothers Teares* revives the conventional grieving mother as patriarchal metaphor: 'It carefully constructs both a good Mother who perpetuates patriarchal hierarchies and an alternate, demonic Mother who absorbs the inherently negative implications of maternal power and disorder'. But there is also a concern about a resurgence of Catholicism, which may be linked specifically to increasing concern about motives at court alongside a more general discomfiture, so that the mother also explicitly figures a beleaguered Protestant nation: 'As a representative of the English Church confronting a Catholic assault, the Mother is as feeble as many in England perceived their country to be in responding to the Papist threat at home and abroad'.[13]

Chris Laoutaris warns against a reading of the proliferation of monuments to mothers as 'a resolutely proto-feminist utterance'. Rather, Laoutaris concludes, 'it allowed the rising classes, in an age of increased social mobility, to base the honour and nobility which they claimed on more than the precarious accoutrements of heraldry'.[14] Thus the mother figures an aspiration to political consolidation, her continued monumental presence restating the rights and demands of the family that she represents. Luckyj meanwhile concludes that, 'while *The Answere of a Mother* and *A Mother's Teares* are anonymous texts that may or may not have been written by women, their performance of motherhood reveals that ... maternity was a potentially explosive site of ideological struggle for English Puritans in the 1620s'.[15] It seems that what Patrick Collinson once termed the 'turning inward' of later Protestantism has its analogy in representations of motherhood, so that the mother's function became once again symbolic of conflict at the heart of the state and church that resonated at local and national levels as the Protestant nation struggled to hold the two together.[16] Frances Dolan's point that 'early modern English culture fiercely debated the extent and value of maternal authority' in seventeenth century England, quoted by Luckyj, attests to the mother's continued capacity to configure and to allegorise, to complicate and to provoke.[17] As England began to divide against itself with increasing complexity, the mother figure remained fundamentally important as an adaptable and yet consistent signifier.

Notes

1. Simon Grahame, 'To the Authour', prefacing Elizabeth Grymeston, *Miscellanea Meditations Memoratives* (London, 1604) in Betty Travitsky, ed., *Mother's Advice Books*, in *The Early Modern Englishwoman* series 1, part 2, vol. 8 (Aldershot: Ashgate, 2001).
2. Jean E. Howard, *The Stage and Social Struggle in Early Modern England* (London: Routledge, 1994), p. 83.
3. Patrick Collinson, *From Iconoclasm to Iconophobia* (Reading: University of Reading, 1986), p. 5.
4. Collinson, From Iconoclasm to Iconophobia, pp. 6 and 35.
5. E. V. Beilin, *Redeeming Eve: Women Writers of the English Renaissance* (Princeton: Princeton University Press, 1987), p. xxiii.
6. Ann Rosalind Jones, 'Nets and Bridles: Early Modern Conduct Books and Sixteenth-Century Women's lyrics', in *The Ideology of Conflict*, eds Nancy Armstrong and Leonard Tennenhouse (New York: Methuen, 1987), p. 60.
7. Juliet Dusinberre, *Shakespeare and the Nature of Women* (London: Macmillan, 1975), p. 15.
8. Margot Heinemann, *Puritanism and Theatre* (Cambridge: Cambridge University Press, 1980), p. 38.
9. Heinemann, *Puritanism and Theatre*, p. 173.
10. Jerzy Limon, *Dangerous Matter: English Drama and Politics 1623/24* (Cambridge: Cambridge University Press, 1986), p. 1.
11. Christine Luckyj, 'Disciplining the Mother in Seventeenth-Century English Puritanism' in Kathryn M. Moncrief and Kathryn E. McPherson, eds, *Performing Maternity in Early Modern England* (Aldershot: Ashgate, 2007), p. 105.
12. Luckyj, 'Disciplining the Mother in Seventeenth-Century English Puritanism', p. 110.
13. Luckyj, 'Disciplining the Mother in Seventeenth-Century English Puritanism', p. 105.
14. Chris Laoutaris, 'Speaking Stones: Memory and Maternity in Shakespeare's *Antony and Cleopatra*', in Moncrief and McPherson, eds, *Performing Maternity in Early Modern England*, p. 166.
15. Luckyj, 'Disciplining the Mother in Seventeenth-Century English Puritanism', p. 114.

16 Patrick Collinson, *From Iconoclasm to Iconophobia* (Stenton Lecture, 1985) (Reading: University of Reading, 1986); *The Birthpangs of Protestant England* (London: Macmillan, 1988); 'The Elizabethan Church and the New Religion' in Christopher Haigh (ed.), *The Reign of Elizabeth I*, (London: Macmillan, 1987).
17 Luckyj, 'Disciplining the Mother in Seventeenth-Century English Puritanism', p. 108.

Bibliography

Abate, C. S., *Privacy, Domesticity and Women in Early Modern England* (Aldershot: Ashgate, 2003).
Adams, H. H., *English Domestic or, Homiletic Tragedy 1575–1642* (New York: Blom, 1965).
Adelman, J., *Suffocating Mothers: Fantasies of Maternal Origin in Shakespeare's Plays* (London: Routledge, 1992).
Aeschylus, *The Oresteia*, trans. Robert Fagles (London: Wildwood House, 1976).
Agamben, G., *Stanzas: Word and Phantasm in Western Culture*, trans. R. L. Martinez (Minneapolis and London: University of Minnesota Press, 1993).
Agamben, G., *The Man Without Content*, trans. G. Albert (Stanford: Stanford University Press, 1999).
Allman, E., *Jacobean Revenge Tragedy and the Politics of Virtue* (London: Associated University Presses, 1999).
Amusson, S. D., 'Gender, Family and the Social Order' in A. Fletcher and J. Stevenson, eds, *Order and Disorder in Early Modern England* (Cambridge: Cambridge University Press, 1985).
Anderson, M., *Approaches to the History of the Western Family 1500–1914* (London and Basingstoke: Macmillan, 1984).
Anon., 'New Custom', in *A Selection of Old English Plays Originally Published by Robert Dodsley in the Year 1744*, 4th edn (London: Reeves and Turner, 1876).
Anon., *A Warning for Fair Women*, ed. C. D. Cannon (The Hague: Mouton, 1975).
Anon., *The Troublesome Raigne of John, King of England*, ed. J. W. Sider (London: Garland, 1979).
Anon., *A Yorkshire Tragedy*, eds A. C. Cawley and B. Gaines (Manchester: Manchester University Press, 1986).
Apter, E., *Feminising the Fetish: Psychoanalysis and Narrative Obsession in Turn-of-the-Century France* (Ithaca and London: Cornell University Press, 1991).
Aries, P. and Duby, G. (gen. eds), *A History of Private Life, Vol. II: Revelations of the Medieval World*, ed. G. Duby, trans. A. Goldhammer (London: Belknap, 1989).

Aries, P. and Duby, G. (gen. eds), *A History of Private Life, Vol. III: Passions of the Renaissance*, ed. R. Chartier, trans. A. Goldhammer (London, Belknap, 1989).
Armstrong, I., 'So What's All This About the Mother's Body? The Aesthetic, Gender and the Polis', *Women: A Cultural Review*, 4:2 (1993), 172–87.
Armstrong, N. and Tennenhouse, L., eds, *The Ideology of Conduct* (London and New York: Methuen, 1987).
Astell, A. W., *The Song of Songs in the Middle Ages* (Ithaca: Cornell University Press, 1990).
Auerbach, E., *Mimesis* (Princeton: Princeton University Press, 1953).
Axton, M., *The Queen's Two Bodies: Drama and the Elizabethan Succession* (London: Royal Historical Society, 1977).
Axton, R., *European Drama of the Early Middle Ages* (London: Hutchinson, 1974).
Badinter, E., *The Myth of Motherhood: An Historical View of the Maternal Instinct*, trans. R. DeGaris (London: Souvenir Press, 1981).
Baker, A. R. H., 'Introduction: On Ideology and Landscape' in A. Baker and G. Biger, eds, *Ideology and Landscape in Historical Perspective*, Cambridge Studies in Historical Geography (Cambridge: Cambridge University Press, 1992).
Baker House, S., 'Literature, Drama and Politics' in D. MacCulloch, ed., *The Reign of Henry VIII: Politics, Policy and Piety*, (London: Macmillan, 1995).
Baldwin, T. W., *William Shakespeare's Small Latin and Less Greek* (Urbana: University of Illinois Press, 1944).
Ballantyne, J. W., 'The Byrthe of Mankynde – Its Authors and Editions', *Journal of Obstetrics and Gynaecology of the British Empire*, 10:4 (1906), 297–325.
Ballantyne, J. W., 'The Byrthe of Mankynde': The Text, *Journal of Obstetrics and Gynaecology of the British Empire*, 12:3 (1907), 175–94.
Bamber, L., *Comic Women, Tragic Men: A Study of Gender and Genre in Shakespeare* (Stanford: Stanford University Press, 1982).
Barthes, R., *Image, Music, Text*, trans. S. Heath (London: Flamingo, 1984).
Baskins, C. L., 'Griselda, or the Renaissance Bride Stripped Bare by her Bachelor in Tuscan Cassone Painting', *Stanford Italian Review*, 10:2 (1991), 153–75.
Bath, M., *Speaking Pictures: English Emblem Books and Renaissance Culture* (London and New York: Longman, 1994).
Beadle, R., *The Cambridge Companion to Medieval English Theatre* (Cambridge: Cambridge University Press, 1994).
Becker, L. M., *Death and the Early Modern Englishwoman* (Aldershot: Ashgate, 2003).
Beckwith, S., *Christ's Body: Identity, Culture and Society in Late Medieval Writings* (London: Routledge, 1993).
Beilin, E., *Redeeming Eve: Women Writers of the English Renaissance* (Princeton: Princeton University Press, 1987).

Beilin, E., ed., *The Early Modern English Woman: A Facsimile of Essential Works*, series 1, *Printed Writings 1500–1640*, part 2, vol. 12, *Protestant Translators: Anne Lock Prowse and Elizabeth Russell* (Aldershot: Ashgate, 2001).
Belsey, C., *The Subject of Tragedy* (London: Methuen, 1985).
Belsey, C., *Shakespeare and the Loss of Eden: The Construction of Family Values in Early Modern Culture* (Basingstoke: Macmillan, 1999).
Bendelow, G. and Williams, S. J., eds, *Emotions in Social Life: Critical Themes and Contemporary Issues* (London: Routledge, 1998).
Benjamin, A. and Osborne, P., *Walter Benjamin's Philosophy* (London: Routledge, 1994).
Berkowitz, D. S., *Humanist Scholarship and Public Order: Two Tracts Against the Pilgrimage of Grace by Sir Richard Morison* (Washington: Folger Shakespeare Library, 1984).
Bettelheim, B., *The Uses of Enchantment: The Meaning and Importance of Fairy Tales* (London: Penguin, 1976).
Bevington, D., *From Mankynd to Marlowe* (Cambridge, Mass.: Harvard University Press, 1962).
Bevington, D., *Tudor Drama and Politics* (Cambridge, Mass.: Harvard University Press, 1968).
Binns, J. W., 'Seneca and Neo-Latin Tragedy in England', in C. D. N. Costa, ed., *Seneca* (London: Routledge and Kegan Paul, 1974).
Boas, F. S., *An Introduction to Tudor Drama* (Oxford: Clarendon Press, 1933).
Boccaccio, G., *The Decameron*, trans. Richard Aldington, vol 2 (London: Folio Society, 1957).
Bradley, A. C., *Shakespearean Tragedy* (London: Macmillan, 1904).
Brant, C. and Purkiss, D., eds, *Women, Texts and Histories 1575–1760* (London: Routledge, 1992).
Bristol, M. D. and Marotti, A. F., eds, *Print, Manuscript, Performance: The Changing Relations of the Media in Early Modern England* (Columbus: Ohio State University Press, 2000).
Brooke, P., *Reading for the Plot* (Oxford: Clarendon Press, 1984).
Bryan, W. F. and Dempster, G., eds, *Sources and Analogues of Chaucer's Canterbury Tales* (Chicago: Chicago University Press, 1941).
Buci-Glucksmann, C., *Baroque Reason: The Aesthetics of Modernity*, trans. P. Camiller (London: Sage, 1994).
Bullough, G., *Narrative and Dramatic Sources of Shakespeare, Vol. III: Early English History Plays* (London: Routledge and Kegan Paul, 1960).
Bynum, C. W., *Jesus as Mother: Studies in the Spirituality of the Higher Middle Ages* (Berkeley: University of California Press, 1982).
Byrne, M. St. Clare, ed., *The Lisle Letters: An Abridgement* (London: Secker and Warburg, 1983).
Callaghan, D., *Women and Gender in Renaissance Tragedy* (Hemel Hempstead: Harvester Wheatsheaf, 1989).
Camden, W., *Annales* (London, 1625).
Cawley, A. C., ed., *Everyman and Medieval Miracle Plays* (London: Dent, 1990).

Caygill, H., 'Benjamin, Heidegger and the Destruction of Tradition' in A. Benjamin and P. Osborne, eds, *Walter Benjamin's Philosophy* (London: Routledge, 1994).
Chambers, Sir E. K., *The Elizabethan Stage*, vols 1, 2, 3 and 4 (Oxford: Clarendon Press, 1974).
Chambers, Sir E. K., *The Medieaval Stage*, vol. 2 (London: Oxford University Press, 1903).
Chappell, W., ed., *The Roxburghe Ballads*, 9 vols (London: The Ballad Society, 1869).
Charnes, L., ' "So Unsecret Ourselves": Notorious Identity and the Material Subject in Shakespeare's Troilus and Cressida', *Shakespeare Quarterly*, 40 (1989), 413–40.
Chartier, R. (ed.), *A History of Private Life, Vol. III: Passions of the Renaissance* (gen. eds P. Aries, and G. Duby), trans. A. Goldhammer London: Belknap, 1989).
Chaucer, G., *The Clerk's Prologue and Tale*, ed. J. Winny (Cambridge: Cambridge University Press, 1966).
Chaucer, G., *Canterbury Tales*, ed. A. C. Cawley (London: J. M. Dent and Sons Ltd., 1978).
Church of England Homilies (1562) (London: Society for Promoting Christian Knowledge, 1908).
Church of England, *Private Prayers put forth by Authority during the Reign of Queen Elizabeth* (Cambridge: Cambridge University Press, 1851).
Cleaver, R., *A Godlie Forme of Household Government* (1589) (London, 1600).
Clemen, W., *English Tragedy before Shakespeare* (London: Methuen, 1967).
Clinton, E., Countess of Lincoln, *The Countess of Lincoln's Nursery* (Harleian Misc. vol. 4, Oxford, 1622).
Cole, D., *Suffering and Evil in the Plays of Christopher Marlowe* (Princeton: Princeton University Press, 1962).
Collinson, P., 'The Elizabethan Church and the New Religion' in C. Haigh, ed., *The Reign of Elizabeth I*, (London: Macmillan, 1987).
Collinson, P., *From Iconoclasm to Iconophobia* (Stenton Lecture 1985), (Reading: University of Reading, 1986).
Collinson, P., *The Birthpangs of Protestant England* (London: Macmillan, 1988).
Comensoli, V., *'Household Business': Domestic Plays of Early Modern England* (Toronto: University of Toronto Press, 1996).
Connell, D., *Sir Philip Sidney: The Maker's Mind* (Oxford: Clarendon Press, 1977).
Costa, C. D. N., ed., *Seneca* (London: Routledge and Kegan Paul, 1974).
Cox, J. D., *Shakespeare and the Dramaturgy of Power* (Princeton: Princeton University Press, 1989).
Craik T. W., ed., *The Revels History of Drama in English*, vol. 2 (London: Methuen, 1980).

Crawford, P., 'The Sucking Child', *Continuity and Change*, 1 (1986) 23–54.
Cunliffe, J. W., *The Complete Works of George Gascoigne*, vol. 1 (Cambridge: Cambridge University Press, 1907).
Danson, L., *Shakespeare's Dramatic Genres*, Oxford Shakespeare Topics (Oxford: Oxford University Press, 2000).
Davenport, E., 'The Representation of Robin Hood in Elizabethan Drama: George a Greene and Edward I' in L. Potter, ed., *Playing Robin Hood: The Legend in Performance* (London: Associated University Presses, 1998).
Davenport, W. A., *Fifteenth-century English Drama* (Cambridge: D. S. Brewer, 1984).
Davidson, C., *Visualising the Moral Life* (New York: AMS Press, 1989).
Davies, R. T., *Medieval English Lyrics* (London: Faber, 1963).
Davies, R. T., *The Corpus Christi Plays of the Middle Ages* (London: Faber, 1972).
Dekker, T., Chettle, H. and Haughton, W., *Patient Grissil: A Comedy*, repr. from the black letter edn of 1603 (London: Shakespeare Society, 1841).
Doane, J. and Hodges, D., *From Klein to Kristeva: Psychoanalytic Feminism and the Search for the 'Good Enough' Mother* (Ann Arbor: University of Michigan Press, 1992).
Dod, J. and Cleaver, R., *A Godlie Forme of Houeholde Government: For the ordering of private families according to the direction of God's word* (London, 1561).
Dodds, M. H., 'Early Political Plays', *The Library*, series 3, vol. 4 (1913).
Dodsley, R., and Hazlitt, W. C., eds, *A Selection of Old English Plays*, 4th edn (London: Reeves and Turner, 1876).
Dollimore, J., *Radical Tragedy: Religion, Ideology and Power in the Drama of Shakespeare and his Contemporaries* (Brighton: Harvester, 1984).
Donne, J., 'Deaths Duell' in *Selected Prose*, ed. N. Rhodes (Harmondsworth: Penguin, 1987).
Doran, M., *Endeavours of Art* (London: Wisconsin University Press, 1954).
Drakakis, J., ed., *Antony and Cleopatra*, New Casebooks (London: Macmillan, 1994).
Drakakis, J., ed., *Shakespearean Tragedy* (London: Longman, 1992).
Duby, G. (ed.), *A History of Private Life, Vol. II: Revelations of the Medieval World* (gen. eds P. Aries and G. Duby), trans. A. Goldhammer (London: Belknap Press, 1989).
Duckworth, G., ed., *The Complete Roman Drama* (New York: Random House, 1942).
Dugdale, G., *A true discourse of the practises of Elizabeth Caldwell, Ma: Ieffrey Bownd, Isabell Hill widow, and George Ferneley, on the parson of Ma: Thomas Caldwell, in the County of Chester, to have murdered and poisoned him, with diuerse others* (London: James Roberts, 1604).
Durston, C., *James I* (London: Routledge, 1993).
Dusinberre, J., *Shakespeare and the Nature of Women* (London: Macmillan, 1975).
Eccles, A., *Obstetrics and Gynaecology in Tudor and Stuart England* (London: Croom Helm, 1982).

Eisenstein, E., *The Printing Press as an Agent of Change*, vols 1 and 2 (Cambridge: Cambridge University Press, 1979).
Eliot, T. S., *The Sacred Wood: Essays on Poetry and Criticism* (London: Methuen, 1920).
Eliot, T. S., 'Coriolan II', in *Collected Poems 1909–1967* (London: Faber & Faber, 1974).
Erasmus, 'The New Mother' (1526, Basel), in *The Colloquies of Erasmus*, trans. C. R. Thompson (Chicago: University of Chicago Press, 1965).
Ewbank, I.-S., 'George Peele and the Importance of Spectacle', in E. G. Hubbard, ed., *The Elizabethan Theatre V* (London: Macmillan, 1975).
Farmer, J. S. (ed.), *Anonymous Plays, Comprising Jack Juggler, King Darius, Gammer Gurton's Needle, New Custom, Trial of Treasure* (Guildford: Charles W. Traylen, 1966).
Farmer, J. S., *Recently Recovered 'Lost' Tudor Plays, With Some Others* (Guildford: Charles W. Traylen, 1966).
Farnham, W., *The Medieval Heritage of Elizabethan Tragedy* (Oxford: Basil Blackwell, 1970).
Feldman, S. D., *The Morality-Patterned Comedy of the Renaissance* (The Hague: Mouton, 1970).
Ferguson, M. W., Quilligan, M. and Vickers, N. S., eds, *Rewriting the Renaissance: The Discourses of Sexual Difference in Early Modern Europe* (Chicago: University of Chicago Press, 1986).
Fildes, V., *Wet Nursing: A History from Antiquity to the Present* (Oxford: Basil Blackwell, 1988).
Findlay, A., *Playing Spaces in early Women's Drama* (Cambridge: Cambridge University Press, 2006).
Finke, L. A., 'Painting Women: Images of Feminity in Jacobean Tragedy', *Theatre Quarterly*, 36:3 (Oct. 1984).
Fleische, M. H., *Iconography of the English History Play* (Salzburg: Universität Salzburg, Institut für Englische Sprache and Literatur, 1974).
Foucault, M., *The History of Sexuality* (Harmondsworth: Penguin, 1976).
Foxe, J., *Acts and Monuments*, vol. 6 (London: Burnside and Seeley, 1846).
Freeman, R., *English Emblem Books* (New York: Octagon Books, 1966).
French, M., 'Chaste Constancy in Hamlet', in M. Coyle, ed., *William Shakespeare, Hamlet*, (London: Macmillan, 1992).
Freud, S., *The Interpretation of Dreams*, trans. J. Strachey, The Penguin Freud Library vol. 4 (Harmondsworth: Penguin, 1985).
Gardiner, H. C., *Mysteries' End: An Investigation into the Last Days of the Medieval Religious Stage* (Hamden, Conn.: Archon Books, 1967).
Garner, S. N., Kahane, C. and Sprengnether, M., eds, *The Mother Tongue: Essays in Feminist Psychoanalytic Interpretation* (Ithaca and London: Cornell University Press, 1985).
Gascoigne, G. and Kinwelmarshe, W., *Jocasta* in *The Complete Works of George Gascoigne*, vol. 1, ed. J. W. Cunliffe (Cambridge: Cambridge University Press, 1907).

Gebert, C., *An Anthology of Elizabethan Dedications and Prefaces* (New York: Russell and Russell, 1996).
Gibson, G. McMurray, *The Theatre of Devotion: East Anglian Drama and Society in the Late Middle Ages* (Chicago: University of Chicago Press, 1989).
Gittings, C., *Death, Burial and the Individual in Early Modern England* (London: Croom Helm, 2001).
Glenister, T. W., 'Facts, Fantasies and Foetuses', *Medical History*, 8 (1964), 15–30.
Gold, B. K. M., Allen, P. and Platter, C., *Sex and Gender in Medieval and Renaissance Texts: The Latin Tradition* (Albany: State University of New York Press, 1997).
Golden, L., *Aristotle's Poetics: A Translation and Commentary for Students of Literature*, with a commentary by O. B. Hardison (Englewood Cliffs, NJ: Prentice Hall, 1968).
Gouge, W., *Of Domesticall Duties, Eight Treatises* (London: John Haviland for Willian Blayden, 1622).
Grantley, D. and Taunton, N., eds, *The Body in Late Medieval and Early Modern Culture* (Aldershot: Ashgate, 2000).
Greg, W. W., ed., *Respublica* (London: Early English Texts Society, 1952).
Griswold, W., *Renaissance Revivals: City Comedy and Revenge Tragedy in the London Theatre 1576–1980* (Chicago and London: University of Chicago Press, 1986).
Guillemeau, J., *The Happy Deliverie of Women* (London, 1612).
Hackett, H., *Virgin Mother, Maiden Queen: Elizabeth I and the Cult of the Virgin Mary* (London: Macmillan, 1995).
Haigh, C., *English Reformations: Religion, Politics and Society under the Tudors* (Oxford: Clarendon Press, 1993).
Haigh, C., ed., *The Reign of Elizabeth I* (London: Macmillan, 1987).
Halliwell, J. O., ed., *Ludus Coventriae* (London: Shakespeare Society, 1841).
Halliwell, S., *The Poetics of Aristotle: Translation and Commentary* (London: Duckworth, 1987).
Happé, P., *English Drama before Shakespeare* (London: Longman, 1999).
Happé, P., ed., *The Complete Plays of John Bale*, vol. 1 (Cambridge: Cambridge University Press, 1985).
Happé, P., ed., *English Mystery Plays* (Harmondsworth: Penguin, 1985).
Harbage, A., *Annals of English Drama 975–1700* (London: Methuen, 1964).
Harré, R. and Gerrod Parrott, W., eds, *The Emotions: Social, Cultural and Biological Dimensions* (London: Sage, 1996).
Hattaway, M., *Elizabethan Popular Theatre* (London: Routledge, 1982).
Heelas, P., 'Emotion Talk across Cultures' in R. Harré and W. Gerrod Parrott, eds, *The Emotions: Social, Cultural and Biological Dimensions* (London: Sage, 1996).
Heinemann, M., *Puritanism and Theatre: Thomas Middleton and Oppositional Drama under the Stuarts* (Cambridge: Cambridge University Press, 1980).

Heisch, A., 'Queen Elizabeth and the Persistence of Patriarchy', *Feminist Review*, 4 (1980), 45–56.
Herrnstein Smith, B., 'Narrative Versions, Narrative Theories' in W. J. T. Mitchell, ed., *On Narrative* (Chicago: University of Chicago Press, 1981).
Hillman, R., 'Out of Their Classical Depth: From Pathos to Bathos in Early English Tragedy, or, The Comedy of Terrors', in *Thêta 7: Théâtre Tudor* (2007), 17–38.
Hobby, E., ed., *The Midwives Book, or the Whole Art of Midwifry Discovered: Jane Sharp* (Oxford: Oxford University Press, 1999).
Hobby, E., ed., *The Birth of Mankind, Otherwise Named The Women's Book* (Aldershot: Ashgate, 2008).
Hoby, M., *The Diary of Lady Margaret Hoby*, ed. Dorothy M. Meads (London: Routledge, 1930).
Hoffer, P. C. and Hull, N. E. H., *Murdering Mothers: Infanticide in England and New England 1558–1803* (New York: New York University Press, 1984).
Holderness, G. and Loughrey, B., *The Tragicall Historie of Hamlet Prince of Denmarke* (Hemel Hempstead: Harvester, 1992).
Home, D. H., *The Life and Minor Works of George Peele* (New Haven: Yale University Press, 1952).
Hook, F. S., *The Dramatic Works of George Peele* (New Haven and London: Yale University Press, 1961).
Hopkins, L., 'With the Skin Side Inside: The Interiors of The Duchess of Malfi', in Corinne S. Abate, ed., *Privacy, Domesticity and Women in Early Modern England* (Aldershot: Ashgate, 2003).
Horstmann, C., ed., *The Lives of Women Saints of our Countrie of England* (London: Early English Texts Society, 1886).
Howard, J. E. and Rackin, P., *Engendering a Nation: A Feminist Account of Shakespeare's English Histories* (London: Routledge, 1997).
Howard, Jean E., *The Stage and Social Struggle in Early Modern England* (London and New York: Routledge, 1994).
Hussey, M., ed., *The Chester Cycle of Mystery Plays* (London: Heinemann, 1979).
Ingram, M., *Church Courts, Sex and Marriage in England, 1570–1640* (Cambridge: Cambridge University Press, 1987).
Jardine, L., *Still Harping on Daughters: Women and Drama in the Age of Shakespeare* (Brighton: Harvester, 1983).
Jed, S., *Chaste Thinking: The Rape of Lucretia and the Birth of Humanism* (Indiana: Indiana University Press, 1989).
Jones, A. R., 'Nets and Bridles: Early Modern Conduct Books and Sixteenth-Century Women's Lyrics', in N. Armstrong and L. Tennenhouse, eds, *The Ideology of Conduct* (New York: Metheun, 1987).
Jones, M., 'Early Moral Plays and the Earliest Secular Drama' in L. Potter, ed., *The Revels History of Drama in English*, vol. 1 (London: Methuen, 1983).

Julian of Norwich, *Revelations of Divine Love*, trans. C. Wolters (Harmondsworth: Penguin, 1966).
Kahn, C., 'The Absent Mother in King Lear', in K. Ryan, ed., *King Lear*, New Casebooks (London: Macmillan, 1993).
Kahn, C., *Man's Estate: Masculine Identity in Shakespeare* (Berkeley: University of California Press, 1981).
Kahn, C., *Roman Shakespeare: Warriors, Wounds and Women* (London: Routledge, 1997).
Kahn, V., ' "The Duty to Love": Passion and Obligation in Early Modern Political Theory', *Representations*, 68 (1999), 92–113.
Kaplan, E. A., *Motherhood and Representation* (London: Routledge, 1992).
Kay, S. 'Women's Body of Knowledge: Epistemology and Misogyny in the Romance of the Rose' in S. Kay and M. Rubin, eds, *Framing Medieval Bodies*, (Manchester: Manchester University Press, 1994).
Kehler, D., 'The First Quarto of *Hamlet*: Reforming Widow Gertred', *Shakespeare Quarterly*, 46:4 (1995), 398–413.
Kempe, M., *The Book of Margery Kempe*, trans. B. A. Windeatt (Harmondsworth: Penguin, 1985).
Kent, J. R., 'Attitudes of Members of the House of Commons to the Regulation of "Personal Conduct" in Late Elizabethan and Early Stuart England', *Bulletin of the Institute of Historical Research*, 46 (1973), 46–71.
Keyishian, H., 'Griselda on the Elizabethan Stage', *Studies in English Literature 1500–1900*, 16:2 (spring 1976), 253–61.
King, J. N., *Tudor Royal Iconography* (Princeton: Princeton University Press, 1989).
King, P. M., 'Morality Plays' in R. Beadle, ed., *The Cambridge Companion to Medieval English Theatre* (Cambridge: Cambridge University Press, 1994).
Kinney, A. F., ed., *Renaissance Drama: An Anthology of Plays and Entertainments* (Oxford: Blackwell, 1999).
Kinservik, M. J., 'The Struggle over Mary's Body: Theological and Dramatic Resolution in the N-Town Assumption Play', *Journal of English and German Philology*, 95 (1996), 190–203.
Klein, M., *The Selected Melanie Klein*, ed. J. Mitchell (London: Penguin, 1986).
Knights, L. C., *How Many Children had Lady Macbeth?* (Cambridge: Minority Press, 1933).
Knott, J. R., 'John Foxe and the Joy of Suffering: Characterising Protestant Martyrs and their Experience in Acts and Monuments', *Sixteenth Century Journal*, 27:3 (1996), 721–34.
Knowles, R., *Shakespeare's Arguments with History* (Basingstoke: Palgrave, 2002).
Knutson, R. L., 'Play Identifications: *The Wise men of Chester and John a Kent and John a Cumber; Longshanks* and *Edward I*', *HLQ* 47 (1984), 1–11.
Krier, T. M., *Birth Passages: Maternity and Nostalgia, Antiquity to Shakespeare* (Ithaca: Cornell University Press, 2001).

Kristeva, J., 'Motherhood According to Giovanni Bellini' in J. Kristeva, *Desire in Language: A Semiotic Approach to Literature and Art*, trans. L. S. Roudiez (New York: Columbia University Press, 1980).
Kristeva, J., *Powers of Horror: An Essay on Abjection*, trans. L. S. Roudiez (New York: Columbia University Press, 1982).
Kristeva, J., *Black Sun: Depression and Melancholia*, trans. L. S. Roudiez (New York: Columbia University Press, 1989).
Kyd, T., *The Spanish Tragedy*, ed. P. Edwards, Revels Plays (Manchester: Manchester University Press, 1977).
Laoutaris, C., 'Speaking Stones: Memory and Maternity in Shakespeare's *Antony and Cleopatra*, in K. M. Moncrieff and K. E. McPherson, eds, *Performing Maternity in Early Modern England* (Aldershot: Ashgate, 2007).
Le Goff, J. and Nora, P., eds., *Faire de l'histoire*, vol. 1, *Nouveaux problèmes* (Paris: Gallimard, 1974).
Leggatt, A., *Shakespeare's Political Drama* (London: Routledge, 1988).
Limon, J., *Dangerous Matter: English Drama and Politics 1623/24* (Cambridge: Cambridge University Press, 1986).
Loades, D., *Mary Tudor: A Life* (Oxford: Basil Blackwell, 1989).
Loades, D., *The Reign of Mary Tudor* (London: Longman, 1991).
Loomba, A., *Gender, Race, Renaissance Drama* (Manchester: Manchester University Press, 1989).
Lordi, R. J., ed., *Richardus Tertius by Thomas Legge* (London: Garland, 1979).
Luckyj, C., 'Disciplining the Mother in Seventeenth-Century English Puritanism' in K. M. Moncrief and K. E. McPherson, eds, *Performing Maternity in Early Modern England* (Aldershot: Ashgate, 2007).
MacCulloch, D., ed., *The Reign of Henry VIII: Politics, Policy and Piety* (London: Macmillan, 1995).
Macdonald, M., *Mystical Bedlam* (Cambridge: Cambridge University Press, 1981).
Macfarlane, A., *Marriage and Love in England 1300–1840* (Oxford: Basil Blackwell, 1986).
Macfarlane, A., *The Family Life of Ralph Josselin* (Cambridge: Cambridge University Press, 1970).
Machyn, H., *The Diary of Henry Machyn of London 1550 to 1563*, ed. J. Gough Nichols (London: Camden Society, 1848)
Mack, M., *Rescuing Shakespeare* (Oxford: International Shakespeare Association, 1979).
Marlowe, C., *The Works of Christopher Marlowe*, ed. C. F. Tucker Brooke (Oxford: Clarendon Press, 1910).
Marshall, T., review of V. Comensoli, *'Household Business'* in *Renaissance Forum*, 4:1. www.hull.ac.uk/reforum/v4no1/marshall.htm, accessed 10 June 2009.
Matchinske, M., *Writing, Gender and State in Early Modern England* (Cambridge: Cambridge University Press, 1988).
McEachern, C., *The Poetics of English Nationhood 1590–1612* (Cambridge: Cambridge University Press, 1996).

McGrath, A. E., *Reformation Thought: An Introduction*, 2nd edn (London: Blackwell, 1993).
Mclaren, D., 'Fertility, Infant Mortality and Breastfeeding in the Seventeenth Century', *Medical History* 22 (1978), 378–96.
McLeish, K., *Aristotle's Poetics* (London: Nick Hern, 1999).
McLuskie, K., *Renaissance Dramatists* (Hemel Hempstead: Harvester Wheatsheaf, 1989).
McLuskie, K., *Dekker and Heywood*, English Dramatists (London: Macmillan, 1994).
McPherson, K. E. and Moncrief, K. M., eds, *Performing Maternity in Early Modern England* (Aldershot: Ashgate, 2007).
Medwall, H., *The Plays of Henry Medwall*, ed. Alan H. Nelson (Cambridge: D. S. Brewer, 1980).
Mendell, D. W., *Our Seneca* (New Haven: Yale University Press, 1941).
Metzger, M. L., 'Controversy and "Correctness": English Chronicles and the Chroniclers, 1553–1568', *Sixteenth Century Journal*, 27 (1996), 437–51.
Middleton, T., *A Chaste Maid in Cheapside*, ed. A. Brissenden, New Mermaid edn (London: Ernest Benn, 1968).
Middleton, T., *Five Plays*, ed. B. Loughrey and N. Taylor (London: Penguin, 1988).
Miller, N. J. and Yavneh, N., eds, *Maternal Measures: Figuring Caregiving in the Early Modern Period* (Aldershot: Ashgate, 2000).
Mitchell, J., *Psychoanalysis and Feminism* (Harmondsworth: Penguin, 1990).
Mitchell, W. J. T., *On Narrative* (Chicago: University of Chicago Press, 1981).
Moncrief, K. M. and McPherson, K. E., eds, *Performing Maternity in Early Modern England* (Aldershot: Ashgate, 2007).
Montrose, L. A., 'Idols of the Queen: Policy, Gender, and the Picturing of Elizabeth I', *Representations*, 68 (1999), 108–61.
Mulder-Bakker, A. B., 'The Metamorphosis of Women: Transmission of Knowledge and the Problem of Gender', *Gender and History*, 12:3 (2000), 642–64.
National Gallery, *The Image of Christ* (catalogue of Seeing Salvation exhibition) (London: National Gallery Company Ltd, 2000).
Neale, J. E., *Elizabeth I and her Parliaments 1559–1601*, vol. 1 (London: J. Cape, 1953).
Neely, C. T., *Broken Nuptials in Shakespeare's Plays* (New Haven: Yale University Press, 1985).
Neill, M., *Issues of Death: Mortality and Identity in English Renaissance Tragedy* (Oxford: Clarendon Press, 1997).
Newman, K., *Fashioning Femininity and English Renaissance Drama* (Chicago: University of Chicago Press, 1981).
Newton, T., ed., *Seneca, His Tenne Tragedies* (New York: Spenser Society, 1967).
Nora, P., 'Le Retour de l'événement' in J. le Goff and P. Nora, eds, *Faire de l'histoire*, vol. 1, *Nouveaux problèmes* (Paris: Gallimard, 1974).

Oberman, H. A., *Masters of the Reformation* (Cambridge: Cambridge University Press, 1991).
Onega, S. and Garcia Landa, J. A., *Narratology: An Introduction* (Harlow: Longman, 1996).
Orgel, S., ed., *The Winter's Tale*, Oxford Shakespeare (Oxford: Clarendon Press, 1996).
Ornstein, R., *The Moral Vision of Jacobean Tragedy* (Wisconsin: University of Wisconsin Press, 1960).
Palmer, D. J., 'Marlowe's Naturalism', in B. Morris, ed., *Christopher Marlowe*, Mermaid Critical Commentaries (London: Ernest Benn, 1968).
Paris, B. J., *Bargains with Fate: Psychological Crises and Conflicts in Shakespeare and His Plays* (New York: Plenum Press, 1991).
Park, K., *Secrets of Women: Gender, Generation and the Origins of Human Dissection* (New York: Zone Books, 2006).
Parker, R., *Torn in Two: The Experience of Maternal Ambivalence* (London: Virago, 1995).
Parry, G. J. R., *A Protestant Vision: William Harrison and the Reformation of Elizabethan England* (Cambridge: Cambridge University Press, 1987).
Paster, G. K., *The Body Embarrassed: Drama and the Disciplines of Shame in Early Modern England* (Ithaca: Cornell University Press, 1993).
Patterson, A., *Censorship and Interpretation: The Conditions of Reading and Writing in Early Modern England* (Madison: University of Wisconsin Press, 1984).
Patterson, A., *Reading Holinshed's Chronicles* (Chicago: University of Chicago Press, 1994).
Pearsall, D., ed., *William Langland: Piers Plowman, The C Text* (Exeter: University of Exeter Press, 1994).
Pearson, J., *Tragedy and Tragicomedy in the Plays of John Webster* (Manchester: Manchester University Press, 1980).
Peele, G., *King Edward the First* in *King Edward the First by George Peele 1593* (London: Malone Society, Oxford University Press, 1911).
Peele, G., *The Old Wife's Tale*, ed. C. Whitworth, New Mermaid edn (London: A. and C. Black, 1996).
Peele, G., *The Dramatic Works*, ed. F. S. Hook, J. Yoklavich, R. Mark Benbow and E. Blistein, 2 vols. (New Haven and London: Yale University Press, 1970).
Penny, D. A., 'Family Matters and Foxe's Acts and Monuments', *Historical Journal*, 39:3 (1996), 599–618.
Phillip, J., *The Commodye of pacient and meeke Grissil*, eds R. B. Mckerrow and W. W. Greg, (London: Malone Society, 1909).
Pollock, L., *Forgotten Children* (Cambridge: Cambridge University Press, 1983).
Poole, A., *Coriolanus*, Harvester New Critical Introductions to Shakespeare (Hemel Hempstead: Harvester Wheatsheaf, 1988).

Postlewate, L. and Hüsken, W., eds, *Acts and Texts: Performance and Ritual in the Middle Ages and the Renaissance* (Amsterdam: Rodopi, 2007).
Potter, L., 'The Plays and Playwrights' in *The Revels History of Drama in English Vol. II, 1500–1576* (London: Methuen, 1980).
Potter, L., ed., *The Revels History of Drama in English*, vol. I (London: Methuen, 1983).
Powicke, Sir M., ed., *The Thirteenth Century 1216–1307* (Oxford: Clarendon Press, 1962).
Prestwich, M., *Edward I* (London: Methuen and Berkeley: University of California Press, 1988).
Prior, M., ed., *Women in English Society 1500–1800* (London: Methuen, 1985).
Prouty, C. T., *George Gascoigne: Elizabethan Courtier, Soldier and Poet* (New York: Blom, 1942).
Pugliatti, P., *Shakespeare the Historian* (Basingstoke: Macmillan, 1996).
Purkiss, D., *The Witch in History* (London and New York: Routledge, 1996).
Rackin, P., *Stages of History: Shakespeare's English Chronicles* (London: Routledge, 1991).
Ribner, I., *The English History Play in the Age of Shakespeare* (London: Methuen, 1965).
Rich, A., *Of Woman Born: Motherhood as Experience and Institution* (London: Virago, 1977).
Richards, J. M., ' "To Promote a Woman to Beare Rule": Talking of Queens in Mid-Tudor England', *Sixteenth Century Journal*, 28 (1997), 101–21.
Richardson, C., *Domestic Life and Domestic Tragedy in Early Modern England: The Material Life of the Household* (Manchester: Manchester University Press, 2006).
Richmond-Garza, E., ' "She Never Recovered Her Senses": Roxana and Dramatic Representations of Women at Oxbridge in the Elizabethan Age' in B. K. Gold, P. A. Miller and C. Platter, eds, *Sex and Gender in Medieval and Renaissance Texts: The Latin Tradition* (Albany: State University of New York Press, 1997).
Ricoeur, P., *Time and Narrative*, vols 1 and 2, trans. K. McLaughlin and D. Pellauer (Chicago: University of Chicago Press, 1984).
Ridley, J. G., *The Life and Times of Mary Tudor* (London: Weidenfeld and Nicolson, 1973).
Robbins, D., unpub. essay, University of Kent, 2002.
Roberts, S., 'Lying among the Classics: Ritual and Motif in Elite Elizabethan and Jacobean Beds' in L. Gent, ed., *Albion's Classicism: The Visual Arts in Britain 1550–1660* (New Haven and London: Yale University Press, 1995).
Roberts, S., *William Shakespeare: Romeo and Juliet* (Plymouth: Northcote House and British Council, 1998).
Robertson, D. W. and Huppé, B. F., *Piers Plowman and the Scriptural Tradition* (New York: Octagon, 1969).
Rose, J., 'Sexuality in the Reading of Shakespeare: *Hamlet* and *Measure for Measure*', in J. Drakakis, ed., *Alternative Shakespeares*, vol. 1, (London: Routledge, 1985).

Rose, M. B., 'Where are the Mothers in Shakespeare? Options for Gender Representation in the English Renaissance', *Shakespeare Quarterly* 42:3 (1991), 291–314.
Rossiter, A. P., *Angel with Horns and Other Shakespeare Lectures*, ed. G. Storey (London: Longman, 1961).
Saccio, P., *Shakespeare's English Kings* (Oxford: Oxford University Press, 1977).
Sacks, E., *Shakespeare's Images of Pregnancy* (London: Macmillan, 1980).
Sackville, T. and Norton, T., *Gorboduc or Ferrex and Porrex*, ed. I. B. Cauthen, Jnr. (Lincoln: University of Nebraska Press, 1970).
Schenk, W., *Reginald Pole: Cardinal of England* (London: Longman, 1950).
Schmidt, A. V. C. (ed.), *William Langland: The Vision of Piers Plowman* (London: Dent, 1978).
Seznec, J., *The Survival of the Pagan Gods* (Princeton: Princeton University Press, 1953).
Shakespeare, W., *Richard II*, ed. P. Ure, The Arden Shakespeare (London: Methuen, 1964).
Shakespeare, W., *Hamlet*, First Quarto, 1603, Facsimile (Oxford: Clarendon Press, 1965).
Shakespeare, W., *The Complete Works*, ed. P. Alexander (London: Collins, 1965).
Shakespeare, W., *Romeo and Juliet*, ed. T. J. B. Spencer, New Penguin edn (London: Penguin, 1967).
Shakespeare, W., *The Merchant of Venice*, ed. W Moelwyn Merchant (Harmondsworth: Penguin, 1985).
Shakespeare, W., *The Winter's Tale*, ed. J. H. P. Pafford (London and New York: Routledge, 1989).
Shakespeare, W., *Titus Andronicus*, ed. J. Bate (London: Routledge, 1995).
Shakespeare, W., *The Winter's Tale*, ed. S. Orgel, Oxford Shakespeare (Oxford: Claredon Press, 1996).
Shakespeare, W., *King Henry VI Part II*, ed. by R. Knowles (Walton-on-Thames: Thomas Nelson and Sons Ltd., 1999).
Shakespeare, W., *Coriolanus*, ed. L. Bliss (Cambridge: Cambridge University Press, 2000).
Shakespeare, W., *King Henry VI Part II*, ed. John D. Cox and E. Rasmussen (London: Thompson Learning, 2001).
Shakespeare, W., *Pericles*, ed. S. Gossett (London: Arden Shakespeare, 2004).
Sharpe, J. A., *Early Modern England: A Social History* (London: Arnold, 1987).
Shaw, B., *Shaw on Shakespeare*, ed. E. Wilson (London: Cassell Penguin, 1961).
Shepherd, S., *Amazons and Warrior Women: Varieties of Feminism in Seventeenth-century Drama* (Brighton: Harvester, 1981).
Sidney, Sir P., *Defense of Poesy*, ed. D. M. Macardle (London: Macmillan, 1919).
Sidney, Sir P., *Defense of Poesy*, ed. G. Shepherd (London: Thomas Nelson and Son, 1965).

Sidney, Sir P., *A Defence of Poetry*, ed. J. A. Van Dorsten (Oxford: Oxford University Press, 1966).
Singh, S., *Family Relationships in Shakespeare and the Restoration Comedy of Manners* (Oxford: Oxford University Press, 1983).
Smith, B. H., *Traditional Images of Charity in Piers Plowman* (The Hague: Mouton, 1996).
Smith, H. L., 'Humanist Education and the Renaissance Concept of Woman' in H. Wilcox, ed., *Women and Literature in Britain 1500–1700*, (Cambridge: Cambridge University Press, 1996).
Smith, L. and Taylor, J. H. M., eds, *Women and the Book: Assessing the Visual Evidence* (Toronto: University of Toronto Press, 1996).
Smith, R., 'The Dilemma of Shakespeare's Gertrude' in M. Coyle, ed., *Hamlet: Contemporary Critical Essays* (London: Macmillan, 1992).
Spector, S., ed., *The N-Town Play*, vol. 2, (Oxford: Early English Texts Society, Oxford University Press, 1991).
Stanton, A. R., 'From Eve to Bathsheba and Beyond: Motherhood in the Queen Mary Psalter' in L. Smith and J. H. M. Taylor, eds, *Women and the Book: Assessing the Visual Evidence* (Toronto: University of Toronto Press, 1996).
Studeley, R., 'Medea', in *Seneca His Tenne Tragedies*, ed. T. Newton (1581, New York: Spenser Society, 1887, repr. 1967).
Sturgess, K., *Three Elizabethan Domestic Tragedies* (Harmondsworth: Penguin, 1969).
Sutton, D. F., hypertext critical edn of Alabaster's *Roxana*, www.philological.bham.ac.uk/alabaster (1998).
Tavormina, M. T., *Kindly Similitude: Marriage and Family in Piers Plowman* (Cambridge: D. S. Brewer, 1995).
Thomas, K., *Religion and the Decline of Magic* (London: Weidenfeld and Nicolson, 1971).
Thomas, K., *Man and the Natural World* (London: Penguin, 1987).
Thomas, K. and Pennington, D., eds, *Puritans and Revolutionaries* (Oxford: Clarendon Press, 1978).
Tittler, R., *The Reign of Mary I* (London: Longman, 1983).
Traub, V., *Desire and Anxiety: Circulations of Sexuality in Shakespearean Drama* (London: Routledge, 1992).
Travitsky, B., *The Paradise of Women: Writings by Englishwomen of the Renaissance* (Columbia University Press: New York, 1989).
Travitsky, B., ed., *Mother's Advice Books* in *The Early Modern Englishwoman* series 1, part 2, vol. 8 (Aldershot: Ashgate, 2001).
Trill, S., Chedgzoy, K. and Osborne, M., *Lay By Your Needles Ladies, Take the Pen: Writing Women in England 1500–1700* (London and New York: Arnold, 1997).
Turner, R., *De morbis foemineis: the woman's counsellour* (London, 1686).
Twycross, M., 'Kissing Cousins: The Four Daughters of God and the Visitation in the N-Town Mary Play', *Medieval English Theatre*, 18 (1996), 99–141.

Utley, F. L., 'Five Genres in The Clerk's Tale', *Chaucer Review*, 6 (1972), 198–228.
Vanhoutte, J. A., 'Engendering England: The Restructuring of Allegiance in the Writings of Richard Morison and John Bale', *Renaissance and Reformation*, 20:1 (1996), 49–77.
Warner, M., *Monuments and Maidens: The Allegory of the Female Form* (London: Picador, 1985).
Warner, M., *From the Beast to the Blonde* (Cambridge: Cambridge University Press, 1994).
Warner, M., *Alone of All Her Sex: The Myth and Cult of the Virgin Mary* (London: Picador, 1995).
Warner, M., *Fantastic Metamorphoses, Other Worlds* (Oxford: Oxford University Press, 2002).
Warner, M., *Phantasmagoria* (Oxford: Oxford University Press, 2006).
Watkins, G., *The Miseries of Enforced Marriage* (1607), Malone Society (Oxford: Oxford University Press, 1963).
Watt, T., *Cheap Print and Popular Piety 1550–1640* (Cambridge: Cambridge University Press, 1991).
Wayne, V., *The Matter of Difference: Materialist Feminist Criticism of Shakespeare* (Hemel Hempstead: Harvester Wheatsheaf, 1991).
Wayne, V., 'Advice for Women from Mothers and Patriarchs' in *Women and Literature in Britain 1500–1700* (Cambridge: Cambridge University Press, 1996).
Webb, J. B., *Shakespeare's Erotic Word Usage* (Hastings: Cornwallis Press, 1989).
Webster, J., *The Duchess of Malfi*, ed. E. M. Brennan, New Mermaid edn (London and Tonbridge: Earnest Benn Ltd., 1973).
Weikel, A., 'The Marian Council Revisited' in J. Loach and R. Tittler, eds, *The Mid-Tudor Polity c.1540–1560*, (London: Macmillan, 1980).
Weil, J., *Christopher Marlowe, Merlin's Prophet* (Cambridge: Cambridge University Press, 1977).
Wells, S. and Taylor, G., *The Oxford Shakespeare: The Complete Works* (Oxford: Clarendon Press, 1988).
White, P. W., *Theatre and Reformation* (Cambridge: Cambridge University Press, 1993).
Wickham, G., *Early English Stages*, vol. 2 1576 – 1600, part 1, (London: Routledge and Kegan Paul, 1963).
Wickham, G., *Shakespeare's Dramatic Heritage: Collected Studies in Medieaval, Tudor and Shakespearean Drama* (London: Routledge and Kegan Paul, 1969).
Wilcox, H., ed., *Women and Literature in Britain 1500–1700* (Cambridge: Cambridge University Press, 1996).
Wiles, T. J., *The Theatre Event: Modern Theories of Performance* (Chicago and London: University of Chicago Press, 1980).
Willbern, D., 'Rape and Revenge in *Titus Andronicus*', *English Literary Renaissance*, 8 (1978), 159–82.

Willis, D., *Malevolent Nurture: Witch-hunting and Maternal Power in Early Modern England* (Ithaca and London: Cornell University Press, 1995).
Wimsatt, J., 'The Blessed Virgin and the Two Coronations of Griselda', *Mediaevalia*, 6 (1980), 187–207.
Woodbridge, L., *Women and the English Renaissance* (Brighton: Harvester Press, 1984).
Wright, W. A., ed., *English Works of Roger Ascham* (Cambridge: Cambridge University Press, 1970).
Wrightson, K., 'Infanticide in Early Seventeenth Century England', *Local Population Studies*, 15 (1975), 10–21.
Wrightson, K., *English Society 1580–1680* (London: Hutchinson & Co., 1982).
Wynne-Davies, M., ' "The Swallowing Womb": Consumed and Consuming Women in Titus Andronicus', in V. Wayne, ed., *The Matter of Difference: Materialist Feminist Criticism of Shakespeare* (Hemel Hempstead: Harvester Wheatsheaf, 1991).
Zimmerman, S., ed., *Erotic Politics: Desire on the Renaissance Stage* (London: Routledge, 1992).

Index

Adams, Henry Hitch 148
Adelman, Janet 5, 68, 97, 113, 115, 161, 168, 170, 172, 178, 184, 187, 188, 190, 191, 204
adultery 129, 140n, 149, 150, 151, 202, 203, 205
Agamben, Giorgio 1, 11
Alabaster, William, *Roxana* 61–4, 65
Anon:
  New Custom 44n
  Nice Wanton 80, 131, 132, 104n, 141n, 144, 162n, 201
  Respublica 12, 35–8, 53, 54, 58
  Warning for Fair Women, A 14, 147–52, 154
  Wisdom 11, 26, 27
  Yorkshire Tragedy, A 14, 152–4
Anselm of Canterbury. 7, 25, 45n
Apter, Emily 63
Aries, Philippe 210
Armin, Robert, 143, 162n
Ascham, Roger 57
Astell, Ann 20, 21
audience 22, 33, 36, 56, 90, 119, 120, 123, 203
Auerbach, Eric 82
Axton, Marie 38, 41, 53, 58, 59, 89, 90, 94
Aylmer, Bishop John 42

Bacon, Francis 2
Badinter, Elizabeth 4, 115
Bale, John 81, 48n, 49n, 132
  Kyng Johan 30–6, 53–5, 59, 80, 98
bastardy *see* illegitimacy
Bate, Jonathan 64, 66, 67
Bath, Michael 2, 105n, 203

Becker, Lucinda 197, 198, 203, 216
Beilin, Elaine 223
Belsey, Catherine 199, 201, 203, 210–12
Bernard of Clairvaux, St. 24, 25, 45n
Bettleheim, Bruno 122
Bevington, David 27, 29, 36, 37, 88, 89, 92, 94, 95, 99
Bliss, Lee 179, 181, 190
Body, mother's 13, 27, 33, 34, 58, 65, 68, 70–4, 86, 97, 111, 118, 120, 130, 146, 150, 172, 204, 208, 211, 212
  see also Mary, mother of Jesus
  blood 100, 205, 206, 207, 214
  breast(s) 7, 23, 24, 38, 46n, 92, 94, 112, 113, 116, 118, 120, 123, 127, 128, 133, 181
    see also milk
  corruption and possession 93, 94, 150, 172, 178, 206
  metaphor 5, 7, 20–5, 31, 32, 37, 38, 39, 59, 63, 66, 187–8
  violence to body 25, 61–4, 192, 94, 154, 156, 177
  womb 7, 9, 42, 56, 64, 66, 72, 79, 86, 107n, 112–14, 124, 133, 190, 191, 214
    see also pregnancy
Bradley, A. C. 3, 4, 169, 172
breastfeeding *see* nursing
Buci-Glucksman, Christine 172
Bynum, Caroline 24

Caldwell, Elizabeth 143, 197
caudle 26

Index

Castan, Nicole 147
Chaucer, Geoffrey 43n, 117
childbirth and lactation 89, 92, 128
  lying in 91, 150, 160
  pain 7, 8, 56, 58, 59, 70, 100, 111, 112, 226, 123, 207, 209, 222
  linked to beasts 101, 116, 121, 133
children and childhood 27, 30, 32, 36, 37, 99, 100, 102, 103, 124, 126, 129, 131, 133, 135, 147, 148, 151–3, 155, 161, 168, 182, 188, 190, 200, 201
Christ as mother or nurse 7, 24, 25, 45n
Chronicles
  Hall 80, 82, 83, 95, 96, 99, 101
  Holinshead 80, 81, 147
churching 9, 10, 42n, 94
Clinton, Elizabeth 115, 121, 134, 202
Clytemnestra 12, 54, 113
Collinson, Patrick 15, 223, 225
Comensoli, Viviane 140n 150, 152, 154
costume for mother figure 26, 27, 43n, 84, 88, 117, 120, 146
Cranmer, Archbishop Thomas 30
Crashawe, Elizabeth 212, 213
Crawford, Patricia 198, 199
Cromwell, Thomas 29
Cycle plays
  Assumption plays now lost 29, 46n
  Chester *Noah's Flood* 21
  Chester *Purification* 21
  N-Town *Assumption* 29, 46n
  N-Town *Death of Herod* 113
  N-Town *Nativity* 22, 23
  Wakefield *Herod the Great* 21–2
  Wakefield *Last Judgement* 23
  Wakefield *Second Shepherd's Pageant* 21, 158

dead or dying mother 73, 74, 94, 123, 199, 202, 203
  execution 121, 150, 151, 159, 198
  tombs 210, 214–16
Dekker, *Patient Grissil* 13, 118, 125–9, 153

Deutsch, Helen 5
Dod, John and Robert Cleaver 48
Dollimore, Jonathan 167, 172, 175, 178, 185, 189
Dudale, Gilbert 197
Dusinberre, Juliet 224

Ecclesia and Church as mother 20, 31, 48n, 225
Eliot, Thomas Stearns 167, 169, 170, 172
Elizabeth I 12, 40–3, 53, 124, 129, 208, 209
emblem 2, 11, 12, 15n, 33, 58, 59, 69, 87, 102–4, 153, 157, 180, 207, 210, 213
England allegorised as mother 30–3, 88, 225
Erasmus, Desiderius 9, 17n, 115

Findlay, Alison 145, 148, 161
Fleische, Martha Hester 3, 87
Foucault, Michel 23
Foxe, John, 31, 33, 34, 42, 47n

Gascoigne, George, *Jocasta* 12, 52, 57, 60, 79, 82
Gibson, Gail McMurray 26, 29
Gittings, Claire 197
Gouge, William, 114–16, 200, 201, 202, 206, 207
gossips 21, 139n, 160
Grymeston, Elizabeth 196–9, 200, 203
Guillemeau, Jacques 114, 115, 132, 133, 134

Hackett, Helen 42, 51n
Haigh, Christopher 30, 38
Happé, Peter 26, 27
Hattaway, Michael 68–70
Heinemann, Margot 155, 224
Heisch, Alison 40, 41
Henry VIII 29, 30, 36, 42, 46n, 47n
Henslowe, Phillip 85, 129
Heywood, Thomas 99
  A Woman Killed with Kindness 150, 163n, 196, 202, 203
Hildegarde of Bingen 20, 21
Hobby, Elaine ix, 9, 16n

Hoby, Lady Margaret 8, 220n
Howard, Jean 222
  with Phyllis Rackin 79, 86, 95,
    96, 98

illegitimacy 99, 158, 159, 162n, 202
infanticide 3, 62, 158, 159, 202
Italian influence 55, 60, 64, 74
  Cinthio *Orbecce* 60
  Dolce *Giocasta* 57, 59
  Groto *La Dalida* 61

Jardine, Lisa 63, 64, 67, 171
James I 109, 182, 204, 208, 209
Jewel, John 93
Jocelin, Elizabeth 196–8, 203, 223
Jones, Ann Rosalind 201, 223
Julian of Norwich 11, 19, 20, 25

Kaplan, E. Ann 129
Katherine of Aragon 29, 35, 46n
Kay, Sarah 23, 24
Kehler, Dorothea 170–1
Kempe, Margery 11, 25, 26
King, Pamela 27, 46n
Klein, Melanie 130
Krier, Theresa 210
Kristeva, Julia 1, 5, 60, 136, 176,
  177
Kyd, Thomas, *The Spanish Tragedy*
  61, 68

Langland, William, *Piers Plowman*
  21, 26
labour *see* pregnancy
lactation *see* breasts; childbirth
lament, mother's 69, 103, 122, 123,
  154
Laoutaris, Chris 198, 210–12, 215,
  216, 225
Luckyj, Christina 201, 208, 209,
  224–6
Legge, Thomas
  Richardus Tertius 82–4, 86, 92, 95
Lyly, John 7

Mack, Maynard 3
Marlowe, Christopher
  Tamburlaine I 70–2, 73
  Tamburlaine II 70–4

Marston, John, *Antonio's Revenge*
  141n
Mary Magdalene 27
Mary, mother of Jesus
  antitypes 21, 90, 157
  body, 22, 23, 29, 111, 112
  see also body of mother
  Madonna lactans 112, 113
  see also breasts
  bride of Christ 20
  church 21
  polis 20–1
  virginity 20–3
Mary I 12, 33–9, 40, 93, 94, 124
McEachern, Claire 208
Mcloskey, Susan 5
McLuskie, Kathleen 69, 126, 149
McPherson, Kathryn 10
Medwall, Henry, *Nature* 11, 27
Middleton, Thomas, *A Chaste*
  Maid in Cheapside 8, 14,
  155–61
midwives 160
  doubting midwife 22, 23
  male midwife 137n
milk, mothers 24, 38, 94, 114, 116,
  120, 127, 205, 207
  see also breasts
moral plays and types 26, 30,
  36, 48n, 53–60, 2, 80,
  94, 116, 117, 119, 121–6,
  131, 132, 134, 149, 160,
  168, 169, 201
Morison, Richard 29, 33

Nature as mother 23, 24
Neely, Carol Thomas 6
Newman, Karen 4, 5, 144
Noah and his wife 90, 157
  see Mary, Mother of Jesus:
    antitypes: Cycle Plays
No natural mother but a monster
  (ballad) 159
Nora, Pierre 91
nurse and nursing 2, 207, 56, 128,
  152, 153, 156, 207
  dramatic character 12, 56, 121–3,
    130, 132–6, 160
  maternal 9, 113, 114, 115, 116,
    120, 127, 134, 181, 204

metaphor 7, 25, 42, 67, 86, 106n, 131, 132, 188, 208
wet nursing 9, 113, 115, 116, 133, 135, 161

Orgel, Stephen 205

Park, Katherine 60, 64–6, 92, 186, 205, 207, 212
Parker, Roszika 4
Paster, Gail Kern 113, 114, 134, 157
Peachum, Henry 66, 67
Peele, George
    Edward I 84–95, 111
    Ballad sources 89
pelican in her piety 207, 219n
Phillip, John, *The Commodye of pacient and meeke Grissil* 118, 119–25, 159
pregnancy 29, 89, 90, 111–13, 116, 120, 150, 204, 206, 214
    false 38–9
Pole, Cardinal 34, 36, 38, 39
Proctor, John 37–8
Pugliati, Paola 79, 81
Purkiss, Diana 92–4

Rackin, Phyllis 99
Raynalde, *The Byrthe of Mankynde* 6, 7, 17n, 114
Reformation 9, 11, 12, 19, 20, 28–30, 32, 38, 40, 43, 116, 119, 171, 222, 223
revenge 55, 62, 66–9, 93, 101, 102, 170, 173, 175, 178, 179
Richardson, Catherine 143, 146, 154, 160
Ricoeur, Paul 83, 107n
Roberts, Sasha 134, 135, 160
Romance of the Rose 11, 23, 24, 27
Rose, Jacqueline 170
Rose, Mary Beth 4, 5, 6, 212

Sackville and Norton, *Gorboduc* 53–7, 59

Seneca
    Medea 54, 62, 121
    Phaedra 55
    Troades 82
Shakespeare, William
    Comedy of Errors, The 111
    Coriolanus 167, 179–92
    Hamlet 3, 167–79, 191, 192
    Henry VI Part 3, 92, 96, 97–104
    Merchant of Venice, The 1
    Pericles 156
    Richard II 85, 86
    Romeo and Juliet 13, 111, 130–7, 155, 156
    Titus Andronicus 61, 64, 65–8
Sharpe, James A 151
Sidney, Sir Philip 7, 52, 53, 61
Snyder, Susan 130, 132
Song of Songs 20, 24, 26
stepmother 122, 123, 135, 136
Stubbes, Philip 79, 146
suicide 69, 71, 72

Thomas, Keith 9, 116, 144
tradition 11, 19, 20, 28
travesty 92, 156, 157, 161
Travitsky, Betty 198, 200, 210
Trubowitz, Rachel 134

Vanhoutte, Jacqueline 29–33

Watkins, George 152
Wayne, Valerie 198, 223
Warner, Marina 20, 23, 28, 93, 94, 113, 211
Webster, John, *The Duchess of Malfi* 14, 15, 212–16
wet nursing *see* nursing
Willis, Deborah 93–6, 98, 99, 102, 168
witches and malevolence 92–5, 168
Wickham, Glynn 36, 224
Woodbridge, Linda 119
Woodford, Donna 205
Wrightson, Keith 158
Wycliffe, John 19

EU authorised representative for GPSR:
Easy Access System Europe, Mustamäe tee 50,
10621 Tallinn, Estonia
gpsr.requests@easproject.com

www.ingramcontent.com/pod-product-compliance
Lightning Source LLC
Chambersburg PA
CBHW061439300426
44114CB00014B/1753